The Economics of Social Security

The Economics of Social Security

Edited by

ANDREW DILNOT
and
IAN WALKER

OXFORD UNIVERSITY PRESS

1989

Oxford University Press, Walton Street, Oxford OX2 6DP

Oxford New York Toronto
Delhi Bombay Calcutta Madras Karachi
Petaling Jaya Singapore Hong Kong Tokyo
Nairobi Dar es Salaam Cape Town
Melbourne Auckland
and associated companies in
Berlin Ibadan

Oxford is a trade mark of Oxford University Press

Published in the United States
by Oxford University Press, New York

British Library Cataloguing in Publication Data
The Economics of Social security.
1. Great Britain. Social security benefits—
For accountancy
I. Dilnot, A.W. II. Walker, Ian, 1945–
368.4'00941
ISBN 0–19–828699–6
ISBN 0–19–828698–8 (pbk.)

Library of Congress Cataloging in Publication Data
The Economics of social security/edited by Andrew Dilnot and Ian Walker.
p. cm.
Bibliography: p. Includes index.
1. Social security—Great Britain. 2. Great Britain—Economic
conditions—1945– 3. Great Britain—Economic policy—1945–
I. Dilnot, A.W. II. Walker, Ian, 1945–
HD7165.E26 1989 368.4'0094—dc 19 88–36507
ISBN 0–19–828699–6—ISBN 0–19–828698–8 (pbk.)

Computerset by
Promenade Graphics Ltd

Printed in Great Britain
by Biddles Ltd.
Guildford and King's Lynn

Preface

This book developed from a conference organized by the Institute for Fiscal Studies in April 1988. The conference, on 'The Economics of Social Security', coincided with the introduction of the new UK social security system. All of the papers presented at the conference are reproduced here, alongside a number of other relevant papers published by IFS in the recent past. Finance for this project has come from the Economic and Social Research Council (grant number WB002220009).

We are very grateful to all of the contributors to this volume, who have kept to very tight deadlines and patiently answered all our questions. Finally, we must thank Chantal Crevel-Robinson for typing much of the material contained here, and Judith Payne for copy-editing and preparing the book for publication; both worked with great speed, accuracy and patience.

Contents

List of Tables

List of Figures

Introduction: Economic Issues in
Social Security

ANDREW DILNOT AND IAN WALKER*

1. Introduction

The cost of social security in the UK in 1988–9 will be some £48.5 billion, accounting for around one-third of total public expenditure, and exceeding total revenue from income tax. The social security programme costs more than twice as much as the second most expensive area, defence. Over 20 million of the 56 million individuals in the UK receive some form of social security benefit. Given the scale of the social security system, it seems likely that its effects on the individuals who experience it must be significant, for good and bad. Our aim in this book is to bring together a number of recent contributions to the debate about the economic effects of social security programmes. In this introductory chapter, we discuss briefly some of the history of social security in the UK, consider the objectives of a social security system, and describe some of the important theoretical issues in this area of economics.

2. Development

Provision for the poor and destitute was essentially a local responsibility until the Poor Law Commission of 1834 (Checkland and Checkland (1974)). This, and subsequent legislation, unified the administration and structure of the many local schemes which had previously existed. The motivation of the Commission was to a large extent the prevention of any public subsidy to the idle. Able-bodied individuals were only given assistance within the workhouse, where conditions were deliberately set so as to be worse than those faced by the lowest-paid employees. The post-1834 Poor Law would administer 'outdoor relief', that is assistance to those not

Andrew Dilnot is a Programme Director at the Institute for Fiscal Studies, and Ian Walker is a Professor at the University of Keele and a Research Associate at the Institute for Fiscal Studies.

in a workhouse, to the sick, disabled, or elderly, since these groups could
not be expected to work. Even one hundred and fifty years ago, the question of how to avoid social security induced unemployment was worrying
policy-makers.

Although the Poor Law of 1834 did signal the start of centralized public
provision of social security, non-state bodies continued to play a major role
in caring for the poor. In 1861, charities in London received income of
around £2.5 million, more than expenditure under the Poor Law there in
that year. Indeed, towards the end of the nineteenth century, there was
considerable opposition to the idea of state provision of social security.
Friendly societies had for a long time organized provision for old age
amongst the slightly better off groups, and the emerging trade unions
derived power and status from their insurance schemes. Even the chari-
table organizations saw their role as threatened by expanded state provision.

The period at the end of the nineteenth century saw the beginning of a
more modern view of poverty. Booth (1902–4) in London and Rowntree
(1902) in York estimated that up to 30 per cent of all families were 'without
adequate support'. Perhaps as important as the numbers in poverty, the
major causes were argued not to be idleness, but old age, injury, sickness,
low wages, or unemployment. These studies formed the background to a
series of debates and Commissions discussing policy towards the poor,
which culminated in the legislation of the 1906 Liberal Government.

A national scheme for pensions was implemented from 1910, closely followed by the 1911 National Insurance Act. Social insurance was seen to be
a way of reconciling the desire of some members of the Government to be
more involved in the plight of the poor with the prevailing views of individual responsibility and non-interventionist government policies. The State
would provide benefits, but only in return for contributions from the individual. The 1911 Act introduced compulsory insurance against sickness
and unemployment, although only seven industries were covered for
unemployment, and the level and duration of benefit payments were again
set low enough to discourage voluntary unemployment. Unemployment
insurance was extended to almost the whole population in 1920.

Very soon, however, the post-war boom turned to slump, and by 1922 22
per cent of the insured population were unemployed. The burden this
imposed on the system far exceeded its resources, while those whose eligibility was exhausted because of lengthy unemployment faced extreme
poverty. The Government's response was the introduction of a supplementary income-related benefit, which grew to cover more individuals than the
insurance benefits by the depth of the depression in the early 1930s. An
expensive, but ultimately inadequate, system of contributory benefits now
operated in tandem with a non-contributory means-tested system which

had not been planned for and the administration of which caused major problems for both government and claimants. The Second World War swept all these problems aside, but it was in response to them that the Beveridge Report, published in December 1942, was commissioned.

The Beveridge Report was enthusiastically welcomed, and followed in 1944 by White Papers (HMSO (1944a and 1944b)) which reflected its main principles and formed the basis of the post-war legislation on social security. The scheme was firmly based on the concept of social insurance, by which Beveridge meant a system in which all individuals would make flat-rate contributions to a scheme which would provide flat-rate benefits. These benefits would be paid in the event of the contingencies identified as causing poverty: sickness, unemployment, old age, disability, and maternity. A safety net of means-tested National Assistance would provide for those few whose needs were not met by the insurance benefits, but the insurance benefits were to be set at a level sufficient to provide an adequate standard of living. Only those with incomplete contribution records or exceptional needs would have to rely on National Assistance.

There were two main problems. The first was simply that the scheme was expensive. The costs were high when the scheme was introduced, but the long-term implications as rights to benefit became fully established were more serious still. It might have been possible to contain costs if the benefit level had remained constant in real terms, as Beveridge intended. However, the post-war period saw benefit levels more than double in real terms. The second difficulty was that the nature of social insurance schemes, with benefit entitlement related to past contribution, requires that the potential causes of poverty are identified in advance. The Beveridge Report and the subsequent legislation made very little provision for poverty amongst either those in work or lone-parent families. These two groups are now covered by the most complex and ineffective parts of the social security system, which have grown up as *ad hoc* responses to unexpected problems.

As costs rose, the level of contributions was increased. Yet as the contribution was flat-rate, increases bore heavily on those on low incomes. This led to pressure for a shift to graduated contributions; in 1960 the National Insurance (NI) contribution became part graduated, in 1975 the last element of flat-rate contribution was abolished for the main class of NI contributions. As a way of defusing opposition to increased contributions, higher benefits were promised, including earnings-related benefits. Thus the two fundamental Beveridge principles of flat-rate contributions and flat-rate benefits were abandoned as a result of the high cost of social insurance.

While costs rose, 'new' categories of poor, especially those in work with children and lone parents, grew in importance. These presented new problems. The unemployed, the sick, and the elderly have lost the chance of earning their own income, and are therefore very likely to need support. For the great bulk of those in work, this is not the case. Whereas unemployment and poverty are likely to be highly correlated, employment and poverty are not. The characteristic of the poor in work which identifies them as poor is their low income. Thus to deal with poverty amongst this group, income-related benefits were required. Since these had not been planned for, and were introduced without a coherent strategy, the resulting system and the relationship between the many benefits which eventually coexisted were incoherent. This led to problems of low take-up, high administrative cost, potential disincentive effects, and a good deal of confusion. Many changes were made; those affecting the unemployed are catalogued and analysed by Tony Atkinson and John Micklewright (Ch. 1, this volume). By the early 1980s, little remained of Beveridge's ideal but the name and the common but erroneous belief that the UK social security system was still based on his report. That the Beveridge ideal collapsed was the inevitable consequence of the desire to increase benefit levels in line with the increase in the general standard of living, and the impossibility of identifying in advance all causes of poverty. Social insurance had failed before the Second World War, but Beveridge and the governments of the 1940s chose to close their eyes to that fact.

The problems within the social security system became a more important focus of public attention during the early 1980s. The increase in unemployment led to higher expenditure at a time when government was attempting to reduce the role of the State in economic activity. Higher unemployment also coincided with worries about the impact of social security on incentives. Growth in numbers of recipients of supplementary benefit is discussed by Jonathan Bradshaw and Meg Huby (Ch. 3, this volume). At the same time, poverty amongst some groups seemed to be on the increase. All of this pointed to the need for a review of the system. Such a review was set up in the summer of 1984 by the then Secretary of State for Health and Social Security, Norman Fowler; hence their now commonly accepted name, the Fowler Reviews.

Evidence, both written and oral, was taken from many individuals and organizations, and a Green Paper (DHSS (1985a)) was published in June 1985. This was followed by a White Paper (DHSS (1985b)) in December 1985, the 1986 Social Security Act, and the eventual implementation of the proposals in April 1988. The apparent aims were simplification, a redirection of resources towards poor families with children, and the encouragement of private provision for retirement. That the reforms were to aim to reduce total social security expenditure, albeit slightly, somewhat restricted the scope for radical changes in structure, while implying that the changes that were made resulted in a good many losers. The review process is discussed in some detail in Ruth Lister's contribution to this volume (Ch. 12), the nature and impact of the reforms in Andrew Dilnot and Steven Webb's (Ch. 14) and also in Andrew Dilnot and Graham Stark's (Ch. 9). Michael Portillo gives a government perspective on the reforms (Ch. 11).

3. Possible Objectives

Far too often, social security policy is discussed without a serious consideration of why we have a social security system and what we want it to achieve. In the UK, for example, there has been a lengthy debate as to whether universal or means-tested benefits are the most desirable form of payment, with all too little attention given to the reasons for having benefit payments at all. This is underlined by Richard Berthoud (Ch. 4, this volume) in the case of housing benefits. Beveridge had a clear idea of what a social security system should do. He expected flat-rate, subsistence-level benefits to be paid to those who had made flat-rate contributions, provided that they experienced particular contingencies. He was not interested in poverty amongst those at work, or redistribution across the life cycle, or in 'relative' poverty. Post-war governments were committed to all of these, and yet attempted to use Beveridge's structure to achieve such a system.

Economists tend to consider the rationale for government social security provision in terms of market failure. One set of problems is associated with the inability of the market to provide appropriate forms of insurance and/ or the unwillingness of individuals to consume such insurance. A second set of problems relates to the failure of the market to ensure a socially optimal distribution of income. The question of whether or not the market is capable of providing appropriate forms of insurance is in principle an empirical one. The traditional view is that the provision of unemployment insurance, for example, by the market mechanism would present serious difficulties. However, the growth of private pension provision and private sickness insurance suggests that there may be some areas where the private sector can at least share the role of insuring against loss of income. These issues are discussed in more detail as they relate to pension provision in the contribution by John Creedy and Richard Disney (Ch. 13), and to the provision of sickness insurance in that by Richard Disney and Steven Webb (Ch. 2). In addition to the possible inability of the market to provide effective insurance, problems may be caused by unwillingness on the part of individuals to consume it. The most obvious example of such a problem would be myopia when considering pension provision. It may well be that 25-year-old individuals would not make any voluntary provision for their retirement, but that they would regret their failure to do so when they reached retirement age. In such a case, a paternalistic government might feel it necessary to institute compulsory membership of a state pension scheme.

The second set of problems outlined above related to failure to achieve a socially optimal distribution of income. If social welfare as a whole is a function of the distribution of income, and especially of poverty and inequality, the government might reasonably redistribute income through the tax and social security systems in an attempt to move towards a more desirable income distribution. In part, this may take the form of redistribution across the life cycle, as well as from rich to poor: given imperfect capital markets, individuals may not be able to shift income from relatively prosperous periods of the life cycle to relatively impoverished periods such as those of child-rearing and old age.

In principle it would be possible to classify all UK social security benefits under one or more of these reasons for state provision. What appears to be lacking is an adequate consideration of which objectives should have priority, and of whether the current mix of benefit regimes is likely to achieve these objectives most effectively.

4. Theoretical Background

The rationale for social security identified above was founded on two possible sources of market failure: individuals are, for whatever reason, unable or unwilling to insure fully against all possible contingencies, and second, the market mechanism fails, in any case, to produce the socially desirable distribution of income across households. In the first case, state intervention takes the form of providing the insurance the market fails to supply or forcing the individual to consume the insurance that he or she is unwilling to purchase voluntarily. In the second case, a form of market failure to the extent that the socially desirable income distribution is a public good, state intervention is to provide some kind of income support. The form this takes varies from income support where entitlement is tested against original income (means-tested benefits), to income support that is provided in a way that is entirely unrelated to household living standards (flat-rate benefits). Using an income test for establishing the level of entitlement to income support is essentially straightforward taxation. Income support payments could also be tested against particular contingencies that are correlated with low living standards—for example, disability, old age, unemployment. The motivation for contingent social security rather than means-tested benefits is that the former are less likely to give rise to adverse incentive effects. That is, if entitlement is related to a characteristic that is not under the recipient's control then there is no dead-weight loss in providing such contingent support. Thus, for example, income support

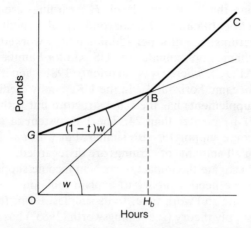

Figure 1 Stylized income support scheme

targeted on the disabled is unlikely to give rise to individuals causing self-inflicted disability.

In contrast, financial support tested against income may cause a disincentive effect to the extent that income may be under the recipient's control via his or her labour supply decision. The disincentive effect of income support may also arise in some types of contingent benefits. Thus provision for the elderly may cause individuals to save less during their working life. Similarly, income support for the unemployed may cause unemployed individuals to search less intensively for a new job and/or demand a higher-paying new job; while employed individuals may take less care over behaviour that may lead to their dismissal—poor timekeeping, for example. The same type of phenomenon may also be associated with income support contingent on sickness: compulsory sickness insurance may reduce self-insuring behaviour such as eating a healthy diet.

Thus the common problem associated with all forms of income support, whether means-tested against income or contingent on particular characteristics or eventualities, is the possibility that individuals change their behaviour to take advantage of the support on offer. The same problem is more commonly encountered in the form of work disincentives associated with high marginal income tax rates and has been the subject of considerable empirical attention. Below we consider a simplified income support system to illuminate the disincentive issue.

Figure 1 shows a simplified income support system that gives £G per individual less a proportion t of any existing earnings, wH, where w is the wage per hour and H is the number of hours worked. Thus the relationship between income and the effort required to earn it is given by the line GBC.

At hours less than the break-even level, H_b, earnings are insufficient to exhaust the benefit entitlement of G; beyond H_b, all benefit entitlement is exhausted and earnings rise at w per additional hour worked.

This simple scheme approximates the US Aid for Families with Dependent Children (AFDC), where t was .66 prior to 1981 when it was increased to 1.0 (i.e. GB became horizontal). In the UK, family credit (and the old family income supplement) has the same structure but with an additional condition that H be greater than 24. The UK system of supplementary benefit (now income support) is also similar, but with $t = 1$ and with the exception that small amounts of earnings are disregarded.

In order to investigate the impact of such an income support scheme on work incentives, we need a theory to explain individual time allocation between leisure time and work time. In its simplest form, traditional neo-classical labour supply theory (see Killingsworth (1983)) has it that individuals will be more prepared to work an additional hour the greater the wage per hour, since the higher the wage the more worth while it is to take an hour of leisure time. Similarly the theory implies that the higher is an individual's unearned income the lower will be the desire to work long hours, since the need for earned income to maintain a reasonable level of consumption is diminished.

These simple propositions are derived from a framework which assumes that individuals have an objective (or utility) function, U, that depends (positively) on income, Y, and (negatively) on hours of work, H. That is, individuals want to maximize $U(Y,H)$, where $U_Y>0$ and $U_H<0$,[1] subject to the budget constraint given by the relationship between hours and earnings as in Figure 1. The most convenient way to depict $U(Y,H)$ is by 'indifference curves', defined as combinations of Y and H that yield equal utility (or U). Thus in Figure 2, U^* is the highest level of utility that is attainable given the constraint OC since, given the assumptions, utility increases as one moves to the north-west in the figure. That is, H^* is the utility-maximizing hours given the constraint OC, since it corresponds to the point where the highest indifference curve is tangential. Notice that the optimum level of hours will depend on the position and slope of the budget constraint and on the shape of the indifference curves. Shifting OC vertically upwards (via some lump-sum transfer, say) would decrease H^*. Increasing w is more complicated since it makes an additional hour of work more worth while but it raises the amount of income earned at the existing hours and so reduces the need for long hours. Thus an increase in w could increase or decrease hours depending on the relative strength of these two forces (i.e. on the shape of the indifference curves). Thus the essence of

[1] Subscripts indicate partial differentiation. It is also conventional to assume that $U_{YY}<0$, $U_{HH}<0$ (diminishing marginal utility), and $U_{HY}<0$ (convexity).

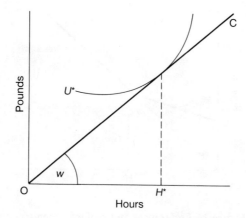

Figure 2 Preferences and the budget constraint

this theory is that labour supply decisions depend on the wage, w, and income, Y, i.e. $H = H(w,Y)$. Notice that since the utility-maximizing choice of H depends on w and Y, the *maximum* level of utility attainable depends, indirectly, on w and Y. That is, if $H = H(w,Y)$ and $U = U(H,Y)$ then the maximum value of U, V say, is given by $V = U(H(w,Y),Y) = V(w,Y)$. This maximum value function is known as the indirect utility function and it is the most convenient way of describing individual preferences for many purposes. Indeed, the indirect utility function has a particularly useful property that the labour supply function can be derived from the indirect utility function as $H(w,Y) = V_w/V_Y$; that is, as the ratio of the derivatives of V. Moreover, a knowledge of the indirect utility function allows us to identify the separate elements of the incentive issue, as we demonstrate below.

Figure 3 shows that preferences determine whether or not a particular individual with a wage w will choose to participate in the social security programme. In the absence of the income support scheme, the individual would choose to work H^0 hours which exceed the break-even point. However, with the introduction of the income support scheme, given by the section of the constraint GB in Figure 3, the utility-maximizing position becomes H^1 hours where the individual's earnings will give rise to an entitlement to income support. Notice that this entitlement only arises because the individual chooses to reduce his labour supply and hence earnings in response to the availability of income support. That is, the generosity of the income support system gives rise to an incentive problem.

The indirect utility function is particularly useful in analysing this aspect of the incentive effect of social security. The maximum utility attainable in the absence of social security is $V^0 = V(w,0)$, where w is the wage in the

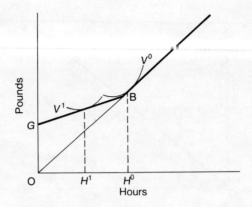

Figure 3   Preferences and welfare dependency

absence of social security, and the level of income in the absence of any earnings is zero. The maximum obtainable utility under the social security system is $V^1 = V((1-t)w,G)$, where G is the income level when earnings are zero and $(1-t)w$ is the marginal wage rate. Thus welfare dependency is chosen if $V((1-t)w,G) > V(w,0)$. Notice that since $V_Y > 0$, an increase in G increases the likelihood that this condition will be satisfied. Similarly, since $V_w > 0$, a decrease in t increases the likelihood that the condition be satisfied. Thus, in either case, an increase in the generosity of the social security system increases its attractiveness. The relationship of the size of this disincentive effect to preferences is explained in the Appendix, where it is shown that the strength of the disincentive effect depends on the curvature of the indifference curves. Inspection of Figure 3 also suggests the importance of the shape of indifference curves. Suppose the curve labelled V^0 were close to right-angled; then it would lie everywhere above the constraint GB and welfare dependency would not be chosen. A measure of the curvature of indifference curves is known as the substitution effect, S, which essentially indicates the extent to which the willingness for individuals to sacrifice additional time in return for additional income changes as the real wage changes.

In the Appendix we demonstrate that $dV = V^1 - V^0 > 0$ if the amount of benefit entitlement $B = G - twH > (wt)^2S$, where H here is the level of hours that would arise in the absence of a welfare system. That is, the straighter are the indifference curves (the bigger is S) the more likely it is that an individual with a given B will choose to go onto welfare. For example, if S were zero, indifference curves in Figure 3 would be right-angled and welfare dependency would only occur if $B > 0$ at the level of earnings and hours that would have occurred in the absence of social security. Thus the first component of the incentive issue is that the more generous the social security system (bigger G or smaller t) the more it makes sense for individuals who are not on it to reduce their earnings so as to generate an entitlement.

We abstract from problems of stigma and hassle that may be associated with means-tested benefits which could give rise to the possibility that individuals fail to take up a positive entitlement. See Moffitt (1983), Blundell, Fry, and Walker (1988), and the contribution by Vanessa Fry and Graham Stark (Ch. 10) for models that incorporate aspects of this important feature of social security. Stephen Jenkins and Jane Millar (Ch. 7) consider the theoretical case for thinking that means-tested benefits, because their complicated nature may give rise to uncertainty about entitlements among the poor, may suffer from low take-up.

The second aspect of the incentive story is that welfare recipients face high marginal tax rates that cause a disincentive to work. This fact is familiar from the literature on income taxation and labour supply (see, for example, Atkinson and Stiglitz (1980, Ch. 13)). In the contribution by Ravi Kanbur and Michael Keen (Ch. 5), this basic theory is extended to consider non-linear taxation. Since the overlap between the tax system and the welfare system makes the overall tax and benefit system non-linear, this is of considerable practical importance. The effect of the marginal tax rate on labour supply is conventionally addressed using the compensated labour supply curve, i.e. the relationship between H and w holding utility constant at some level. The most convenient vehicle for analysing compensated labour supply is the household expenditure function which is formed by 'inverting' the indirect utility function. That is, if $U = V(w,Y)$ then $Y = E(w,U)$. The interpretation of the expenditure function is the minimum income required to attain the level of utility U at the wage w. The usefulness of this function stems from its property that the compensated labour supply curve is given by $H^c(w,U) = E_w$, the wage derivative of the expenditure function, so that the slope of H^c is E_{ww} which is also the substitution effect S. The efficiency (or dead-weight) loss of a change in tax rate, dt, is the area to the left of the compensated supply curve minus the change in government revenue, as depicted in Figure 4 (which assumes for simplicity that the supply curve is linear). The efficiency loss of raising the tax rate is given by the shaded area; since $dH^c = E_{ww} \times dt$ and $S = E_{ww}$ we get, by simple geometry, that the loss is equal to $S(dt)^2/2$. Thus this second aspect of the incentive issue surrounding social security suggests that decreasing t has beneficial incentive effects.

Thus the upshot of these two elements of the incentive issue is that they counteract each other. While a decrease in t reduces the disincentive effect for existing welfare dependants, it makes welfare more attractive for those whose current income is just above the break-even point. Thus the trade-off is between a high tax rate on a small number of claimants against a

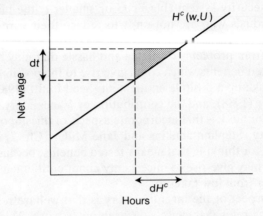

Figure 4 Efficiency, compensated labour supply, and the tax rate

lower tax rate that penetrates higher up the wage distribution. It is not clear on any a priori grounds where on this trade-off is most desirable from an efficiency point of view.

Here we have considered just the hours of work dimension of incentives. In fact, labour supply has many aspects: human capital investment in education and health, retirement and the life cycle timing of participation in general, effort and promotion, etc. It could well be that these dimensions are in practice more important than hours of work, but these aspects are under-researched because of the absence of reliable data on which to base quantitative work. The paper by Robert Moffitt and Anuradha Rangarajan (Ch. 6) is an exception since it investigates the impact of welfare dependency on the long-run incentive to acquire human capital to enhance earning ability. Further research along these lines ought to be an urgent priority since there are good grounds for believing that for many individuals, hours of work is not a choice variable and that longer-run dimensions of the supply of work are therefore correspondingly more important.

5. Empirical Evidence

There is a great deal of empirical evidence on the incentive effect of high marginal tax rates. However, the evidence is not particularly conclusive as to the precise magnitude of the effect. Nevertheless, a few regularities have emerged. First, the responsiveness of prime age males to changes in the structure in economic incentives is probably quite small. Second, the labour supply behaviour of married women is relatively responsive to both income and wage changes. From the point of view of the social security system, the greatest areas of our ignorance seem to be those of greatest policy interest. Thus while there is a great deal of evidence on married women and prime age men, there is little evidence for those groups most likely to be affected by the social welfare system. In particular, there is little evidence on single parents (Blank (1985)), relatively little on those near to retirement age (Boskin and Hurd (1978), Zabalza, Pissarides, and Barton (1980), and Burtless and Moffitt (1985)), only one paper that deals with the wives of unemployed men (that by Andrew Dilnot and Michael Kell in this volume (Ch. 8)), and but one study on the disabled (Halpern and Hausman (1986)). Many of the US studies are included in the survey by Moffitt (1987c), but there is no survey available for other countries. In general it would appear that wage effects are not usually very large for these 'minority' groups, and income effects are relatively more important. However, since it is these minority groups that are often to be found facing high marginal tax rates, even small wage elasticities can be important.

Moreover, in addition to our ignorance over the relevant behavioural elasticities, there has been little work conducted on analysing the *implications* of estimated behavioural responses for social and economic policy. More often than not, policy analysis has been conducted in terms of the effect of changes on the average individual in a sample. For example, in Burtless and Moffitt (1985) a 20 per cent cut in social security benefits for the retired reduces the productivity of early retirement for an 'average' man, but it does not tell us how many actual individuals would switch into retirement. The latter kind of policy analysis is somewhat more difficult to conduct since it requires the use of the estimated behavioural model to predict the change in behaviour for each individual in a sample. This course is a particularly difficult one to pursue since the budget constraint is likely to be highly non-linear for social security systems in practice (see Blundell, Meghir, Symons, and Walker (1989) for details of simulation methodology in such circumstances).

However, the issue of the trade-off between the beneficial incentive effects of reduced tax rates in means-tested benefits for programme participants and the detrimental effects on those attracted to become participants has been addressed by Moffitt (1986) for the reform of AFDC in the US in 1981. He concludes that increasing the tax rate (from 66 per cent to 100 per cent) reduced the hours for remaining programme participants but reduced the number of participants, and the two effects broadly balanced each other.

Earlier we argued that the income support that is contingent on some event or characteristic, such as falling sick or being disabled, also gives rise to an adverse incentive effect. There is, in fact, a considerable body of evidence that suggests that income support that is contingent on being unemployed does produce an incentive for individuals to remain unemployed for longer than they otherwise would. For example, Nickell (1979) showed that the elasticity of the duration of a spell of unemployment with respect to the ratio of unemployment benefit to income while in work is 0.6. That is, a 10 per cent increase in benefits relative to earnings increases unemployment duration by 6 per cent. However, Atkinson, Gomulka, Micklewright, and Rau (1984) suggest that this elasticity may not be significantly different from zero. Some time series evidence (Layard and Nickell (1985), for example) also suggests that the severity with which the work availability test in the benefit system is administered has some bearing on the numbers unemployed.

The question of the extent to which public provision of income support for the elderly through the state pension scheme reduces individual incentives to provide for their own old age is a difficult one to address. However, some cross-country comparisons have suggested that the problem could be a severe one (for example, Feldstein (1980) and Feldstein and Pellechio (1979)), while other evidence (e.g. Barro (1978)) suggests that the effect is negligible. The issue is clearly an important and topical one, but there is not yet much agreement on the econometric magnitudes involved. The paper by Richard Disney and Steven Webb (Ch. 2) is very much in the spirit of this literature on private versus public saving in that it attempts to test whether or not there is a trade-off between publicly provided compulsory sickness insurance and occupational schemes.

6. Conclusions

Social security plays a significant role in the economics of most developed countries, and raises important political and economic questions. Our aim in this introduction has been to outline the development and rationale of UK social security, and to introduce some of the most important economic issues. The chapters that make up the remainder of the book address many of these same questions with a wide range of approaches. Recent years have seen rapid growth in research in this area, and we now know much more than we did even ten years ago. None the less, there continues to be uncertainty about both the role and the impact of social security programmes; the scope for further research is enormous.

Appendix

Since $V^0 = V(w,0)$ and $V^1 = V((1-t)w,G)$, dV can be expressed as the following second-order Taylor series expansion:

$$dV = V_y G + V_w(-wt) + \tfrac{1}{2} V_{yy} G^2 + \tfrac{1}{2} V_{ww}(-wt)^2 \tag{1}$$
$$+ V_{wy} G(-wt),$$

where G is the loss in lump-sum income involved in moving from welfare recipiency to non-recipiency and $(-wt)$ is the reduction in the wage. Since, from Roy's Identity (see Killingsworth (1983, p. 15)), $H = V_w/V_y$ it follows that $H_w = (V_{ww} - HV_{wy})/V_y$ and $H_y = (V_{wy} - HV_{yy})/V_y$. Moreover, the Slutsky Equation says that $S = H_w - HH_y$. Thus, we have that

$$S = (V_{ww} - 2HV_{wy} + H^2 V_{yy})/V_y. \tag{2}$$

Multiplying and dividing (1) throughout by V_y, we get

$$dV = V_y [B + \tfrac{1}{2} (wt)^2 (V_{ww} - 2V_{wy}(G/wt) + V_{yy}(G/wt)^2)/V_y], \tag{3}$$

where $B = G - wtH$ is the amount of welfare payable at hours H. Since $H_b = G/wt$, we can substitute this in (3) and then substitute (2) evaluated at the break-even hours to get

$$dV = V_y[B + \tfrac{1}{2} (wt)^2 S_b]$$

where S_b is (2) evaluated at H_b.

1

Turning the Screw: Benefits for the Unemployed 1979–88

TONY ATKINSON AND JOHN MICKLEWRIGHT[*]

1. Introduction

The high level of unemployment in Britain in the 1980s has put the benefit system for the unemployed under a degree of strain not previously experienced in post-war years and not envisaged by those who drew up much of the relevant legislation. It would be natural therefore to expect that the system has been subjected to detailed scrutiny. However, this is not the case. Notably, the 1985 Green Paper on the reform of social security (DHSS (1985a))—which preceded the benefit changes introduced in April 1988—devoted very little space to the problems of coping with high unemployment and simply proposed 'to leave the present arrangements for unemployment benefit as they are' (Cmnd 9517, para. 10.2). In contrast to the inter-war depression, there has been no Royal Commission on unemployment insurance, no new machinery such as the Unemployment Assistance Board, and certainly no collapse of a government over failure to agree on a cut in benefits for the unemployed.

If there has been little public debate about the adequacy of income support for the unemployed, this does not mean that the system has remained untouched. As we show in this paper, there have in fact been many changes in the benefit system for the unemployed over the past 10 years. Some of these are well known, such as the abolition of earnings-related National Insurance benefit and the taxation of short-term benefits. Others have been given less publicity and the cumulative impact of the different changes does not seem to have been widely recognized. Although many of the measures are limited in their individual impact, the great majority have

* Tony Atkinson is a Professor at the London School of Economics. John Micklewright is a Lecturer at Queen Mary College, London.

This paper was presented at a conference on 'The Economics of Social Security', organized by the Institute for Fiscal Studies, held on 15 April 1988.

The research reported has been carried out as part of the Economic and Social Research Council Programme on Taxation, Incentives, and the Distribution of Income. The authors are grateful to Holly Sutherland for her help with the data and to Andrew Dilnot and Ian Walker for their comments on the first version.

made the system less generous and have weakened the role of unemployment *insurance* as opposed to unemployment *assistance*. The total effect of the Conservative Government's actions is such that the structure of benefits for the unemployed in 1988 is quite different from that in 1979. It is a matter of concern that little by little the system has undergone major changes of principle without any widespread public recognition. As was noted by the Social Security Advisory Committee in 1981 in its first report, 'a major shift from contributory to means-tested non-contributory benefit appears to be taking place without public debate on its implications' (para. 3.6).

Our first purpose in this paper is simply to catalogue the changes over the last 10 years and to place them in their historical context. The mere length of the list of measures affecting the benefits of the unemployed between 1979 and 1988 is in itself indicative. Our Appendix, which may not be comprehensive, itemizes 38 significant changes. In examining this catalogue, we consider first in Section 2 National Insurance unemployment benefit, and then in Section 3 the income-tested assistance provided by supplementary benefit (now income support) and housing benefit.

Our second purpose is to quantify the effect of the changes on the incomes of the unemployed. Just how much has the screw been tightened? Discussion of the effect of the benefit system frequently employs hypothetical calculations of the entitlement of people with particular family and household characteristics. These calculations cannot, however, capture the myriad of characteristics that exist in the population nor, crucially, do they reflect the fact that entitlement itself may be changed by policy. Changes in the contribution conditions or in the administration of benefit may have a substantial effect, with the result that looking only at the hypothetical levels of benefit for those who do receive may be quite misleading. Similarly, aggregate statistics on numbers in receipt in different years cannot give the full story, since it is not clear whether any changes reflect changes in the benefit system or changes in the composition of the unemployed between the two dates.

Our approach in this paper is to take a sample of actual unemployed people and to compare their incomes under the benefit system as it was in 1979 and as it is after the introduction of income support (IS) in 1988. This approach is similar in spirit to earlier studies by Dilnot and Morris (1983) and Mallender and Ramsden (1984). However, our analysis differs from these in several respects. Dilnot and Morris concentrated on the incentive for the employed to become unemployed, and most of their results related to the position of those in employment (comparing their income with that if they were to quit their jobs). In contrast, we are concerned exclusively with the position of those already unemployed. Mallender and Ramsden looked at the effects of changes between 1978 and 1982 using a sample of the male inflow into unemployment, focusing on the impact in the early months of unemployment. In our analysis we consider a sample of the stock of the unemployed, including both men and women and covering all durations of unemployment. Moreover, in contrast to both these studies, we look solely at incomes out of work and do not compare these with incomes when employed. This allows us to concentrate on the effects of changes in unemployment benefits without the analysis having to take account of changes to incomes in work.

The methods by which these calculations are carried out, using a version of the LSE tax and benefit model TAXMOD, are described in Section 4. The findings with regard to unemployment insurance and the erosion of National Insurance are given in Section 5. Section 6 shows the total effect of both National Insurance and income-tested benefits. The main conclusions are summarized in Section 7.

2. Changes in Unemployment Insurance 1979–88

The present 'two-tier' structure of benefits for the unemployed—a flat-rate insurance benefit paid subject to contribution and other conditions, supported by a second tier of income-tested assistance—is essentially the same as that introduced in the Unemployment Act of 1934. Although it is widely believed that the Beveridge Report led to major changes in unemployment benefit, his principal recommendation of an unlimited duration for insurance benefit was not accepted. Although a third, earnings-related, tier was introduced in 1966, this was one of the first casualties of the Thatcher Government. The basic structure in 1988 is therefore little different from that half a century earlier.

What have changed are the details of the schemes. The last decade has seen many changes in both insurance and income-tested benefits for unemployed workers—many more than we realized when we began to list them. What began as a relatively short appendix turns out to include 17 significant changes for National Insurance unemployment benefit (UB) alone. Some of the changes have received a lot of attention, such as the abolition of the earnings-related supplement (ERS) and the taxation of benefits. Others may be less familiar, such as the change in the linked spells rule, the abolition of reduced rates of benefit, the abatement for occupational pensions, the introduction of the equal treatment provisions required by the European Community, and the change in the contribution conditions contained in the Social Security Bill 1988.

The changes affecting National Insurance (NI) UB are listed in Table 1.1. Where possible, we indicate the direction of the effect of the measures on the net incomes of the unemployed. We highlight below those that we consider to represent major changes in emphasis.

- The abolition of ERS has meant that Britain is the only member of the European Community with no element of unemployment benefits linked to past earnings, and one of only four OECD countries in this position (the others are Australia, New Zealand, and Iceland).
- The abatement of UB for occupational pensions has introduced an element of personal means-testing into National Insurance unemployment benefit for the first time.
- The abolition of reduced rate NI benefit taken with that of ERS ends the principle of better benefit for better contributors embodied in legislation since the introduction of National Insurance benefit in 1911.
- The equal treatment provisions mean that UB now treats husbands and wives symmetrically with respect to claiming for a dependant.
- The more than fourfold increase in the maximum disqualification period from NI benefit (and reduction in supplementary benefit—SB) in the case of voluntary quitting, industrial misconduct, or refusal of a job offer, has changed a parameter of the benefit system that had been in operation for much of the century (the original 1911 Act, the two major inter-war Acts of 1920 and 1934, and the post-Beveridge 1946 Act all stipulated a 6-week figure).
- The new contribution conditions contained in the 1988 Social Security Bill mean that benefit entitlement depends on paid (rather than paid or credited) contributions in the two preceding tax years; this strikes at the system introduced by Beveridge, and returns us to a situation similar to that 50 years ago.

Considering the individual measures in Table 1.1, we see that in certain cases they have improved the position of the unemployed. The equal treatment provisions extend the range of choice open to unemployed couples. The redefinition of voluntary redundancy in 1985 was designed to make sure that workers are not regarded as having left their job voluntarily even when they volunteer or agree to be made redundant.

In other cases, the effect may have been positive or negative. An example is provided by the change in the linked spells rule, which reduced the period of linking from 13 weeks to 8 weeks. This disadvantaged a worker who lost his job again after, say, 9 weeks in that he had a further 3 waiting days before he could receive benefit, but it was an advantage in that a person could 'start a fresh run of unemployment benefit after only eight weeks back at work, instead of thirteen' (Social Security Advisory Committee, First Report, p. 9)). (It is not clear whether this was widely appreciated at the time, since the change also applied to NI sickness benefit where the intention was to reduce the number of people qualifying for invalidity benefit paid at a higher rate.) Another example is the sequence of changes in the method of payment of benefits, particularly following the Rayner Report in 1981, some of which made life easier for the unemployed

Table 1.1 Changes in National Insurance unemployment benefit, 1979–88

Measure	Indication of quantitative importance
Measures favourable to the unemployed	
Equal treatment provisions (7)	
Definition of voluntary redundancy (12)	
Measures whose effect may be positive or negative	
Basis for uprating of benefit (3)	See text.
Linked spells rule (8)	
Earnings rule (9)	
Payment of benefits (14)	Postal charges affect 195,000 claimants, saving £0.6m. (*Hansard*, 10 June 1986, col. 145).
Measures unfavourable to the unemployed	
End of earnings-related supplement (1)	Saving in 1978–9 some £95m. (see text).
Taxation of NI unemployment benefit (2)	Tax yield on benefits paid to unemployed (NI and SB) £375m. in 1986–7 (UBull, 24).
Suspension of statutory indexation (4)	See text.
Abolition of child additions (5)	In November 1984 123,000 men had child dependancy additions (*Social Security Statistics, 1987*, Table 1.40).
Abolition of lower rate benefits (6)	Estimated savings £27m. (SSAC, Fifth Report, 1986–7). 57,000 without SB affected (UBull, 19).
Abatement for occupational pensions (10)	Saving to NI Fund £65m. in 1989–90 (Social Security Bill 1988).
More stringent administration (11)	
Disqualification period (13)	Extension from 6 to 13 weeks estimated to save some £25m.–£30m. (*Hansard*, 1 March 1988, col. 849).
Students (15)	
Full extent normal rule (16)	
Contribution conditions (17)	Saving to NI Fund £380m. in 1990–1 (Social Security Bill 1988).

Notes: The numbers in parentheses refer to sections in the Appendix.
For abbreviations of sources, see beginning of Appendix.

as well as the DHSS, and some of which—such as the liability to pay postal charges—were to the disadvantage of claimants.

We have also included in this indeterminate category changes which initially had a positive effect, but which were later eroded or reversed. The change in the earnings rule, increasing the permitted earnings to £2 a day from 75p in 1982, represented a distinct improvement at the time, but the figure has not changed. So that, whereas it was then possible for an unemployed person to earn up to 53 per cent of the UB daily amount, by 1988 it had fallen to 37 per cent.[1] This is an example of a 'hidden constant' of the social security system, i.e. a parameter which is not regularly updated and which erodes benefit entitlements without people being aware. Another example is the abatement rule for occupational pensions, which was introduced at the level of £35 in 1981 and has remained fixed in money terms. (The introduction of this abatement had, of course, a negative effect which has now got worse.)

Turning to the uprating of benefits, we may note that the effect of the change in basis from 'forecast' to 'historic' depends on the path of inflation. We have, however, recorded the suspension of indexation as a negative entry in the balance sheet. Whatever the actual outcome, the suspension of inflation-proofing of UB represented a loss of certainty for the unemployed. This has been reinforced by government statements. In July 1983, the Prime Minister was asked to give a guarantee that UB would be increased in line with inflation like other NI benefits, and refused to do so. A similar position was taken by the Chancellor of the Exchequer, who in his reply referred to concern about voluntary unemployment. The new provision in the Social Security Act 1986 means that the level of benefit in real terms is now permanently at risk. Even if *ex post* the purchasing power has been maintained (see below), *ex ante* there has been uncertainty.

The movement over time in the real value of UB for a single person is shown by the solid line in Figure 1.1, where the dates plotted are those of upratings, so that these represent the *maximum* real values for the periods in question. Taking the decade as a whole, we see that NI UB increased more or less in line with the retail price index: between November 1978 and April 1987, UB for a single person rose by 99.7 per cent, compared with a rise of 98.3 per cent in the retail price index (HM Treasury (1988, p. 274)). However, the position in individual years displays some variation— the solid line in Figure 1.1 is not horizontal. In particular, there was a fall in the real value in the early years, reflecting the 5 per cent withdrawal in advance of the taxation of benefit, restored in November 1983. The dashed

---

[1] In *Hansard* (6 November 1986, col. 589) the Government gave a figure for the approximate hours of work for a person on half national average earnings represented by the earnings limit. In 1956 this was $2\frac{1}{2}$ hours; in 1965 and 1975, $1\frac{1}{2}$ hours; and in 1985, with the £2 limit, 1 hour.

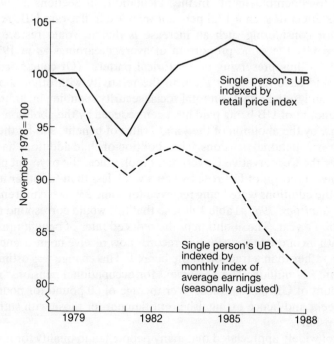

Figure 1.1   The real value of unemployment benefit, 1978–88

line in Figure 1.1 shows the movement in the same UB figure when indexed
by movements in average earnings. Viewed in this way, the level of benefit
has declined markedly, in particular in later years when real wage rises
have been large. By the end of the period, the value of single UB indexed
by earnings had fallen by a fifth.

The majority of the measures listed in Table 1.1 were quite clearly unfavourable to the unemployed. The abolition of ERS is a prominent
example. Although it was not widely lamented due to the somewhat arcane
mechanics of the scheme, the sum of money involved was substantial, and
if re-allocated to an increase in the flat-rate UB, could have allowed a significant improvement. In November 1978, 156,000 men were receiving ERS
with an average of £9.34 and there were 53,000 women with an average of
£6.49 (*Social Security Statistics, 1982*, Table 1.50). This corresponds to
expenditure at an annual rate of some £95 million, compared with total
expenditure on NI unemployment benefit in the year 1978–9 of £632
million (same source, Table 44.04). If the money had been allocated to
raising the flat-rate UB, then it appears that the latter could have been
raised by around 17.5 per cent without changing the total spent on NI

benefits for unemployment. In the calculations in Sections 5 and 6, we show the effect of such a 17.5 per cent increase in flat-rate UB. A second reason for considering such an increase is that it would restore UB to approximately the same proportion of average earnings as in 1978—see Figure 1.1—thus preserving the historical pattern. (Of course, consideration would have had to be given to the relativity with other short-term benefits, and to the effects on total social security spending including SB.)

The amount of UB being paid has been reduced by the abolition of child additions, by the abolition of the $\frac{1}{2}$ and $\frac{3}{4}$ rates of benefit, and by the abatement for occupational pensions. The abolition of child additions has meant that since the Conservative Government took office, the payment per child in families in receipt of UB rose by 85p a week less than for other families. In 1984 the additions were being received for some 230,000 children (*Social Security Statistics, 1987*, Table 1.40), so that this would correspond to some £10 million a year. The abolition of the reduced rates of benefit means that those with incomplete contribution records now receive no insurance benefit at all, rather than a fraction of the benefit. This change was estimated to save some £27 million. The abatement for occupational pensions[2] reduces the amount of UB paid to those over the age of 60 pound for pound over £35 a week, and hence extinguishes entitlement for those with sufficiently large pensions.[3]

It is not widely appreciated that many people fail to qualify for insurance benefit on account of insufficient contributions (*Social Security Statistics* gives no information on the reasons for non-receipt). In May 1986, over 800,000 of the 3 million people unemployed had insufficient contributions to receive any UB, a figure not much less than the 1.07 million who had exhausted their period of entitlement (*Hansard*, 28 November 1986, col. 405).[4] The new contribution conditions to be introduced in 1988 will substantially worsen this position. The estimated saving to the NI Fund in 1990–1 is £380 million. Those affected will include people with lengthy contribution records. A man may have been employed for 30 years and still not qualify for UB during a second spell of unemployment, since the crediting of contributions during the first spell will not now count towards the relevant condition for UB.

Entitlement may also be lost as a result of the extended disqualification

---

[2] It should be pointed out that previous governments had considered this change which was suggested by a report of the National Insurance Advisory Committee in 1968 (Cmnd 3545).

[3] The meaning of 'occupational pensions' is open to interpretation. According to Rowland (1988, p. 37), 'arrangements are widely interpreted as occupational pensions. The term has been held to include payments not actually made out of an occupational pension fund'.

[4] In Atkinson and Micklewright (1985, Ch. 4), we provide an analysis of unpublished administrative data on reasons for non-receipt of UB for unemployed men in each year 1972–9.

period, set in 1911 at 6 weeks, which has been increased to 13 weeks and then, only 18 months later, to 26 weeks. The Social Security Advisory Committee (Sixth Report, p. 14) comments on the recent extension to 26 weeks that:

disqualification from unemployment benefit for 6 months, with reduced income support entitlement, is a harsh penalty and one which should therefore be applied with care. We regret that voluntary unemployment is an area in which claimants may be assumed 'guilty' until they can prove their 'innocence' in that where the benefit officer suspects voluntary unemployment he or she may suspend payment of benefit pending a decision by the adjudication officer on disqualification.

The way in which disqualification works in practice has been described by Rowland (1988):

The issues in these cases are never as clear cut as the legislators would wish, as employers and employees usually have different views about the reasons for dismissals or resignations. Cases are investigated by the writing of letters which takes a long time and during that time benefit is suspended and any income support paid at a reduced rate. . . . Even if the decision to disqualify has been made by the date of the tribunal hearing, the tribunal are invariably unable to consider that question as the adjudication officer does not have the right set of papers at the hearing. The end result is that many people are disqualified for much longer than should be the case because they are not sufficiently articulate on paper, and then tribunals only consider their cases some months after the events have happened if the claimants can keep their enthusiasm going for long enough to make a second appeal.

Some of the changes listed in Table 1.1 affected relatively small numbers of people. For example, the announcement of the abolition of the reduced rates of UB said that the number without SB eligible for the $\frac{3}{4}$ rate was 36,000 and the number eligible for the $\frac{1}{2}$ rate was 21,000. As we emphasized in the introduction, the cumulation of such small changes may, however, have a sizeable impact. Moreover, the different measures interact. For example, the tighter contribution conditions mean that more people will have incomplete contribution records in the relevant periods and hence that the removal of the reduced rates of benefit will be more significant.

The measures that have been taken in recent years are one of the reasons why the number of UB recipients has fallen and is predicted to fall in the next few years. This is not of course the only explanation, but it is noteworthy that the Public Expenditure White Paper projections (HM Treasury (1988, Table 15.6)) show the number of recipients as falling from 755,000 in 1988–9 to 635,000 in 1990–1 on the basis of the conventional assumption of *constant* unemployment. Administrative data show that UB recipients as a *proportion* of the total benefit recipients have fallen. Again there are other factors in operation, including the changing duration mix of the unemployed. This is one reason why the calculations in Sections 5 and 6 have been undertaken, since they hold constant the composition of the population.

3. Changes in Income-Tested Benefits for the Unemployed 1979–88

Income-tested assistance to the unemployed, unlike that in many other countries, is not a separate scheme but forms part of the general programme of income support. It is intended to act as a 'safety net', and hence it is often suggested that any cuts in NI UB are simply offset by a corresponding increase in the safety net payment under SB/IS. So that for those receiving SB, the abolition of ERS may not have entailed any overall loss of net income (12.5 per cent of male ERS recipients in November 1980 were also receiving SB (*Social Security Statistics, 1985*, Table 1.32)). There are, however, important reasons why this is too optimistic a view:

1. In some cases the cuts in NI are complemented in SB/IS: for example where a person is disqualified from NI UB there is a 40 per cent voluntary unemployment deduction in SB/IS.
2. SB/IS is assessed on a family basis rather than an individual basis. Total family income may be such that the person is not eligible. Families with incomes not far above the SB/IS level will therefore lose from reductions in UB. An unemployed person may not be entitled to IS because his or her partner is in full-time work, even if total family income is below the IS level.
3. A sizeable fraction of those entitled to SB do not claim their entitlement. The official figure quoted in the Public Expenditure White Paper (HM Treasury (1987, p. 244)) is that the take-up rate for the unemployed in 1983 was 81 per cent. This means that some one in five are not receiving their entitlement, and, even though take-up measured in value terms may be higher, the safety net evidently has holes.

It is also the case that changes have been made to SB/IS over the period 1979–88—including of course the renaming—and that the majority of these have reduced the effectiveness of the safety net. These measures are summarized in Table 1.2. In addition to the two major reforms in the past decade, there have been a series of less sweeping measures, some of them specifically directed at the unemployed.

The effects of the reform of supplementary benefit in November 1980, and of the replacement of supplementary benefit by income support in April 1988, are not easily summarized, in that there were many different changes, some of which operated in different directions as far as the unemployed are concerned. The reduction, in 1980, in the number of scales for children, for instance, represented a real improvement for younger chil-

Table 1.2 Changes in supplementary benefit/
income support affecting the unemployed,
1979–88

Measures favourable to the unemployed
Long-term SB rate (19)
Equal treatment provisions (21)

*Measures whose effect may be positive or
negative*
1980 reform of SB (18)
Part-time study (27)
Introduction of IS in 1988 (30)

Measures unfavourable to the unemployed
Taxation of benefit (2)
Students (15)
More stringent administration (20)
Non-householder housing cost addition (22)
Voluntary unemployment deductions (23)
Disqualification period (24)
Board and lodgings (25)
School-leavers (26)
Heating additions (28)
Mortgage interest (29)
Social Fund (31)
16- and 17-year-olds (32)

Note: The numbers in parentheses refer to sections in
the Appendix.

dren in the new ranges. On the other hand, the introduction of an absolute
capital cut-off meant that a number of the unemployed lost their entitlement to SB. In 1988, the raising of the capital limit, accompanied by the
reintroduction of a tariff income for capital between £3,000 and £6,000, is
to the benefit of a number of potential claimants. On the other hand, the
limitation of rates assistance to 80 per cent, and the loss of water rates,
have not been compensated in all cases by the new IS scales. And the
exclusion under IS of people whose partner is in full-time work (basically
defined as 24 hours a week) reduces the opportunities open to the unemployed. (Previously, receipt of SB was reduced on account of the partner's
earnings but not precluded—see Dilnot and Kell (Ch. 8, this volume).)

The measures introduced at other dates are also mixed in their effects. The
extension of the long-term rate to unemployed men aged 60 and over provided substantial benefit to this group, estimated to number 40,000 (Social
Security Advisory Committee (SSAC), First Report, p. 27) benefiting from

the extension in 1981, coupled with the later extension of automatic entitlement to the lower rate heating addition. But the majority of the measures are unfavourable to the unemployed. For example, under SB, there has been the raising of the age for the non-householder housing cost addition, the measures taken to limit board and lodging payments, and the fact that, for owner-occupiers aged under 60, only 50 per cent of mortgage interest is taken into the calculation for the first 16 weeks on benefit, a change introduced in January 1987 and retained in the income support scheme. In addition, there were a number of measures parallel to those described for NI benefit; these include the taxation of SB with effect from 1982, and the lengthening of the disqualification period. The latter has been just one of a number of measures that represent a continuing attempt to administer the receipt of both benefits more stringently. In this, the Government's response to high unemployment has been similar in nature to the inter-war period. The 1988 White Paper, *Training for Employment* (Department of Employment (1988)), highlights the Government's view that 'significant numbers of benefit claimants are not genuinely available for work' and this is labelled as one of the 'three major problems' to be faced if unemployment is to be reduced (p. 4). Availability testing has concentrated on closer scrutiny of the initial claim, which now involves an additional questionnaire on availability,[5] and use of the Restart scheme. From April 1988 all unemployed people are called to Restart interviews every 6 months.

Like supplementary benefit, housing benefit has been through two major sets of changes—the new scheme legislated in the Social Security and Housing Benefits Act 1982 and introduced in November 1982 and April 1983, and the reforms made in the Social Security Act 1986 which came into effect in April 1988 along with the introduction of income support. In addition there have been a series of cuts in housing benefit via increases in the tapers and non-dependant deductions, which have not been fully offset by changes in the opposite direction, such as the increase in the real value of the child's needs allowance. These changes have to be seen against a background of substantially faster increases in levels of rents and rates than in the retail price index.

In describing the changes in this section, we have not considered the payments made by such 'special employment measures' as the Youth Training Scheme or the Community Programme. It is certainly the case that large numbers of people without work are dependent on the income that these

---

[5] The problems that claimants may face are described by Rowland (1988, p. ix): 'those least articulate are at a disadvantage, and administrators do not seem to realise that the completion of forms does not always give a realistic picture of events. Thus parents may well not have made detailed arrangements for the care of their children in the event of their obtaining employment, but they may also know that in the short term arrangements can be made informally through family and friends and longer-term arrangements can be sorted out then. The lack of precision does not appeal to administrators.'

Table 1.3 Changes in housing benefit
affecting the unemployed, 1979–88

Introduction of new HB in 1982 (33)
Changes in tapers (34)
Non-dependant deductions (35)
Changes in needs allowances (36)
Minimum payments (37)
Social Security Act 1986 (38)

Note: The numbers in parentheses refer to
sections in the Appendix.

schemes provide and that the increase in the coverage of these schemes has been a prominent feature of the labour market in the 1980s. However, as we describe in the next section, we exclude persons on these schemes from the definition of unemployment.

Finally, we have concentrated on the position of the unemployed, but a number of the measures discussed above have of course major implications for other groups in the population.

4. Modelling the Effects on the Unemployed

In the rest of this paper we are concerned with modelling the effects of the policy changes between 1979 and 1988 described above on the incomes of families containing an unemployed person. For this purpose we use the TAXMOD model constructed at LSE (for further details see Atkinson and Sutherland (1988)). The data we use are a sample of actual families drawn from the 1982 UK Family Expenditure Survey (FES). We take those families interviewed in the 1982–3 tax year before the November benefit uprating.

An important preliminary is to make clear our definition of 'unemployed'. The definition adopted here is intended to approximate, as far as possible, the International Labour Organization (ILO)/OECD definition, which requires that people are:

- without a paid job;
- available to start work in the next 2 weeks;
- have either looked for work at some time in the past 4 weeks or are waiting to take up a job.

In terms of FES definitions, this can be approached most closely by taking those who are 'out of employment but seeking or about to start work' excluding those who are receiving a TOPS or YOPS (in 1982) allowance.

This excludes a number of those (in 1982) in receipt of NI unemployment benefit, and it is well known that the ILO/OECD definition leads to a different classification from the Department of Employment's claimant count (see, for example, the *Employment Gazette*, January 1988, p. 30).

Our concern is with the effect of the changes on the net incomes of the unemployed families measured at one date. Our calculations are therefore for the current position, not for income over the course of a year (for discussion of this aspect, see Nolan (1987)). The focus on *family* incomes means that we may be including in the 'unemployed families' those where the husband is unemployed but the wife has high earnings (or vice versa), so that the family as a unit is in one of the top income ranges (evidence about this is also provided by Nolan (1987)). We should also note that there are a sizeable number with no recorded income at all in the current period.

Calculations are made first of the net incomes arising from the benefit system in October 1988 (taken as representing the tax year 1988–9);[6] we then put history into reverse and ask how the incomes of the unemployed families would be changed if we were to introduce in 1988–9 the measures that were in force in 1978–9. The aim of this comparison is to show the effect, for a constant population, of the policy changes over the decade.

There are a number of aspects of this exercise that need to be emphasized. First, the data that we use are drawn from neither of the two tax years we focus on: 1978–9 or 1988–9. However, we update the characteristics of the 1982 sample of unemployed families that influence benefit entitlement. Thus, housing costs, wages, and other income are updated by appropriate retail price sub-indices and indices of earnings, pensions, etc. Second, when modelling the 1978–9 benefit system we hold fixed the characteristics of the unemployed sample of families as predicted for 1988–9; the only variables being changed are the policy parameters. We are not investigating what would happen if we returned to 1978–9 levels of unemployment. Third, we should stress that we are not attempting to predict any changes in behaviour that would be induced by the policy changes (this applies equally to our calculations for 1988–9 and 1978–9). Fourth, the calculations at both dates clearly depend on a number of assumptions about benefit receipt, an aspect of the analysis on which we now elaborate.

Our strategy is to take as much account as is feasible of the information on benefit receipt recorded in the 1982 FES data. For example, if an unemployed person is not recorded as receiving National Insurance UB in 1982, then we do not assume receipt in 1988, unless there is reason to believe that there would be eligibility as the result of the policy changes (an example

[6] The version of TAXMOD used is 6.2. This does not include the increase in the capital cut-off for housing benefit to £8,000 announced subsequent to the introduction of the April 1988 scheme.

Table 1.4 Calculated distribution of net income in 1988: unemployed and whole population

Range of net income (upper limit in £ per week)	Unemployed		Whole population	
	%	Cumulative %	%	Cumulative %
25	14.1	14.1	2.7	2.7
40	29.4	43.5	4.8	7.5
55	9.5	52.9	6.8	14.3
70	7.2	60.2	8.7	23.0
85	4.9	65.0	7.3	30.4
100	5.8	70.8	7.6	38.0
115	5.0	75.8	6.4	44.4
130	3.8	79.6	6.0	50.4
145	3.6	83.1	5.4	55.8
160	2.3	85.5	5.0	60.8
175	1.6	87.1	4.1	64.9
190	2.9	90.1	4.5	69.4
205	2.0	92.1	3.8	73.2
220	2.1	94.1	3.6	76.8
235	1.5	95.6	3.2	80.0
250	0.6	96.2	2.8	82.8
–	3.8	100.0	17.2	100.0

would be the equal treatment provisions, although these are not covered by the model). But if reduced rate UB is identified as being received in 1982, then we do not allow receipt in 1988, this being one of the changes that has occurred. Our assumptions about take-up of means-tested benefits use information recorded on receipt in 1982, together with a random element, but of course we are hampered where there was no eligibility at that date. We assume the take-up rates for the new benefits to be the same as for SB in the case of IS and the same as family income supplement in the case of family credit.

The TAXMOD model uses a system of grossing-up factors to produce an estimate of the population from the FES sample data (the sample has 538 tax units containing an unemployed person). The results of the calculations with the 1988–9 system are shown in Tables 1.4 and 1.5 in two different ways. In Table 1.4 we show in the second column the distribution of unemployed families by range of total net income (i.e. income including all benefits, including housing benefit, minus income tax and NI contribution); and for comparison the distribution of all families is given alongside. This makes no adjustment for differences in family size; it also takes no account of housing costs. In Table 1.5 we show the distribution of net resources, defined as net income minus housing costs, the latter including

Table 1.5 Calculated distribution of equivalent net resources in 1988: unemployed and whole population

Range of equivalent net income (upper limit as percentage of scale)	Unemployed		Whole population	
	%	Cumulative %	%	Cumulative %
80	21.2	21.2	4.3	4.3
90	13.6	34.7	2.4	6.8
100	5.7	40.4	1.3	8.1
110	26.1	66.4	4.1	12.2
120	5.6	72.0	2.5	14.7
130	3.4	75.4	3.3	18.0
140	2.4	77.8	6.5	24.5
160	2.7	80.5	5.8	30.3
180	1.3	81.8	4.3	34.6
200	1.6	83.4	4.1	38.7
240	4.3	87.7	8.6	47.3
–	12.3	100.0	52.7	100.0

Note: The scale is based on net resources of £31.70 per week for a single person and £50.72 for a couple, plus £12.68 per child.

water rates. Net resources are then expressed relative to a scale obtained by taking £31.70 a week for a single person (the SB scale rate for 1987–8 uprated by 4.2 per cent) and using the following equivalence scale:

couple	1.6
+ per child	0.4

(these being based broadly on the SB equivalences).

These calculations of the position in 1988–9 provide a base against which we can compare the effects of a return to the 1978–9 policy parameters. It is clear that the net incomes of the unemployed are typically much lower. The median net income is some £50 a week, compared with a figure of £130 a week for the whole population (which includes the unemployed). Put another way, half the unemployed families have net income of less than £50 per week, compared with only one in eight in the population as a whole. The proportions below £40 show an even more marked comparison, being 43.5 per cent for the unemployed and 7.5 per cent in the whole population. However, the table does show that a significant number of unemployed families have much higher incomes, where for example there is one partner in work or substantial income from another source. This illustrates the variety of circumstances faced by the unemployed. For example, nearly one in ten tax units have incomes above £200 per week although the figure for the population as a whole is, not surprisingly, much higher (a quarter).

Turning to the calculations of resources relative to the equivalence scale described above, we see from Table 1.5 that a third of the unemployed families are at only 90 per cent of the scale or less, compared with only 7 per cent in the population as a whole. Two-thirds are below 110 per cent of the scale (many of those close to the scale are likely to be receiving IS). The comparison further up the distribution is now more marked: only two in ten unemployed families have net resources greater than 160 per cent of the scale, compared with seven in ten in the whole population.

5. The Erosion of National Insurance Benefit

In this section we concentrate on the effects of the changes that have taken place in National Insurance benefit. What would be the incomes of the unemployed in 1988–9 if National Insurance benefit were paid under the rules prevailing in 1978–9 (with benefits uprated by the rise in the retail price index) but assuming the *current* system of means-tested benefits, i.e. income support/post-April 1988 housing benefit? We should stress at the outset that we do not provide a full answer to this question. Several of the changes described in Table 1.1 are very difficult to model adequately, such as the treatment of voluntary redundancy. Notably, we have not attempted to re-create the workings of the now defunct earnings-related supplement (this being a much harder exercise than several observers have appreciated; see Micklewright (1985)). Instead, we have increased the real value of flat-rate benefit payable in 1978–9 by a uniform 17.5 per cent. This is the amount we identified in Section 2 as being possible if the total ERS being paid at the time had been redistributed to all unemployed NI benefit recipients and would restore the level of flat-rate UB in relation to average earnings. Finally, we have not included measures due to take effect after October 1988, including the lowering of the age for the occupational pension abatement and the tightening of the contribution conditions which will have a major impact.

The measures covered by our calculations (together with their reference number in Table 1.1) are: the taxation of benefit (2),[7] the abolition of child additions (5), the abolition of lower rate benefits (6), the abatement for occupational pensions (10), and the lengthening of the disqualification period (13). While we account for neither of the two measures in Table 1.1 which we labelled as being definitely favourable to the unemployed, we also exclude a number of changes that have been unfavourable, and as a result we do not think that we have overstated the comparison.

We calculate the gross cost of reversing these changes in NI benefit to be

---

[7] Although we do not take account of the effect on weekly incomes of tax refunds that might be payable during unemployment.

Table 1.6 Effect on unemployed of returning UB system from 1988 to 1979

Range of net income in 1988 (upper limit)	Average gain (£ per week)	Percentage of gainers
25	3.86	13.2
40	1.72	30.5
55	0.84	12.4
70	2.23	22.4
85	1.84	18.1
100	2.83	17.1
115	3.82	17.8
130	0.80	13.5
145	2.09	11.2
–	2.90	28.8
Average	2.33	22.1

Range of equivalent net resources (upper limit as percentage of scale)	Average gain (£ per week)	Percentage of gainers
80	3.48	20.2
90	0.44	3.9
100	1.08	13.9
110	1.96	30.2
120	2.30	14.9
130	1.03	17.2
140	0.89	15.4
150	3.21	39.9
160	2.75	25.7
–	3.58	31.5
Average	2.33	22.1

£417 million. This cost refers to the unemployed sample studied here. As noted earlier, some NI recipients are not covered, so that the total cost is higher. However, increases in NI benefit lead to some saving in means-tested benefits. There is also the loss of income tax revenue. Taking these into account, the net cost is £370 million for the unemployed sample studied here. (The net cost of the measures apart from the 17.5 per cent rise is £160 million.) No net gain in income (or, in 0.2 per cent of cases, a loss)[8] is experienced by 78 per cent of unemployed families, this occurring where there is no NI benefit entitlement or where the increases in NI benefit are insufficient to

[8] A loss may arise where entitlement to SB ceases and, as a result, passported benefits are lost.

Table 1.7 Effect on unemployed of returning UB system from 1988 to 1979: breakdown of average gain by family and household characteristics

	Average gain (£ per week)		
Head of household	2.57	1.98	Non-head of household
Owner	3.53	1.77	Tenant
Married	3.19	1.76	Single
Children	2.02	2.43	No children
Wife works	6.22	1.97	Wife does not work

extinguish the receipt of IS. A gain of up to £6 per week accrues to 14 per cent of the unemployed, while 8 per cent gain more than this figure. Table 1.6 shows the average gain (taking zeros and losses into account) and the percentage of families which gain in the range analysed in Tables 1.4 and 1.5 (we have combined the higher ranges), where the results are shown separately for net income and equivalent net resources. Looking at net income, we see that the second greatest proportion of gainers is to be found in the highest income range, but that the largest average gain is experienced by families in the lowest range. One of the smallest average gains and lowest percentage of gaining families is in the range £40–£55 which contains the median. The impression of the greatest gains being at both ends of the distribution is reinforced by the results for equivalent net resources.[9]

Table 1.7 analyses the average gain in a different way, distinguishing between different family and household characteristics. It shows that in terms of net income, a return to the 1978–9 NI benefit system would benefit householders more than non-householders, owners more than tenants, couples more than single persons, and those with no children more than those with some (it should be remembered that there is no adjustment for family size in these calculations). The average gain for those units with a working wife is particularly notable.

Our concern in this paper is with the effect of policy changes on the levels of income of the unemployed. We should, however, note one—no doubt unintended—consequence of the shift away from insurance benefits since 1979, which is the rise in the marginal tax rate faced by working wives whose husbands are unemployed. The independent basis inherent in NI UB does not lead to the family being penalized if the wife earns more (unless the dependant's addition is thereby lost), whereas the family assessment under SB means that she faces a high tax rate. Moreover, the marginal tax rate was raised when NI UB became taxable, since this reduced

[9] If we had modelled the entitlement to ERS as such, the gains at the upper end would probably have been greater.

the allowances which could be set against the earnings of bread-winner wives. Our calculations show that 8 per cent of wives in paid work would have faced a lower marginal tax rate if the 1978-9 NI system had been in force, and that the average marginal tax rate would have been 2 percentage points lower. This may well have affected work decisions—which we assume here to be unchanged (see Dilnot and Kell (Ch. 8, this volume) for discussion of male unemployment and women's work).

6. The Total Effect

The erosion of insurance benefit has been accompanied by changes in the income-tested benefits which also affected the incomes of the unemployed. In this section we show the additional effects of the changes that have taken place in SB/IS and housing benefit. As before, we cannot model all of the changes that have taken place. Those included (with their reference numbers in Tables 1.2 and 1.3) are: taxation of SB (2), 1980 reform (18), long-term SB rate (19), non-householder housing cost addition (22), voluntary unemployment deductions (23), disqualification period (24), heating additions (28), mortgage interest (29), income support (30), 1982 housing benefit (33), tapers (35), needs allowances (36), minima (37), and 1988 measures (38). In a number of cases, these relate to only a small number of cases in the sample, and this should be borne in mind when considering the results.

There are certain people who would be worse off with the 1978–9 system. This applies, for example, to unemployed men aged 60 and over who bene-fited from the long-term scale. It applies to families with children in the younger part of the post-1980 age ranges who enjoyed a real increase as a result of that reform. Both of these measures mean that the SB paid would have been lower. On the other hand, the payment of rates and mortgage interest in full, the payment of water rates, the restoration of the housing costs addition for non-householders aged under 25, and the return to the 1979 treatment of capital income, would all have increased the SB in pay-ment. Netting out the amount transferred from certificated housing benefit, SB payments are estimated in the model to be some £100 million higher for the families covered. The total effect is that the unemployed covered in our analysis would have received £465 million more than under the present policy, or an average of £2.92 a week.

It should be noted that a return to the 1978–9 SB system could have implications for many groups besides the unemployed, and that the overall cost would be very much larger.

The effect of the total package on families in different ranges of net income is given in Table 1.8. This shows that those losing from a return to the system of 1978–9 (as modelled here) are a minority—about one in five. The majority would have gained. One in twelve would have gained more

Table 1.8 Effect on unemployed of returning UB and SB/IS from 1988 to 1979

Range of net income in 1988 (£ per week)	Percentage of families in range	Average gain (£ per week)	Percentage of gainers	Percentage of losers
25	14.1	5.01	55.6	5.7
40	29.4	2.54	77.9	19.6
55	9.5	4.15	77.6	12.9
70	7.2	2.89	71.0	14.1
85	4.9	2.47	60.6	30.5
100	5.8	2.19	40.8	51.6
115	5.0	2.85	28.4	49.4
130	3.8	−1.45	17.9	74.8
145	3.6	1.33	32.9	27.9
–	16.9	2.87	31.0	3.2
Average		2.92	57.0	20.1

Range of equivalent net resources (upper limit as percentage of scale)	Percentage of families in range	Average gain (£ per week)	Percentage of gainers	Percentage of losers
80	21.2	6.54	63.1	6.2
90	13.6	3.71	100.0	0.0
100	5.7	3.01	76.8	10.5
110	26.1	0.83	55.2	44.2
120	5.6	2.26	46.5	47.9
130	3.4	−2.21	25.2	61.2
140	2.4	−8.34	21.5	78.5
150	0.5	5.31	64.9	0.0
160	2.2	2.75	25.7	0.0
–	19.5	3.65	33.5	0.0
Average		2.92	57.0	20.1

than £10 a week—see Table 1.9. The percentage of gainers is above average in the lower ranges of net income (below £85 a week) and there are fewer losers in the ranges of equivalent resources below 110 per cent of the scale. It is not surprising that there are no losers among families with equivalent resources in excess of 140 per cent of the scale, since they are not affected by the changes in income-tested benefits. There is also a smaller percentage of gainers (a third) in the top group.

Table 1.9 Extent of gains and losses in returning UB and SB/IS from 1988 to 1979

Limit of range (£ per week)	Percentage of families
Losses	
> 10.00	1.7
4.00–10.00	10.4
< 4.00	8.0
No change	22.9
Gains	
< 4.00	27.4
4.00–10.00	21.1
> 10.00	8.5

It should be re-emphasized that the coverage of these calculations is incomplete and subject to qualifications. We have covered only 20 out of the 38 measures listed in the Appendix which are in force in 1988. We have not, for example, taken account of the Social Fund and the fact that in 1986 2 million exceptional needs payments were made to the unemployed with an average rate of £82 (*Social Security Statistics, 1987*, p. 216). We do not allow for the changes affecting the benefit entitlement of 16- and 17-year-olds currently being debated, or those to be introduced in October 1988 or later, such as the change in contribution conditions. Moreover, there are features which are not modelled or only approximated. These include the effect of exceptional circumstances additions, which are not included in the 1978–9 SB calculations and hence understate the gain from a return to this system: the average value of these additions per unemployed person in 1978 indexed to 1988 is £0.37 (*Social Security Statistics, 1978*, Tables 34.43 and 1.32). They include the problem of take-up, where the model needs to be refined. None the less, we feel that the calculations provide a useful guide to the orders of magnitude involved in the changes covered.

7. Conclusions

The Green Paper on the reform of social security which preceded the April 1988 benefit changes was presented by the Government as 'the most extensive reform of social security since Beveridge'. In the case of the unemployed, however, the Green Paper paid scant attention to the financial problems of coping with unemployment, problems that concerned Beveridge throughout much of his professional life. Notwithstanding, the Government has felt able to borrow from Beveridge to provide justification for some of its policies towards the unemployed. His proposal that benefit after a certain duration of unemployment should be made conditional on attendance at a work or training centre has seen considerable airing in relation to the denial of income support to 16- and 17-year-olds. In its recent White Paper, *Training for Employment* (Department of Employment (1988)), the Government quoted Beveridge's support for the 'enforcement of the citizen's obligation to seek and accept all reasonable opportunities of work'.

In praying Beveridge in aid of their policies, the Government must have hoped that readers would not go back to the original source, since this makes clear that Beveridge envisaged a quite different system of benefits for the unemployed from that we see today. The paragraph concerned (§130) refers explicitly to insurance benefits being made adequate for subsistence *without other means*; and indeed the paragraph opens with the trenchant statement that: 'To reduce the income of an unemployed or disabled person, either directly or *by application of a means test*, because the unemployment or disability has lasted for a certain period, is wrong in principle' (Beveridge (1942, p. 57, our italics)). The post-war National Insurance benefit for the unemployed has never incorporated this recommendation, and there has always been a substantial proportion of the unemployed who have exhausted their entitlement to insurance benefit or who have been debarred by the contribution conditions. None the less, the period prior to 1979 did represent a time when there was a presumption in favour of a contributory system paying benefit as of right. Since 1979, however, there has been a major shift away from insurance benefit towards reliance on income-tested assistance for the unemployed. Without public debate, there has been a shift in principle underlying income support for the unemployed. The role of insurance benefits has been eroded by the tightening of the contribution conditions, the extension of the disqualification period, the restriction of benefits to students, the abolition of the lower rate benefits, and the abatement for occupational pensions; their value has been reduced by the taxation of benefits; and the abandonment of statutory indexation has made the position of recipients insecure. As we have seen, these measures add up to a substantial reduction in the amount of National Insurance benefit paid to the unemployed. At the same time, the generosity of income-tested assistance has been reduced in a number of respects, and the overall loss to the unemployed covered in our analysis for 1988—from just the measures included in the modelling—is nearly £500 million or some 7 per cent of the predicted total benefit expenditure for the unemployed (HM Treasury (1988, Table 15.8)).

We have not considered the reasons why these changes have been made,[10] but it is clear that most have stemmed from the Government's belief that the benefit system it inherited in 1979 constituted a major disincentive to work and that the generosity of benefit needed to be reduced (e.g. Department of Employment (1985)). In our view, this belief is misguided and is not supported by the evidence, which does not in general indicate a large and significant disincentive to return to work, as we and others have argued elsewhere (e.g. Atkinson, Gomulka, Micklewright, and Rau (1984), Narendranathan, Nickell, and Stern (1985), and Micklewright (1986)). And the disincentive most likely to be serious is that concerning the labour supply of the wives of unemployed men, and here we have seen that recent policy has worsened rather than improved the position.

There has been a major change in emphasis, amounting to the covert abandonment of the insurance principle as far as the unemployed are concerned. However, it is not our intention to fight the corner of particular pieces of earlier legislation. Rather, we are concerned that the change in policy towards income support for the unemployed appears to have taken place without any serious discussion of the relative merits of social insurance and the income-tested alternative. Social insurance is clearly different in that there is no significant problem of non-take-up, so that the benefit is effective in reaching those for whom it is intended. Social insurance is based largely on individual entitlements, rather than a family means test, and hence is in line with the trend towards independence in the field of personal taxation. The contribution conditions for social insurance provide an incentive for labour force participation and for people to take 'regular' as opposed to 'marginal' employment (Atkinson and Micklewright (1988)).

Appendix: A Catalogue of Changes in Benefits for the Unemployed 1979–88

This Appendix describes the changes affecting the unemployed which took place between 1979 and 1988 in National Insurance unemployment benefit, referred to as UB, in income support (IS), which was previously supplementary benefit (SB), and in housing benefit (HB). Only a brief account is given of the individual measures; we do not, for example, give a blow-by-blow account of the controversy surrounding SB payments for board and lodging. It should be emphasized that the coverage is not intended to be exhaustive. We do not include measures affecting job training schemes, but it should be noted that the payments made under such schemes may be basically similar (indeed, when the new Job Training Scheme supplement

---

[10] The political economy of unemployment insurance is discussed in Atkinson (1988).

was introduced, it was technically SB and participants continued to be entitled to passported benefits).

The order of the measures is broadly chronological.

The references for each change include the following abbreviations: NWB (*National Welfare Benefits Handbook* published by the Child Poverty Action Group (CPAG)), SSAC (Social Security Advisory Committee), SSN (*Social Security Notes* published by the Department of Health and Social Security), UBull (*Unemployment Bulletin* published by the Unemployment Unit), and WRB (*Welfare Rights Bulletin* published by CPAG).

National Insurance (NI)

(1) Abolition of Earnings-Related Supplement (ERS)   The Social Security (No. 2) Act 1980 abolished ERS. The 15 per cent rate of ERS was reduced to 10 per cent in January 1981, and from January 1982 no new claims could be made for ERS. As a result, no ERS was payable after June 1982.

(2) Taxation of UB and SB   The income tax treatment of the unemployed has been changed in two respects: tax refunds are not paid till after the resumption of work, or the end of the tax year if that is sooner, and UB and SB have become taxable. The first was implemented with effect from April 1982. The taxation of benefits was announced in the 1980 Budget as coming into effect at this date, but it was deferred to July 1982, partly on account of Civil Service industrial action. The provisions are included in Section 27 of the Finance Act 1981 and the details are given in Income Tax (Employments) No. 13 Regulations 1982. On the termination of the benefit claim, or the end of the tax year if that comes sooner, the claimant's tax position is calculated, taking account of the benefit received, and any net refund due is made. Where there is a net liability, this would normally be collected by an adjustment of the PAYE code. The taxable benefits are the UB for the claimant plus the addition for one adult dependant, and any SB (for the claimant and adult dependant) paid in lieu of UB. Additions for children are not taxable. In the case of a bread-winner wife, the tax office will only transfer the balance of the married man's allowance after subtracting UB at the standard rate for the rest of the tax year (WRB, 49, August 1982).

(3) Basis for Uprating of Benefit   The uprating of short-term NI benefits has been modified in two important respects. The first concerns the calculation of the inflation rate. The Social Security Act 1975 required the Secretary of State to forecast the inflation rate, a forecast which naturally was

not always accurate. As a result, in November 1981, there was a claw-back
of a 1 per cent overestimate of the inflation rate for the previous period; a 2
per cent underestimate was made good in November 1982. In the March
1983 Budget it was announced that there would be a reversion to a historic
basis, with the uprating announced in June on the basis of inflation up to
the end of May. The 1985 Social Security Act gave provision for a move to
an April uprating from 1987, with a transitional uprating in July 1986.

(4) Suspension of Statutory Indexation   The second change to uprating
concerned the extent to which NI short-term benefits would in fact be
inflation-proofed. The Social Security (No. 2) Act 1980 suspended for 3
years the duty of the Secretary of State to index-link short-term NI benefits, giving power to increase them by up to 5 percentage points less than
the rate of inflation. In 1980 there was indeed a 5 per cent withholding of
UB pending taxation of UB, which was restored in November 1983. The
Social Security Act 1986 provides for the Secretary of State to vary the
amount of any increase 'if he considers it appropriate, having regard to the
national economic situation and any other matters which he considers relevant' (Matthewman and Calvert (1987, p. 103)).

(5) Abolition of Child Additions   In November 1980 there was a change in
the method of calculating the inflation adjustment for the child's addition;
and this addition was abolished from 26 November 1984, except for claimants over pensionable age.

(6) Abolition of Lower Rate Benefits   In January 1986 it was announced
that the $\frac{3}{4}$ and $\frac{1}{2}$ rates of NI benefit for those not meeting the full contribution conditions were to be abolished and this was implemented under the
Social Security Act 1986 from October 1986.

(7) Equal Treatment Provisions   In accordance with a 1978 European
Community directive, in November 1983 regulations were introduced to
ensure 'equal treatment' of men and women. These allow married women
to claim NI dependency additions. The payment of an addition for a
dependent husband is conditional on the husband earning less than the
amount of the addition.

(8) Linked Spells Rule   From September 1980, the linked spells period
was reduced from 13 weeks to 8 weeks if there was unexhausted entitlement to National Insurance benefit (Social Security (No. 2) Act 1980). If
entitlement had been exhausted then the period remained at 13 weeks. The
significance of the linking is that a person does not have to wait a further 3

waiting days, but the total period of receipt in the linked spells is limited to 52 weeks (SSAC, First Report, p. 9).

(9) Earnings Rule   From March 1982 the regulations were amended to increase from 75p to £2 the amount that an unemployed person could earn per day without losing UB provided that he/she is still available for full-time work on that day (WRB, 47, April 1982). This remains at £2 in 1988. The rules were also eased to allow certain types of voluntary work.

(10) Abatement for Occupational Pensions   From April 1981, a person over the age of 60 and receiving an occupational pension of more than £35 has UB (including increases for dependants) reduced by 10p for every 10p above this level (Social Security (No. 2) Act 1980). The occupational pension abatement is the same in 1988, but the Social Security Bill 1988 reduces the age from 60 to 55 (to be introduced in January 1989).

(11) More Stringent Administration   The operations of Unemployment Review Officers (UROs), responsible for finding out what the claimant is doing to get a job, traditionally based on the supplementary benefit side, were extended to cover those receiving NI unemployment benefit supplemented by SB in 1980. From October 1982, registration for work at a Job Centre became voluntary for unemployed people aged 18 and over. At the same time, unemployment benefit offices took over from Job Centres the task of testing 'availability for work'. In August 1983 the Department of Employment set up Regional Benefit Investigation Teams. In 1984 the DHSS ordered a major drive in 59 areas into social security abuse: UROs questioned 18- to 25-year-olds about why they left jobs; Social Security Policy Inspectorate interviewed young people not joining a YTS scheme. The Restart scheme was introduced nationally in July 1986 with a benefit-monitoring function (UBull, 21). A more stringent availability-to-work test was introduced in October 1986 involving a new questionnaire for new claimants (UBull, 22). A revised questionnaire for new claimants and a new questionnaire for claimants called to Restart interviews were introduced from April 1988 (*Employment Gazette*, January 1988, p. 3). All unemployed people were to be invited to Restart interviews every 6 months for the duration of their claim and all new claims were to be handled by more senior staff than before (White Paper, *Training for Employment*, pp. 38–9).

(12) Definition of Voluntary Redundancy   The Social Security Act 1985 amended the disqualification provisions to ensure that they are not applied to those who volunteer or agree to be made redundant within the meaning of the Employment Protection (Consolidation) Act 1978. Such workers

were no longer subject to disqualification from NI benefit from July 1985 (SSN, 15, October 1985).

(13) Disqualification Period   The Social Security Act 1986 extended the maximum period of benefit disqualification from 6 to 13 weeks, with effect from October 1986 (SSN, 17, July 1986). This applies where there is quitting without just cause, or loss of job through industrial misconduct, or refusal to take suitable work or training offers (the voluntary unemployment deduction). The extension was made 'in view of concern at the number of people leaving their job voluntarily' (HM Treasury (1987, vol. II, p. 246)). The Act gave the Secretary of State the power to alter this period and from 11 April 1988, there was a further increase to 26 weeks. The Act also allows the Secretary to make regulations which will provide that days of disqualification count towards the entitlement to a total of 312 days of benefit (SSN, 17, July 1986). As is noted by the SSAC (Fifth Report, p. 36), this would mean for the UB claimant 'a longer maximum period of disqualification during which no benefit is paid, followed by a shortened entitlement to UB'.

(14) Payment of Benefits   In September 1979 the Social Security (Claims and Payments) Amendment Regulations became effective: UB to be paid fortnightly, except for those on short-time working or who chose to be paid weekly. The Rayner Report on payment of benefits to unemployed people was published in March 1981. In June 1984 it was announced that all new claimants would be paid fortnightly in arrears instead of one week in advance/one week in arrears (*Hansard*, 18 June 1984, col. 20). In April 1986 postal claimants of UB became liable to pay their own postal charges. In April 1987 new rules were introduced governing overpayments. Whereas previously benefit could only be recovered if the claimant failed to use 'due care and diligence', now it may be recovered if payment is due to any misrepresentation or failure to disclose a material fact, even where this was entirely innocent (e.g. where the fact was unknown to the claimant).

(15) Students   From September 1986 regulations were made to remove entitlement by full-time students to UB and SB during the 'grant-aided period', effectively removing entitlement for most students in the short vacations (SSN, 18, October 1986; WRB, 70, February 1986).

(16) Full Extent Normal Rule   This rule prevents those who do not normally work on every working day in the week from claiming UB on their 'off' days. This has caused particular difficulties with part-time Community Programme (CP) workers. Following a decision by a tribunal of Social

Security Commissioners that such persons were not precluded from claiming UB, regulations were introduced with effect from March 1987 preventing such people from claiming UB for days on which they are not employed on a CP scheme (WRB, 79, August 1987).

(17) Contribution Conditions The Social Security Bill 1988 tightens the contribution conditions for NI benefit, with the change planned to take effect from October 1988. The entitlement will depend on the contribution record for the *two* tax years before the start of the benefit year, as opposed to the present one tax year. Class 1 contributions on earnings of at least fifty times the lower weekly earnings limit must have been paid or credited in both tax years; and, for unemployment benefit, Class 1 contributions must have been paid (i.e. *not* credited) on earnings of at least twenty-five times the weekly lower earnings limit in one of the two tax years (as opposed to *any* tax year). Moreover, the rule permitting the aggregation of contributions paid in more than one tax year in order to satisfy the second condition is abolished.

Income Support/Supplementary Benefit and the Unemployed

(See also (2) and (15) above.)

(18) 1980 Reform On 24 November 1980 the SB scheme was revised, with the changes including (introduced in Social Security Act 1980):

  (i) alignment of SB and NI rates;
 (ii) reduction in number of age ranges for children from five to three (previously there had been scales for ages 0–4, 5–10, 11–12, 13–15, and 16–17; these became 0–10, 11–15, and 16–17);
(iii) changes in earnings disregards, and introduction of tapered earnings disregard for single parents;
 (iv) a capital limit of £2,000 (in place of £1,250), which became absolute (rather than tariff income assumed);
  (v) school-leavers denied the right to claim benefit until the end of the vacation following their last term in full-time education (see (26) below);
 (vi) introduction of standard rent share deduction for non-dependent members of the household;
(vii) extra circumstance additions (ECAs) became part of the legal entitlement for those meeting specified conditions;
(viii) introduction of new powers to recover overpayments retrospectively.

(19) Long-Term SB Rate   In November 1981 the long-term SB rate was extended to unemployed men aged 60 or over, provided that they ceased to register for employment, so that if unemployed for more than 1 year, and no longer registering for work, they received the higher long-term rate (SSAC, First Report, pp. 11 and 27). From May 1983, all unemployed men aged 60 and over were no longer required to be available for employment and became entitled to the long-term rate of SB (WRB, 54, June 1983). From November 1985, people in this position qualified automatically for the lower rate of heating addition (WRB, 67, August 1985).

(20) More Stringent Administration   The number of Unemployment Review Officers, responsible for finding out what the claimant is doing to get a job, increased from 300 in 1978 to 880 in 1981 (Rayner Report (1981, p. 26)). In February 1980 the Social Security Minister announced deployment of 1,050 additional staff to carry out a drive to expose social security fraud. Specialist claims control teams controlled by Regional Fraud Section to deal with specific areas including the 'work-shy' were introduced nationally in November 1981 (SSN, 7, July 1983). Total DHSS staff allocated to fraud work increased from 2,044 in 1980–1 to 3,674 in 1986–7 (*Hansard*, 19 June 1986, col. 591; 20 February 1986, col. 315; 24 February 1986, col. 589; and 15 May 1986, col. 533).

(21) Equal Treatment Provisions   As with NI benefit, 'equal treatment' provisions were introduced in November 1983. These allow for one of a couple to be the claimant, according to qualifying conditions and restrictions on the dates at which changes in roles are permitted (SSN, 8, October 1983; WRB, 56 and 57).

(22) Non-Householder Housing Cost Addition   The non-householder fixed housing cost addition was abolished for those aged 16–17 in April 1983 (NWB, twelfth edition, p. 41), for those aged 18–20 in 1984, and for those aged 21–24 in 1986 (this representing a step towards the income support scheme with its lower rates for those aged under 25) (NWB, seventeenth edition, p. 49).

(23) Voluntary Unemployment Deductions   In 1983 the Social Security Policy Inspectorate reported on voluntary unemployment deductions, disclosing widespread misapplication of these rules. These rules apply to those persons disqualified from NI benefit and reduce the SB payable by either 40 per cent or 20 per cent of the personal scale rate (no deduction being made with respect to payments for a partner or children). The lower 20 per cent rate was applied where the full cut would cause hardship (the

so-called 'compassion clause'). From August 1983 the application of the 20 per cent deduction, as opposed to 40 per cent, was restricted to families where someone in the family is pregnant or seriously ill and the claimant's capital is less than £100 (£200 from April 1988) (SSN, 8, October 1983).

(24) Disqualification Period   The extensions of the disqualification period in 1986 and 1988 described for NI benefit also apply to SB where there is a 40 per cent (or 20 per cent) deduction.

(25) Board and Lodgings   In September 1984 the DHSS announced a 6-month freeze on amounts of SB paid to people in board and lodgings. With effect from April 1985, a system of national maxima was introduced, the general discretion to disapply the maxima was removed, and restrictions were introduced to limit the length of time an unemployed person under the age of 26 could claim benefit as a boarder in given locations. Certain parts of these regulations were found by the High Court to be *ultra vires*; they were remade in October 1985 but were subsequently withdrawn. A further set of regulations was produced in November 1985 (SSAC, Fifth Report, Ch. 7; WRB, 76, February 1987; WRB, 78, June 1987).

(26) School-Leavers   Prior to 1980, school-leavers could claim benefit as soon as they left school. In 1980 the concept of a 'terminal date' was introduced, under which benefit could not be claimed until approximately the first Monday of the following term. Easter leavers entered for a summer examination were deemed to be ineligible for benefit until September (SSAC, Second Report, p. 13; Fifth Report, p. 30).

(27) Part-Time Study   The conditions for students taking part-time courses which do not prevent them being available for work have been the subject of a number of changes in regulations. The '21-hour' rule allows people to undertake up to 21 hours of part-time study without prejudice to their entitlement to SB. In 1982 a regulation made clear that the 21 hours referred to supervised study and did not include private study or non-teaching time such as lunch breaks, but this regulation also introduced a qualifying period, requiring that the person had for the previous 3 months been in receipt of SB, UB, or sickness benefit (or an alternative condition during the previous 6 months) (SSAC, Second Report, p. 16; WRB, 49, August 1982). This condition did not apply to 16–18-year-olds whose course was not deemed to be 'full-time'. The definition of the latter was changed in August 1984 to more than 12 hours a week of supervised study excluding homework and meal breaks (WRB, 61, August 1984).

(28) Heating Additions   No awards for central heating additions for SB were made from August 1985 (WRB, 67, August 1985).

(29) Mortgage Interest   Those aged under 60 receive only 50 per cent of the mortgage interest eligible for SB during the first 16 weeks on benefit (WRB, 76, February 1987; WRB, 78, June 1987). Claimants have to make an appropriate application within 4 weeks of the end of the period (or else start a new claim again). This provision was introduced for SB from January 1987 and is retained in the income support scheme.

(30) Income Support   The replacement of SB in 1988 by IS has meant major changes. It replaces the system of short-term and long-term rates, and distinction between householders and non-householders, by personal allowances determining benefit on the basis of age and marital status. There is a flat-rate premium paid to all families with children in addition to age-related scales for children. It replaces the variety of extra payments under SB designed to cater for different dimensions of need (for heating, laundry, special diets, etc.) by premiums for different groups: lone parents, pensioners, the disabled, and other groups. Exceptional needs payments are replaced by the Social Fund (see below). In addition there are the following changes:

  (i) those with capital in excess of £6,000 are not eligible for IS or housing benefit; capital between £3,000 and £6,000 is assumed to produce a weekly income (equal to £1 for each £250, or part thereof, in excess of £3,000) which is taken into account in assessing entitlement;

 (ii) the IS payment no longer includes water rates or residual housing costs (such as maintenance or insurance for owner-occupiers);

(iii) the definition of net earnings is changed (for example, only half of contributions to occupational pension schemes are deducted and there is no provision for work expenses) and higher earnings disregard for couples unemployed for 2 years (and lone parents);

(iv) persons working 24 hours or more per week are defined as being in 'remunerative work' and ineligible for IS; in the case of a couple, there is no entitlement if either partner is ineligible;

 (v) couples have a free choice as to who claims.

In determining the scales for IS

the Government has had regard to the previous levels of supplementary benefit . . . as well as trends in the number of beneficiaries of different types, to the overall support available for various groups from public funds, and to the need to restrain public expenditure. The rates of these benefits include the average amount that the Government expect householders who are income support claimants will have to meet as their minimum contribution to domestic rates in 1988–89. (HM Treasury (1987, vol. II, p. 274))

There is transitional protection for existing SB claimants in April 1988 who would qualify for a lower level of IS. Their benefit is frozen at its current level in money terms until the IS entitlement has been uprated to a higher level.

(31) Social Fund   In April 1988 the new Social Fund replaced supplementary benefit single payments (SSN, 20, February 1988). (In 1987 the Social Fund had begun to make maternity and funeral payments in place of the maternity grant, the death grant, and single payments for these contingencies.) Payments are at the discretion of the Social Fund officers; there is no legal right to help or to an independent appeal if help is refused. The payments are in most cases loans, not grants, the only exception, apart from maternity and funeral payments, being grants being paid for certain community care needs. To repay loans, a claimant's weekly benefit is reduced, normally by 15 per cent. Payments apart from those for maternity or funeral expenses are subject to a cash limit on total expenditure.

(32) 16- and 17-Year-Olds   The Social Security Bill 1988 and the Employment Bill 1988 make major changes in the income support for school-leavers aged under 18. The former removes the general entitlement to IS of 16- and 17-year-olds, allowing only for IS to be awarded on a discretionary basis where 'severe hardship' might occur (this may include those with disabilities and single parents). The Bill also allows parents to continue to receive child benefit for a period after their son or daughter leaves school. The Employment Bill provides for a 'bridging allowance' to be paid to 16- and 17-year-olds who leave jobs or YTS and are waiting for a YTS place, on condition that the claimant has registered for a place on a scheme. The Bill extends the circumstances in which benefit may be withdrawn or reduced for unemployed people leaving or refusing places on job training schemes.

Housing Benefit

(33) Social Security and Housing Benefits Act 1982   Under the system in force in 1979, an unemployed person could receive either SB or HB, with the possibility of an overlap at the beginning of a spell of unemployment where HB continued to be paid. The choice between SB and HB gave rise to the 'better off' problem. Whereas an unemployed person with no other source of income would be better off on SB, a person in receipt of NI benefit, or with a working spouse, could be treated more favourably under HB. This added a major source of complexity and there is little doubt that many claimants received the less advantageous benefit (see Atkinson and Micklewright (1985, p. 37)). The better off problem was eliminated by the

1982 legislation. This transferred the payment of rent and rates assistance to the local authorities, although payments for water rates and for owner-occupiers' mortgage interest (and other costs) continued under SB. Where the unemployed person's resources fell short of his SB calculation of requirements (not including rent and rates), there was entitlement to SB and to certificated HB, paying (normally) 100 per cent rent and rates. Where the resources exceeded requirements, so that the person was not eligible for SB, then standard HB could be claimed. If after receiving HB the net rent and rates were greater than the excess of resources over requirements, then HB supplement could be claimed equal to the difference. There were therefore after 1982 four types of payment for housing: SB payments for water rates and owner-occupiers' costs, certificated HB, standard HB, and HB supplement. There were in addition changes in the tapers, non-dependant deductions, and other parameters of the scheme.

(34) Changes in Tapers   The tapers determine the amount of HB payable where income is above or below the needs allowance. With effect from April 1983, the tapers for claimants below pension age with incomes above the needs allowance were 21 per cent for rent rebates and 7 per cent for rate rebates. These tapers were increased to 26 per cent and 9 per cent from April 1984, and to 29 per cent for rent rebates from November 1984. The taper for rate rebate was further increased to 13 per cent from November 1985, and the rent rebate taper to 33 per cent in April 1987.

(35) Non-Dependant Deductions   From April 1984 changes were made in the non-dependant deductions, extending these to persons aged under 18 and increasing their level. In consequence of the abolition of the fixed housing cost addition to SB for non-householders aged under 21, the deduction was set at zero for persons aged under 21 (25 from 1986) and either receiving SB or attending YTS.

(36) Changes in Needs Allowances   There have been changes in the real value of the needs allowances, including a 50p increase in the real value of the needs allowance for a child in November 1984 and a 95p increase in November 1985 (*Hansard*, 20 May 1986, col. 169).

(37) Minimum Payments   The minimum payment has been increased to 50p a week (*Hansard*, 20 May 1986, col. 169).

(38) 1988 Changes   The Social Security Act 1986 introduced a common basis of assessment for housing benefit and IS (with the exception that HB has a higher single-parent premium) and abolished HB supplement. Where a person's income is below the IS level then HB is paid in full, where this is

100 per cent of rents (unless these are considered 'unreasonable') and 80 per cent of rates, less deductions for non-dependants. Where the income is above the IS level then the rate rebate is reduced by 20 per cent of the excess, not being payable where the net amount falls below 50p a week, and the rent rebate is reduced by 65 per cent of the excess, not being payable where the net amount falls below 50p a week. One major implication of the alignment of HB and IS is that HB has become subject to a capital condition. The fact that the claimant has to meet a minimum of 20 per cent of the rates payment represents a major departure, and has to be judged in conjunction with the introduction of the poll tax.

2

Is There a Market Failure in Occupational Sick Pay?

RICHARD DISNEY AND STEVEN WEBB*

1. Background

In recent years, the Government has introduced a number of major modifications to the social security system in the United Kingdom. A rationale of present social security policy is ' . . . the basic principle that social security is not a function of the state alone. It is a partnership between the individual and the state—a system built on twin pillars' (DHSS (1985a, Cmnd 9517, p. 1)).

The Government has identified two particular components of the social security system where the potential role of individual, private market, contracts is to be enhanced at the expense of public provision. One is that of earnings–related pensions, and major changes have been implemented here in the provisions of the Social Security Act 1986.[1] The second area is that of earnings replacement during short-term sickness. It is the latter which concerns us here.

Since 1979, public provision of short-term sickness benefits has been significantly downgraded. The first change was the abolition of the earnings-related supplement in 1980, which the CBI (1980) estimated to have reduced annual public spending on sickness benefits by £185 million at 1980–1 prices. The second change was the introduction in 1983 of employers' statutory sick pay (SSP) under the Social Security and Housing Benefits Act 1982 for the first 8 weeks of a spell of sickness. From April 1986, under the Social Security Act 1985, SSP was extended to the first 28 weeks of a spell of sickness. As a consequence, sickness benefit eligibility

* Richard Disney is a Professor at Keynes College, University of Kent and a Research Associate at the Institute for Fiscal Studies. Steven Webb is a Research Officer at the Institute for Fiscal Studies.

This paper was presented at a conference on 'The Economics of Social Security', organized by the Institute for Fiscal Studies, held on 15 April 1988 at University College, London. Comments of participants are gratefully acknowledged.

[1] For an appraisal of this pension reform, see Creedy and Disney (Ch. 13, this volume).

has been reduced to a rump of cases, and short-term industrial injury benefit has been abolished.

Statutory sick pay is a benefit paid by employers at one of two rates according to earnings. There are no allowances for dependants. SSP payments are refunded in full by deduction from payments of tax and National Insurance contributions, although it was originally proposed to finance SSP by an across-the-board reduction in the National Insurance contribution (DHSS (1980)).[2] Estimates originally presented by the DHSS suggested that public spending on sickness benefits would be reduced significantly at the time of this reform, largely because, unlike sickness benefit before 1983, SSP is taxable and liable to National Insurance contributions (HMSO (1984) and Committee of Public Accounts (1985)). However, calculations by Disney (1987) suggest that the gain to public funds is rather small, when estimated for the financial year 1986–7.[3] Nevertheless it is apparent in both financial and philosophical terms that these changes reflect a clear diminution of state involvement in short-term earnings replacement during sickness. As a consequence, these changes have involved a reduction in the replacement ratio of public sickness benefits to net earnings for some individuals. Whether the changes imply a significant reduction in the replacement ratio of total sickness benefits to net earnings is an issue that we intend to discuss in this paper.

The primary justification for the introduction of statutory sick pay was presented in the Green Paper which, reflecting the more general policy, argued that ' . . . the state should, wherever possible, disengage itself from activities which firms and individuals can perform perfectly well for themselves' (DHSS (1980, p. 2)).

The presumption that there is extensive private provision of earnings replacement during sickness was explicit in this statement. Although the theoretical arguments for private provision in this area seem reasonably compelling,[4] the Government rested its case for the introduction of SSP largely on empirical evidence drawn from the 1974 DHSS survey of occupational sick pay (OSP) schemes. This survey reported that 80 per cent of males and 78 per cent of females in full-time employment were covered by some kind of OSP scheme (DHSS (1980, Annex A)). Regarding inter-industry differences in coverage, no industry had fewer than half its workforce covered and other industries were close to 100 per cent coverage

[2] Some implications of the shift in the method of refunds are described in Disney (1987, Section IV).
[3] This reduced gain stems largely from the decision to waive the employer's contribution on SSP in preparation for the extension of SSP to 28 weeks, and also because of the upward trend in SSP refunds since 1983.
[4] See Creedy and Disney (1985, Ch. 8).

(ibid., Table 1).[5] Occupational coverage was a little more uneven, but even manual occupations had 74 per cent coverage for men and 56 per cent for women (ibid., Table 2). Furthermore, a large number of employees were said to have generous OSP provision, with full pay received by 66.5 per cent of men and 85.9 per cent of women at the commencement of their spell of sickness (ibid., Table 5). Since not all employers deducted state sickness benefit in calculating OSP entitlements, and sickness benefit was not taxable at this time, some employees had replacement ratios in excess of 100 per cent when sick (even when allowing for the fact that sick pay entitlements may be based on basic pay, not normal pay including overtime and bonuses). Overall, therefore, the case for reducing the public component of sickness benefits, at least for the majority of the sick, seemed compelling.

This argument has received a certain amount of criticism. It has been noted that the DHSS survey of OSP schemes excluded part-time workers and employees on certain kinds of contracts. It may have treated some OSP provisions as automatic entitlements when they were in fact discretionary. More seriously, a major household study undertaken in 1976–7 found that, of those temporarily away from work on grounds of sickness, only 56 per cent had received OSP (Harris et al. (1984, p. 213))—much lower than the near-80 per cent coverage cited by the Green Paper. This discrepancy might stem from faulty recall;[6] the discretionary aspect of OSP schemes described previously; the possibility that the sub-population of the sick from which the 1976–7 survey was drawn had different average characteristics from the population at risk as a whole on which the DHSS sample was based;[7] or a combination of all three factors. Whatever the cause, to the extent that OSP coverage rates among the sick were lower than those suggested by the Green Paper, the case for a reduction in the public component of earnings replacement during sickness might appear to be much weakened.

Nevertheless, simply looking at the proportion of workers covered by OSP is not by itself an adequate guide as to whether private coverage is satisfactory. Coverage need not be 100 per cent in all sectors where there is perfect occupational mobility, where some workers are not risk-averse, and where wages fully reflect differences in fringe benefits as a compensating differential.[8] In a competitive market, the demand and supply of insur-

[5] Coverage was lower in industries such as textiles, leather, and some engineering and metal fabrication, whereas it was close to 100 per cent in white-collar private sector employment and in the public sector generally.

[6] See Atkinson and Micklewright (1983).

[7] This is a standard problem of selectivity; see Maddala (1983). Of course, in this context, it is the conditioned subsample which is more interesting, since whether one has OSP coverage is of importance only when one is sick.

[8] See Hamermesh and Rees (1984, pp. 300–5) and, for some British evidence, Green, Hadjimatheou, and Smail (1985).

ance should be parameterized as functions of the price at which insurance is offered to workers. Equilibrium in the insurance market may not therefore imply 100 per cent coverage.

Although an absence of market failure and less than 100 per cent coverage are not inconsistent, significant disparities in coverage may nevertheless be associated with market failure rather than simply reflect differences in preferences among individuals. Market failure in OSP coverage can occur if insurance is quantity-rationed, particularly where firms are only prepared to offer OSP to select groups of workers and separate private markets are not fully developed. A market failure can also occur if individuals are not fully risk-rated *ex ante*; where, for example, a low-risk individual shares other characteristics with a group of high risks and the insurer offers insurance to that individual only at the high risk premium of the group as a whole. Finally and most simply, high-risk groups may not be able to obtain insurance at a price which they are prepared to pay. Strictly speaking, this is an equity argument for public provision, although the private market is not in equilibrium with a positive supply of insurance, at least to this group, in such circumstances.

The present paper utilizes data drawn from an analysis of the Family Expenditure Survey (FES) in order to determine the characteristics of the sick and the characteristics of recipients of OSP. It seeks to determine whether the degree of OSP coverage in 1974 justified the Government's more optimistic belief concerning private provision of sick pay, and investigates whether the case for reduced public involvement on grounds of adequate private provision is as strong, or stronger, today. In the light of the preceding discussion, the basic contention to be tested is as follows. If those with a high probability of sickness by, say, occupation or industry have a low probability of coverage by OSP, and assuming employees generally desire a high level of earnings replacement during short-term sickness, then a potential for market failure exists. There is then a case for government intervention to provide and maintain the real value of sickness benefits for these individuals. Indeed, in such circumstances there is a strong case for providing public sickness benefits to the whole population at risk on incentive grounds, financed by compulsory contributions or levies. Although SSP is just such a scheme, it can nevertheless be argued that it is suboptimal to reduce the replacement ratio of public sickness benefits to net income in work, as has occurred for some individuals since 1979, when those individuals are quantity-constrained in their coverage by occupational sick pay schemes.[9]

[9] Particular concern in this context has been expressed over the sick who have dependants, especially if they are on the lower rate of SSP (Disability Alliance (1986)). However, it should be noted that SSP recipients are entitled to means-tested benefits where their benefit falls short of the poverty standard.

56   *Disney and Webb*

The plan of the remainder of the paper is straightforward. In the next section, the FES data are described briefly. Probit equations describing the incidence of sickness and OSP coverage are estimated for 1974 in order to allow a direct comparison with the figures used by the DHSS. Section 3 re-estimates the same probits using FES data for 1984. Some striking differences emerge. The trend in OSP coverage between 1974 and 1984 is then explored and the reason for these differences becomes apparent. The final section summarizes the results.

2. Comparing the DHSS Survey and Family Expenditure Survey 1974

The Family Expenditure Survey is now a well-analysed source of data on household expenditure patterns and income receipt, including social security benefits (Kemsley, Redpath, and Holmes (1980) and Atkinson and Micklewright (1983)). The FES reports two questions concerning employee sickness and OSP coverage. First, it asks whether an individual who is currently temporarily away from work due to sickness or injury has also received full or part pay. Second, it contains a 'recall' question as to whether an individual who received state sickness benefit at some time in the FES reference period in addition received some pay from their employer. The first question, which captures a 'snapshot' of uncompleted durations of sickness, has a smaller sample number than the second question, which is a sickness incidence measure conditioned on receipt of state sickness benefit. The second question, however, suffers from two drawbacks: it is only asked from 1980 onwards, and it conditions OSP receipt on state benefit receipt. Thus changes in state benefit eligibility, such as the alteration to the qualifying period rules introduced by SSP, will change the sample composition, and so will preclude any direct comparison. Thus we work with the snapshot.[10]

Descriptive statistics for the 1974 and 1984 samples are described in the Appendix. The 'population at risk' is comprised of those individuals normally in employment, and normal income, as defined in the FES, and which for this group is primarily earnings, forms the basis of the income variable. Those currently temporarily away ill comprise around 2.5 per cent of the sample in both years. Mean proportions in some aggregated occupational and industrial categories are also described, along with the proportion of part-time employees in the sample.

[10] Consistency checks suggested (1) that changes in FES numbers reporting current uncompleted spells of sickness tracked reasonably closely on 'snapshots' of sickness benefit recipients pre-1983 from non-FES sources; (2) that reported receipt of various state benefits, including SSP, coincided approximately with eligibility conditions (primarily duration characteristics); and (3) that those reporting OSP receipt were not simply reporting SSP payments received from the employer (i.e. in no case did the cash amounts tally).

Table 2.1 Probability (temporarily away sick) 1974

Variable	Coefficient	Standard error	t-statistic
Constant	−2.06	0.09	−23.06
Administration	−0.03	0.18	−0.24
Teaching	−0.22	0.27	−0.82
Professional	0.24	0.15	0.16
Shopworkers	−0.00	0.19	−0.01
Skilled manual	0.27	0.10	2.63
Unskilled manual	0.15	0.10	1.60
Normalized income	−0.015	0.006	−2.28
Normalized income squared	−0.00	0.00	−0.90
Heavy	0.10	0.09	1.09
Light	0.11	0.11	1.02
Primary	0.18	0.16	1.08
Public service	0.09	0.13	0.64
Engineering	0.15	0.10	1.51
Part-time	−0.24	0.11	−2.10

Log likelihood			−881.14
Chi-squared (14)			50.58

	Actual total	Correctly predicted	Wrongly predicted
Sick	193	0	193
Not sick	7,683	7,683	0
	7,876	7,683	193

Controls: clerical workers, private service employment, full-time employment.

Table 2.1 describes the results of a probit equation concerning the characteristics of those reporting themselves temporarily away sick in 1974. The equation suggests that occupation is an important determinant of sickness incidence, with manual workers, especially the skilled, having a higher probability of sickness. There is not, however, a significant difference in sickness among non-manual occupations, with clerical workers as the control group. A quadratic term is imposed on the income variable, although in 1974 only the linear term is significant and negative. This result is perhaps not very robust, as a rather different picture emerges in 1984. Furthermore, the results of Creedy and Disney (1985, Figure 8.1), using DHSS data for 1971–3, suggest that there is a negative but weak relationship between incidence of short-term sickness and earnings in this period. Most industrial groupings have higher rates of sickness incidence than the control group of private service employment, but only engineering is close to significance. Part-time employees have a lower probability of absence due to sickness, but this may stem from differences in employment protec tion and flexibility of hours, rather than from differences in personal characteristics.

The most significant term is the constant. This result, together with the inability of the specification to predict any individuals temporarily away sick, stems from the low probability of experiencing sickness among the sample (193 cases out of 7,876). Essentially, in attempting to predict the probability of sickness, no combination of characteristics among the sample individuals is sufficient to raise the probability of sickness above the necessary threshold of 0.5. In summary, therefore, the key result to bear in mind from Table 2.1 is the role of occupation in sickness incidence, with the negative signs on income and part-time employment, and the weak inter-industry differences also worthy of note.

Table 2.2 illustrates the probit of occupational sick pay receipt conditioned on being temporarily away ill.

It is useful first to note the relation of predicted to actual incidence in the bottom part of the table, below the main equation. Only 95 of the 193 individuals sampled report having received OSP at some stage in the current spell of illness—far lower than the 80 per cent or so coverage reported by the DHSS survey for the population at risk as a whole. In addition, the equation in Table 2.2 is much better at predicting cell numbers than was the case in Table 2.1. This stems from the fact that just under half of the sample are covered by OSP. So 83 out of the 98 individuals not receiving OSP are predicted, and 59 out of 95 who do receive it. The equation underpredicts overall OSP receipt somewhat, but the margin of error is not enormous, given the small sample and the relatively small number of variables included.

Among the characteristics which are important in determining OSP coverage, occupation again stands out, with all manual workers as well as shopworkers having lower probabilities of OSP coverage. The income variable is unimportant but there are significant inter-industry differences in OSP coverage. In particular, and as in the DHSS 1974 survey of OSP schemes, light manufacturing industry and engineering have significantly lower coverage rates (remembering that the latter had an above-average rate of sickness, albeit not quite statistically significant). Public service workers have rather better OSP coverage, and part-time employees slightly worse, although interestingly this last coefficient is not significant.

It is now useful to put together the stories told by Tables 2.1 and 2.2. First, OSP coverage among the sick in 1974 was much lower than that reported for the population at risk by the DHSS survey of OSP schemes, although the inter-occupational and inter-industry differences were as predicted by the DHSS survey. Second, exclusion of part-time workers does

Table 2.2 Probability (occupational sick pay coverage, conditioned on sickness) 1974

Variable	Coefficient	Standard error	t-statistic
Constant	2.02	0.47	4.30
Administration	−0.13	0.87	−0.16
Teaching	2.97	341.84	0.01
Professional	−0.22	0.71	−0.30
Shopworkers	−2.10	0.71	−2.97
Skilled manual	−1.98	0.49	−4.08
Unskilled manual	−1.74	0.47	−3.72
Normalized income	0.02	0.02	0.74
Normalized income squared	−0.00	0.01	−0.23
Heavy	−0.58	0.30	−1.92
Light	−0.88	0.37	−2.37
Primary	−0.25	0.49	−0.52
Public service	1.18	0.64	1.85
Engineering	−1.36	0.37	−3.69
Part-time	−0.44	0.40	−1.11

Log likelihood	−94.71
Chi-squared (14)	78.081

	Actual total	Correctly predicted	Wrongly predicted
On OSP	95	59	36
Not on OSP	98	83	15
	193	142	51

Controls: clerical workers, private service employment, full-time employment.

not appear to have biased the DHSS sample. Of the three reasons for the discrepancy between the 1974 DHSS survey and the 1976–7 results described in the previous section, therefore, it is the inclusion of discretionary entitlements rather than exclusions from the population at risk and sample selectivity which seems to be the major cause.[11] Third, there is evidence that some groups with higher-than-average probabilities of being away ill had lower-than-average probabilities of OSP coverage in 1974. This was particularly true of manual workers, and to a lesser extent of some industries such as engineering. Overall, therefore, the results suggest that the Government was too sanguine in 1980 in using the results of the 1974

[11] We intend to test for sample selectivity in future work; that is, whether the probability of OSP coverage among the population at risk is different from that among individuals conditioned on sickness, for both 1974 and 1984.

DHSS survey of OSP schemes to justify the reduction in public provision of short-term sickness benefits. The lower level of coverage among those away ill, and the significant differences in individual risk of sickness and of OSP coverage, raise the possibility of a private market failure at that time.[12] If such a failure existed, it in turn suggested a case for greater rather than less public sector involvement in provision of earnings replacement during sickness. Whether this conclusion is true today is the next issue to be investigated.

3. Sick Pay Incidence and OSP Entitlements in 1984

Although the results of the previous section are useful because they provide a suitable comparison with the DHSS survey of OSP schemes in 1974, it is the present situation which is of greater interest in policy terms. Similar calculations were undertaken therefore using the 1984 FES. Table 2.3 describes the results of a probit equation concerning the characteristics of those reporting themselves temporarily away ill in 1984.

The equation again suggests that occupation is an important determinant of sickness incidence. The higher probability of sickness among manual workers is again clear, with the respective coefficients even more significant. In this equation, professional workers also have higher rates of sickness. The most clear-cut conclusion from the rest of the equation is that almost every coefficient is reversed in sign compared with 1974: income is positive and insignificant while income squared is significant and negative; there is no evidence of higher rates of sickness among employees in manufacturing industry, even engineering; and part-time employment now has a weak positive effect on incidence of sickness.

These conclusions should not be too surprising: there is no reason why labour market variables should have very strong effects on sickness probability, although the comparison of 1974 with 1984 shows that the distinction between manual and non-manual occupations' sickness rates is robust across both samples. Sickness rates may, of course, vary according to personal characteristics, and a regression in the Appendix (Table 2.A4), with slightly different sample size and controls, shows that region, housing ten-

---

[12] If lower OSP coverage among certain groups reflected a pure compensating differential, we might expect the coefficient on the earnings term to be negative and significant in Table 2.2. This is not the case. Alternatively, Nick Barr has suggested that lower earners such as those in manual occupations would have had higher replacement ratios of public benefits to net earnings in 1974 and that the inference to be drawn from Table 2.2 is simply that public benefits substituted for OSP benefits at that time. This may be true, although there is of course no way of testing market failure directly when there is public intervention. Nevertheless, if Barr's explanation were correct, we might perhaps expect a significant positive coefficient on the earnings term in Table 2.2. Again, this is not the case.

Table 2.3 Probability (temporarily away sick) 1984

Variable	Coefficient	Standard error	t-statistic
Constant	−2.15	0.11	−20.73
Administration	0.01	0.18	0.04
Teaching	−0.07	0.24	−0.29
Professional	0.26	0.14	1.84
Shopworkers	0.09	0.22	0.40
Skilled manual	0.42	0.11	3.94
Unskilled manual	0.47	0.15	3.11
Normalized income	0.02	0.02	1.06
Normalized income squared	−0.01	0.003	−3.23
Heavy	−0.14	0.11	−1.29
Light	−0.15	0.13	−1.16
Primary	0.04	0.15	0.27
Public service	0.10	0.10	0.97
Engineering	−0.01	0.12	−0.06
Part-time	0.04	0.13	0.34

Log likelihood −730.97
Chi-squared (14) 53.29

	Actual total	Correctly predicted	Wrongly predicted
Sick	159	0	159
Not sick	6,783	6,783	0
	6,942	6,783	159

Controls: clerical workers, private service employment, full-time employment.

ure, and age, although not gender, have some impact on sickness rates in the 1984 FES.[13] Nevertheless it is the evidence of disparities in occupational sickness rates relative to OSP coverage in 1984 which concerns us here, and the latter provides the next piece of evidence.

Table 2.4 shows the results of the probit of sick pay coverage in 1984.

The first point to note is the great increase in OSP coverage between

[13] There is an interesting side-issue to this analysis of the effect of labour market characteristics on sickness. The shift in financing the SSP scheme from the Green Paper proposal for an across-the-board reduction in the National Insurance contribution to full refund of SSP payments was in response to pressure from trade unions and the CBI concerning the unfair incidence of the former when there were significant inter-industry disparities in sickness rates. The results here, albeit at a highly aggregated level, provide no evidence for clear disparities of this kind. Since full refund implies the potential for serious moral hazard problems (HMSO (1984) and Disney (1987, Section IV)), further evidence on differential sickness rates would be useful.

Table 2.4 Probability (occupational sick pay coverage, conditioned on sickness) 1984

Variable	Coefficient	Standard error	t-statistic
Constant	1.71	0.54	3.17
Administration	6.12	1,079.24	0.01
Teaching	−1.35	1,598.57	−0.00
Professional	5.80	714.31	0.01
Shopworkers	−0.70	0.80	−0.87
Skilled manual	−0.20	0.47	−0.43
Unskilled manual	0.63	0.66	0.94
Normalized income	0.29	0.10	2.82
Normalized income squared	−0.06	0.02	−3.22
Heavy	−0.82	0.46	−1.79
Light	−0.79	0.51	−1.54
Primary	−1.51	0.54	−2.82
Public service	6.59	589.82	0.01
Engineering	−0.83	0.47	−1.76
Part-time	0.76	0.65	1.17
Log likelihood			−54.02
Chi-squared (14)			45.98

	Actual total	Correctly predicted	Wrongly predicted
On OSP	129	124	5
Not on OSP	30	9	21
	159	133	26

Controls: clerical workers, private service employment, full-time employment.

1974 and 1984, with 129 out of 159, or 81 per cent of the sample, covered. Indeed, the model now overpredicts OSP coverage, identifying only 14 individuals with a probability of at least 0.5 of not being covered by OSP. The second important conclusion is that occupation is no longer a significant predictor of OSP coverage, with neither skilled nor unskilled having a significant and negative sign (compare this with Table 2.2). A third interesting conclusion is that other variables, not significant in the sickness incidence equations, continue to be significant in the OSP equations. These are primarily industry variables. All manufacturing industries, especially heavy manufacturing and engineering, continue to have significantly lower OSP coverage than the public sector and private services. Finally, the quadratic in income is now significant, although it was not so in 1974, and the sign on part-time employment is now positive (albeit insignificant), per-

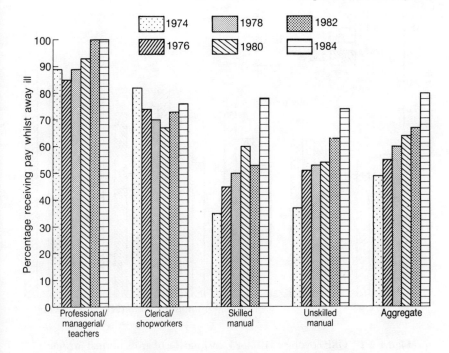

Figure 2.1 OSP coverage, 1974–84: percentage coverage amongst those 'away ill'

haps reflecting the composition of part-time employment largely in public sector and non-manual occupations.

4. Trends in Coverage and Conclusions

What are we to make of this comparison between 1974 and 1984? It was suggested that there was tentative evidence for market failure in 1974. Occupations with higher-than-average rates of sickness had lower-than-average rates of OSP coverage. This relationship has disappeared by 1984, for while it is true that manual workers continue to have higher sickness rates, the disparity in OSP coverage is no longer significant. Why this is so becomes apparent from Figure 2.1, which shows that coverage has increased almost continuously among manual workers since 1974, from just over a third of the sample to over three-quarters.

Since 1982 alone, coverage has increased by about 15 percentage points among manual workers, and interestingly there is no significant difference between skilled workers and the semi-skilled and unskilled combined. Since the effect of the introduction of SSP was to curb the highest replacement ratios, we might have expected a fall in the demand for OSP

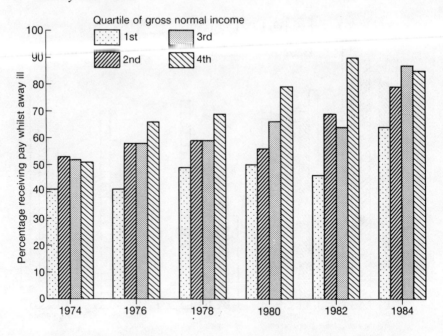

Figure 2.2   OSP coverage, 1974–84: by quartile of gross normal income

coverage, coupled with an attempt by those with better OSP coverage to recoup some of the benefit losses resulting from making the state component of OSP taxable. Instead, we seem to be observing a continued increase in the breadth of coverage, suggesting that the experience of operating SSP may have induced employers who previously relied on state benefits to consider the value of operating their own OSP schemes.

Figure 2.2 presents an analysis of OSP coverage by income quartile. It shows that coverage has increased among all quartiles of the distribution over the period. Until 1982, the third and fourth quartiles (the upper half of the income distribution) showed the steadier increase, but thereafter it is again the lower quartiles which have gained in coverage.

The main disparity which continues to be observed is in OSP coverage by broad industrial grouping. Manufacturing industries have significantly lower coverage rates in both 1974 and 1984. Yet no clear-cut differences in the probability of sickness among industries emerge from the probits. This result raises the possibility that there are individuals working in some industries who are quantity-rationed in OSP coverage. Yet if there are no significant disparities in sickness rates between industries, this lower OSP coverage cannot be attributed to some kind of adverse selection problem stemming from their facing higher probabilities of sickness. Indeed, we may be observing a lower demand for insurance, or employees obtaining compensation in other ways, for example through wage differentials. More detailed work on the interaction between wages, OSP coverage, and sickness incidence would be useful, but the conclusion which emerges from the present analysis is that the signs of market failure observable in 1974 are indistinct by 1984.

Appendix

Table 2.A1. Definition of variables used in probits (based on Family Expenditure Survey definitions)

Variable name	Definition
Administration	Administrative and managerial workers
Teaching	Teachers
Professional	Professional and technical workers
Clerical	Clerical workers (e.g. clerks, commercial travellers)
Shopworkers	Shop assistants
Skilled manual	Skilled manual workers
Unskilled manual	Semi-skilled and unskilled manual workers
Income	Normal gross income, annualized. Measured in £ '000s above or below £1,500 in 1974, £6,000 in 1984.
Heavy	'Heavy' industries—e.g. vehicle manufacture, textiles, timber
Light	'Light' industries—e.g. food and drink manufacture, clothing manufacture, printing/publishing
Primary	'Primary' industries—e.g. agriculture, mining, mineral extraction
Public service	'Service' industries in the public sector—e.g. national government, police, local government, education
Private service	'Service' industries in the private sector—e.g. banking, insurance, communications
Engineering	General engineering, including electrical engineering, mechanical engineering
Part-time	Normal hours less than 31 per week
Temporarily away sick	Employee temporarily absent from work due to sickness or injury; excludes long-term invalids
On occupational sick pay	Receiving full or part pay from employer whilst temporarily away ill
Age	Normalized measure—decades above or below 40
Midlands/North	Includes FES regions: East Midlands, West Midlands, Northern, Yorkshire and Humberside, North Western
Scotland/Wales	Scotland, Wales, Northern Ireland
Council house	Rented from a council or new town authority
Private rented	Non-council rented housing, furnished and unfurnished
Tobacco consumption	Weekly expenditure of household on cigarettes (continuous variable)

Table 2.A2 Descriptive statistics: 1974 means

	Population at risk	Temporarily away sick
Administration	0.07	0.03
Teaching	0.04	0.01
Professional	0.09	0.05
Clerical	0.17	0.14
Shopworkers	0.04	0.03
Skilled manual	0.24	0.34
Unskilled manual	0.33	0.39
Normalized income	0.35	0.09
Normalized income squared	17.55	6.76
Heavy	0.21	0.24
Light	0.10	0.12
Primary	0.03	0.05
Public service	0.07	0.06
Private service	0.47	0.37
Engineering	0.12	0.16
Part-time	0.22	0.17
Temporarily away sick	0.025	n.a.
On occupational sick pay	0.012	0.49
Sample size	$n = 7,876$	$n = 193$

Table 2.A3 Descriptive statistics: 1984 means

	Population at risk	Temporarily away sick
Administration	0.10	0.04
Teaching	0.05	0.03
Professional	0.12	0.11
Clerical	0.18	0.10
Shopworkers	0.05	0.03
Skilled manual	0.43	0.59
Unskilled manual	0.07	0.10
Normalized income	5.71	0.44
Normalized income squared	20.41	8.6
Heavy	0.15	0.14
Light	0.09	0.08
Primary	0.05	0.08
Public service	0.16	0.18
Private service	0.46	0.45
Engineering	0.09	0.11
Part-time	0.25	0.21
Temporarily away sick	0.023	n.a.
On occupational sick pay	0.019	0.81
Sample size	$n = 6,942$	$n = 159$

Table 2.A4 Probability (temporarily away sick): personal and labour market variables, 1984

Variable	Coefficient	Standard error	t-statistic
Constant	−2.19	0.20	−11.12
Administration	−0.30	0.18	−1.65
Teaching	−0.33	0.24	−1.35
Clerical	−0.31	0.14	−2.12
Shopworkers	−0.24	0.22	−1.07
Skilled manual	0.06	0.12	0.53
Unskilled manual	0.07	0.17	0.40
Armed forces	0.14	0.46	0.30
Age	0.05	0.03	1.77
Midlands/North	0.12	0.08	1.56
Scotland/Wales	0.16	0.10	1.59
Normalized income	0.02	0.02	0.94
Normalized income squared	−0.01	0.003	−3.10
Heavy	−0.16	0.11	−1.45
Light	−0.20	0.14	−1.49
Primary	0.05	0.15	0.31
Public service	0.09	0.11	0.87
Engineering	−0.02	0.12	−0.14
Council house	0.21	0.08	2.63
Private rented	−0.20	0.17	−1.18
Female	0.011	0.09	1.14
Full-time	0.06	0.13	0.42
Married	0.17	0.09	1.89
Tobacco consumption	0.07	0.04	1.57

Log likelihood	−720.38
Chi-squared (14)	83.88

	Actual total	Correctly predicted	Wrongly predicted
Sick	160	0	160
Not sick	6,823	6,823	0
	6,983	6,823	160

Controls: professional workers, private service employment, part-time employment, resident in Greater London/south-east/south-west/East Anglia, owner-occupier, male, single.

Note: Sample is larger than in Table 2.3 because of inclusion of members of HM Forces.

3

Trends in Dependence on Supplementary Benefit

JONATHAN BRADSHAW AND MEG HUBY*

1. Introduction

More than one person in seven in Britain is now living in a family dependent for all or part of its income on means-tested social assistance. This
level of dependence on social assistance is certainly the highest of any
country in Europe and has doubled since the mid-1960s.

Beveridge envisaged that the assistance scheme would serve a purely
residual and diminishing role for those who fell through the social insurance
net. In fact, by 1986 8.3 million people were living on supplementary benefit.
They included over two-thirds of unemployed people, over half of all single-
parent families, a fifth of pensioner households, and a substantial minority of
sick and disabled people. Among the families were 2 million school-age children. All these people were dependent on roughly the same low equivalent
income. Some will gain and most will lose from the advent of income support,
but the social security reforms if anything confirm their structural position.
They are detached from the labour force and, given their characteristics and
the state of the labour market, have limited incentive (or opportunity) to
supplement their income with work. They did not benefit from the April 1988
tax cuts. They are increasingly referred to as an underclass experiencing, in
the Secretary of State for Social Services's words, 'the sullen apathy of dependence [rather than] the sheer delight of personal achievement'.

2. Objectives

This paper is devoted to exploring past trends in the numbers on supplementary benefit. It attempts to relate these trends to other factors which

* Jonathan Bradshaw is a Professor and Meg Huby is a Research Fellow in the Department
of Social Policy, University of York.

This paper was presented at a conference on 'The Economics of Social Security', organized
by the Institute for Fiscal Studies, held on 15 April 1988.

The single parents' analysis draws on the MA dissertation of Tony Tarpey. Initial computing
for the pensioners' and unemployed analysis up to 1983 was carried out by Dr Y. Y. Chung.
Bob Lavers carried out a validating generalized least squares analysis of the single-parent data.

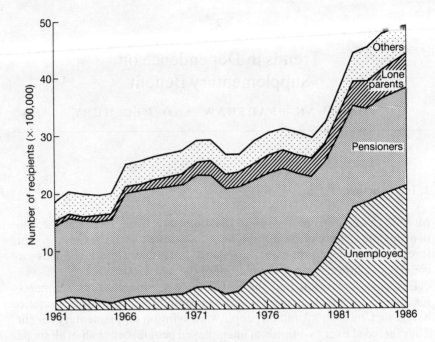

Figure 3.1   Numbers of supplementary benefit recipients, 1961–86, broken down by main groups

prima facie might have been expected to have had an influence. These include:

(a) financial factors—the real level of supplementary benefit and their relationship to insurance benefits and earnings;
(b) demographic factors—the numbers of pensioners or lone parents in the population;
(c) economic factors—the state of labour demand and supply;
(d) policy shifts.

The investigation has been restricted to the three largest groups of supplementary benefit recipients—pensioners, the unemployed, and single-parent families—which between them constitute over 89 per cent of all supplementary benefit claimants in 1986. Figure 3.1 shows how numbers of claimants in these groups have changed between 1961 and 1986.

The two largest groups excluded from the analysis are the sick and disabled, and students. The analysis is of course greatly constrained by available data. Restricting the period of analysis from 1961 to 1986, we examine the claimant groups—pensioners, the unemployed, and lone parents—in turn. Although some factors affecting the numbers of claimants are common to more than one group, the underlying demographic trends are very different.

3. Pensioners

Until 1982 pensioners (recipients and dependants) were the largest group in receipt of supplementary benefit (they were then overtaken by the unemployed). Figure 3.2 reveals a fluctuating pattern with two points where sharper changes took place—an increase in 1965–6 with a fall over 1972–5. The 1965–6 shift could have been due to special efforts made to increase the take-up of National Assistance in 1965 and the measures associated with the change in 1966 from National Assistance to supplementary benefit. The 1972–5 shift was almost certainly due to the introduction of the first national scheme of rent rebates and allowances.

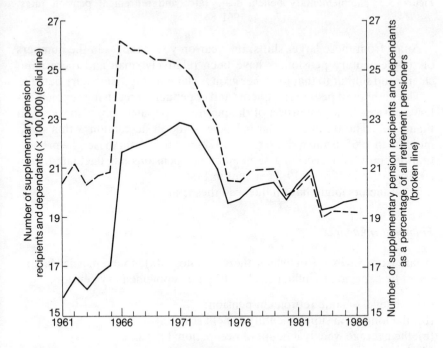

Figure 3.2 Number of supplementary pension recipients and as a percentage of all retirement pensioners, 1961–86

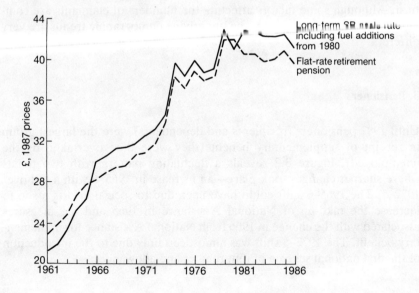

Figure 3.3 Supplementary benefit scale rates and retirement pension rates, 1961–86

Apart from these larger shifts, the year-on-year changes in the numbers of supplementary pensioners have been relatively small and there is no clear trend similar to that for other groups claiming supplementary benefit.

The number of people (recipients and dependants) receiving supplementary pensions as a proportion of the pensioner population is also shown in Figure 3.2. The trend is similar in shape—modest fluctuation with a sharp increase in 1965–6 and a sharp fall in 1972–5. Apart from these, the proportion of pensioners receiving supplementary pensions has fluctuated from 20.5 per cent in 1961 to 19.2 per cent in 1986.

What factors might have influenced these patterns?

Financial Influences

Apart from savings (for which there are no data), four financial factors might be expected to influence eligibility for supplementary pension:

(a) the level of state retirement pension;
(b) the long-term supplementary benefit scale rate;
(c) the average weekly amount of occupational pension;
(d) housing costs.

Figure 3.3 shows that in 1966, with the introduction of supplementary benefit and the 'long-term addition', the rate of supplementary benefit moved ahead of state retirement pension. It remained ahead until falling relatively in 1980, but then increased again in 1981 with the introduction of heating additions. Other things being equal, it would be expected that the higher the rates of supplementary benefit relative to retirement pensions, the more pensioners would be eligible for, and claim, supplementary benefit.

Occupational pensions, graduated pensions, and State Earnings-Related Pensions (SERPS) represent further sources of retirement income. Figure 3.4 shows that the average real value of these increased over the period except during the periods of rapid inflation in 1974 and 1980.

A measure of housing costs can be obtained by using the housing element of the retail price index to estimate the relationship between supplementary pension and housing costs. All other things being equal, it would be expected that as housing costs rise in relation to supplementary pensions, the numbers eligible for supplementary pensions would, until the introduction of housing benefit in 1983, also rise. Housing costs have risen faster than the supplementary benefit scales.

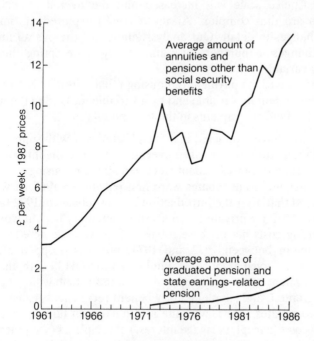

Figure 3.4 Occupational pensions, graduated, and state earnings-related pensions, 1961–86

Demographic Influences

We have investigated the impact of two demographic factors:

(a) the *number of retirement pensioners* has risen from 7.7 million to 10.3 million over the period;
(b) *female pensioners over 75* are more likely to be dependent on supplementary pensions and their number has also risen consistently, from 1.4 million to 2.5 million over the period.

Economic Influences

All other things being equal, it would be expected that when unemployment rises, the opportunities for people over retirement age to delay retirement or supplement their pension with work would decline and the numbers in receipt of supplementary pension would therefore rise.

Influence of Policy

(a) Efforts were made in 1965 to increase the take-up of National Assistance, and the policy change in 1966 introduced supplementary benefit. The assistance scale was increased and the overall effects of the changes are thus complex. Atkinson (1969) explored the impact of these changes in detail. Our analysis allows for the overall impact of these changes in numbers of claimants by representing them by a dummy variable.
(b) The shift due to the payment of housing rebates in 1974 is represented by a second dummy variable and by a variable measuring the numbers of housing benefit recipients in the total population.

   Housing costs have interacted in a complicated way with supplementary benefit and the pattern has changed over time. Prior to the introduction of rent rebates and allowances, tenants received all their housing costs in supplementary benefit. Rate rebates were first payable in 1967. It was originally intended that after the introduction of rent rebates in 1972 (and rent allowances in 1973 for private tenants), supplementary benefit would only include housing costs net of these rebates. This was attempted in a staggered phasing-in between 1972 and 1974, but was dropped after that period. However, local authorities reimbursed the DHSS with an amount roughly equivalent to the rebates and allowances that would otherwise have been granted, and supplementary benefit recipients became 'indirect recipients' of rebates. Then, with the introduction of housing benefit, all the housing costs (except mortgage interest) of recipients of supplementary benefit were transferred as 'certified cases' to local authorities. However, a number of supplementary benefit recipients who would have been made

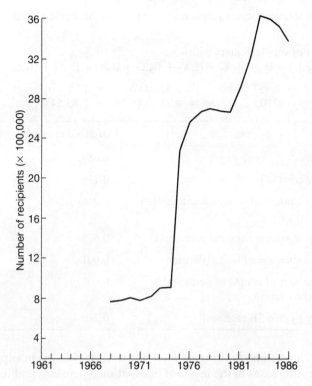

Figure 3.5 Number of recipients of housing benefit, 1961–86

worse off as a result of the transfer continued to receive housing benefit supplement. 'Certificated' pensioners were transferred to housing benefit in autumn 1982, and housing benefit became fully operable in April 1983. This is the reason for the sharp fall in the number of supplementary benefit recipients in 1983. How the number in receipt of housing benefit has moved over the period is shown in Figure 3.5.

The introduction of housing rebates has certainly led to a reduction in the numbers of supplementary pensioners—some were better off claiming rebates, some preferred to go on to rebates, and some already on did not consider it worth while transferring to supplementary benefit.

Table 3.1 gives the results of a multiple regression that was used to derive a model to show how the changes in the number of supplementary pensioners over time have depended on changes in financial, demographic, and policy variables. Generalized least squares regression was used to correct for the effects of auto-correlation of the residuals.

Increases in the numbers of supplementary pensioners have been associated with increases in the number of people of pensionable age in the

Table 3.1 Generalized least squares regression model for supplementary pensioners

Log (number of supplementary pensioners)
(thousands) $= B_0 + B_1X_1 + B_2X_2 + B_3X_3 + B_4X_4 + B_5X_5 + B_6X_6$

Adjusted R^2 = 0.997 Rho = 0.32 DW = 1.76
s.e. regression = 0.021 s.e. rho = 0.22 F(6,19) = 1183.54

Variable		Estimated coefficient	t-statistic
	Constant	6.689	22.56
X_1	Housing costs (£)	0.116	5.57
X_2	Average amount of occupational pension (£)	−0.016	−2.37
X_3	Amount of state retirement pension (£)	−0.026	−5.06
X_4	Total number unemployed (thousands)	−0.001	−5.69
X_5	Total number of people of pensionable age (thousands)	0.001	2.93
X_6	Dummy 1 (1966 SB changes)	0.210	7.72

population, increasing housing costs, and the 1966 changes in supplementary benefit. Increases in the levels of occupational pensions and the retirement pension including graduated pension and SERPS are, predictably, associated with decreases in the numbers of supplementary pensioners. Less easy to interpret is the association between increases in the number of unemployed in the population with decreases in the number of supplementary pensioners. It may be that a fall in the demand for labour is associated with an increase in the number of younger retired people, who are less likely to be eligible for supplementary pensions.

The level of supplementary pension in real terms, the number of women aged 75 or over in the population, the numbers receiving housing benefit, and the dummy variable reflecting the 1974 shift due to the payment of housing rebates do not contribute any significant improvement to the fit of the model, as shown in Table 3.2, and this was also the case when lagged explanatory variables were tried.

4. Unemployed

In the mid-1960s, the unemployed were the smallest group in receipt of supplementary benefit. Now they are the largest, having overtaken pen-

Table 3.2 Effects of adding further variables to the pensions model

Variable added	F change (1,20)	t-statistic for added variable
Long-term SB rate 1987	0.026	−0.161
No. of elderly in population	0.473	−0.730
No. receiving housing benefit	1.031	−1.011
Dummy 2 (1974 changes)	2.467	−1.575

sioners in 1982 (Figure 3.1). Since 1979, the number of unemployed recipients of supplementary benefit has increased very rapidly indeed and they now constitute nearly two-thirds of all people registered unemployed (Figure 3.6).

Once again we examined financial, demographic, economic, and policy-related factors to discover whether any of these could be used to explain adequately the shift in numbers of unemployed supplementary benefit claimants. Only those with contributory records and who have been unemployed for less than a year are entitled to unemployment benefit, and the fewer entitled to unemployment benefit, the more would be receiving supplementary benefit. The number of people receiving unemployment benefit as a proportion of the number unemployed in Great Britain should pick up the effects of lengthening unemployment spells and the consequences of the large increase in the young unemployed without a contributory record.

There has been a fluctuating downward trend in the proportion of unemployed receiving unemployment benefit from a high point of 84.6 per cent in 1963 to 25.5 per cent in 1985. For those in receipt of unemployment benefit, the higher it is in relation to supplementary benefit, the less likely are the unemployed to be eligible for supplementary benefit.

Financial Influences

We first examined a number of financial factors that might affect the numbers of unemployed on supplementary benefit. These included the real level of unemployment benefit in relation to supplementary benefit, various replacement ratios as indicators of financial incentives and the extent of the unemployment trap, and housing costs measured as described for pensioners.

There is considerable literature devoted to assessing whether and to what extent differentials between income in work and benefits affect labour supply decisions. Economic theory would suggest that the higher the replacement ratio, the more people would remain unemployed and the more would be receiving supplementary benefit. It is difficult to produce a

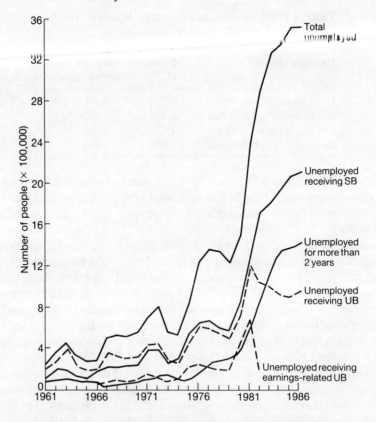

Figure 3.6   Total unemployed, unemployed receiving SB, unemployed receiving UB, and unemployed receiving earnings-related benefit, 1961–86

satisfactory definition of the replacement ratio, but supplementary benefit as a percentage of net average income for a couple with two children has fluctuated between 53.6 per cent in 1961 and 72.1 per cent in 1983.

Economic and Demographic Influences

Total unemployment in the population shows a fluctuating pattern followed by a sharp rise after 1975 (Figure 3.6), when long-term unemployment also increases rapidly. The number of unemployed on supplementary benefit rises and falls with the number of unemployed.

Influence of Policy

The same policy variables as used for pensioners—two dummies and the number of housing benefit recipients—might be expected to affect numbers of unemployed supplementary benefit recipients in similar ways.

Table 3.3 Generalized least squares regression model for unemployed claimant of supplementary benefit

Log (number of unemployed SB recipients)
    (thousands) $= B_0 + B_1X_1 + B_2X_2 + B_3X_3$

Adjusted R^2 = 0.995   Rho   = 0.354   DW   = 1.85
s.e. regression = 0.096   s.e. rho = 0.201   F(3,21) = 1640.29

Variable		Estimated coefficient	t-statistic
	Constant	1.957	1.788
X_1	Log (number of long-term unemployed at time t)	0.846	3.329
X_2	Log (number of unemployed at time t)	0.922	6.072
X_3	Log (number of unemployed at time $t-1$)	-0.980	-3.994

Table 3.3 gives the results of a multiple regression that was used to derive a model to show how the change in the number of unemployed claimants of supplementary benefit has depended on changes in financial, demographic, and policy variables. Again, generalized least squares regression was used to correct for the effects of auto-correlation of the residuals.

The variables that contribute to the best model of changes in the level of dependence of the unemployed on supplementary benefit were all economic and demographic—the number of unemployed and the number of long-term unemployed. Indeed, the fact that the number of unemployed and its lag enter with equal magnitudes and opposite signs suggests that it is spell length that drives supplementary benefit recipiency. It has been seen from Figure 3.6 that the number of unemployed on supplementary benefit rises more or less *pari passu* with increases in unemployment, and so this is not a surprising result. However, what we hoped to find out was, given the numbers of unemployed, how other factors would influence the number on supplementary benefit. What we have found is that, given the trend in the numbers of unemployed, neither the numbers receiving housing benefit, nor the real level of unemployment benefit, nor a variety of measures of the replacement ratio, nor the level of housing costs, nor the two policy changes considered, make a significant impact on the number of unemployed on supplementary benefit (see Table 3.4).

It may be that our equations are wrongly specified and would benefit from quarterly data. We tried lagging the explanatory variables but no additional variables added significantly to the model. There may be other variables that, if they were available, would contribute to the models—the

Table 3.4 Effects of adding further logged variables to the unemployed models

Variable added	F change (1,20)	t-statistic for added variable
log (no. receiving housing benefit)	0.199	0.441
log (dummy 1 (1966 changes))	1.575	1.256
log (dummy 2 (1974 changes))	0.300	0.543
log (UB rates 1987)	1.795	1.433
log (net average income (couple + two children) 1987)	0.670	0.817
log (SB scale rates (couple + two children))	1.423	1.195
log (housing costs)	1.077	1.039

proportion of unemployed who are married women (and therefore not entitled to supplementary benefit) or the proportion of the unemployed who are young people. Also policy changes, particularly unemployed programmes affecting the numbers of young people and the long-term unemployed on supplementary benefit, in the later years of the period covered, may be muddying the picture.

5. Single Parents

The number of lone parents on supplementary benefit has increased almost sevenfold since 1961 (Figure 3.1). This increase is without doubt a reflection of the overall increase in the number of lone-parent families in the population. However, the increase in the number of lone-parent families has not been anything like as fast as the increase in the numbers of lone parents on supplementary benefit (particularly since 1980) (Figure 3.7). The proportion of lone parents on supplementary benefit has therefore risen (Figure 3.8). In 1961, one in six single parents claimed supplementary benefit. By 1986, over half claimed supplementary benefit.

There have been two previous attempts to explain this growing dependence of lone parents on supplementary benefit. In 1974 the Finer Committee report analysed the position up to 1972 and considered that demographic changes were no more than a minor element in accounting for the growth in the number of fatherless families receiving supplementary benefit. It concluded that 'an important factor may have been the improved real value of the supplementary benefit scale rates' and an 'improved general awareness and acceptability of the scheme' (p. 247). In 1978 Hamill at the DHSS set out to update the Finer Committee analysis. Hamill thought that Finer had underestimated the impact of demographic trends, but also pointed to the importance of the changing level of

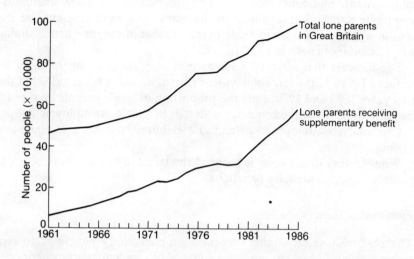

Figure 3.7   Lone parents in Great Britain and lone parents receiving
supplementary benefit, 1961–86

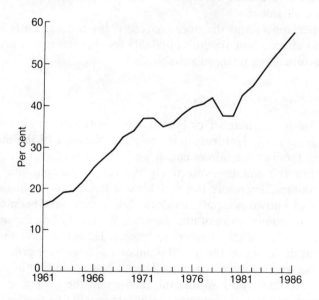

Figure 3.8   Lone parents receiving supplementary benefit, as a percentage of total
lone parents in Great Britain, 1961–86

employment. She concluded that 'The combination of a low unemployment rate and an improvement in the gains from work . . . may be the
reason why there was no increase in the number of lone mothers claiming
supplementary benefit in 1973' (p. 17).

She forecast that after 1978 the rate of increase in numbers might be
reduced by an improved employment situation, and it is the case that the
two years 1973 and 1979 when the proportion of single parents on supplementary benefit declined coincide with falls in female unemployment.

Our analysis attempts to extend and elaborate the work of Finer and
Hamill.

What factors might have influenced the trend in the numbers of single
parents on supplementary benefit?

Financial Influences

The real cash value of the long-term supplementary benefit scale represents a measure of the purchasing power of supplementary benefit over
time. The long-term rate of supplementary benefit is taken because since
1980 single parents have been entitled to the long-term rate after one year
dependent on benefit. This has risen over time from £19.96 in 1961 to
£30.08 in 1986 (in 1987 prices). The average weekly earnings of a female
manual worker are used to represent the earnings potential of a lone
parent in employment.

As for pensioners and the unemployed, rising housing costs might be
expected to affect a lone parent's eligibility for supplementary benefit and
are thus included as a financial variable.

Demographic Influences

The increase in the number of lone parents in the population has been
shown in Figure 3.7. Unfortunately, because estimates of the number of
lone-parent families are infrequent, it was found necessary to interpolate
values between estimates—effectively drawing a straight line through
known estimates. Therefore this variable is a trend line rather than a full
time series of known population values. There may have been structural
changes in the composition of lone parents. We tried using the number of
illegitimate births and the number of divorces. However, after experimen-
tation it was decided that the actual number was a sounder proxy for both
demographic and structural changes. Hamill had noted that in the period
1966 to 1971, there were significant changes in the proportion of lone
mothers with children under five, partly attributable to the fact that the
average age of lone mothers had tended to decrease over this period. However, this trend has stabilized since 1971. There has also been a slight fall in

the number of children per lone-parent family from 1.8 in 1972 to 1.6 in 1984. The median age of lone mothers has also remained fairly constant during the 1970s and 1980s. So overall there appears to have been a good deal of consistency in the structural features of the lone-parent population. The main change has been a doubling in the numbers between 1961 and 1986.

Economic Influences

Registered female unemployment is probably not a good indication of the tightness of the labour market for single parents, since the propensity to register may have changed over time because of changes in National Insurance rules rather than changes in demand for labour. We therefore included total unemployment as an alternative indicator of labour demand (Figure 3.6).

Influences of Policy

The two dummy variables representing policy shifts, together with the numbers of people receiving housing benefit, were again used in the analysis.

The regression analysis was not particularly successful in deriving a sensible model of the numbers of lone parents on supplementary benefit. We found that two factors—the real values of the long-term supplementary benefit scale rates and the level of female unemployment—were associated with the dependence of lone parents on supplementary benefit. However, they had rather different impacts during different periods. Thus up to the mid-1970s, the real value of supplementary benefit scale rates was more important, rising fairly steadily while female unemployment remained low. In the later period, female unemployment rose rapidly and was more influential (Figure 3.9). A model based on these two variables is presented in Table 3.5.

The low Durbin-Watson value in this model suggests that use of generalized least squares has not solved the problem of auto-correlation. We experimented with introducing the variables in various forms (including logging and lagging), without further sensible improvement in this model or alternative versions. Replacing female unemployment with total unemployment failed to produce a better model. Surprisingly, perhaps, not even the numbers of lone parents in the population contributed to any model tried.

Overall, the analysis suggests that there is relatively little room for manœuvre in reducing dependence of lone parents on supplementary benefit. Economic factors are important determinants of the number of lone parents on supplementary benefit, but even with improvements in

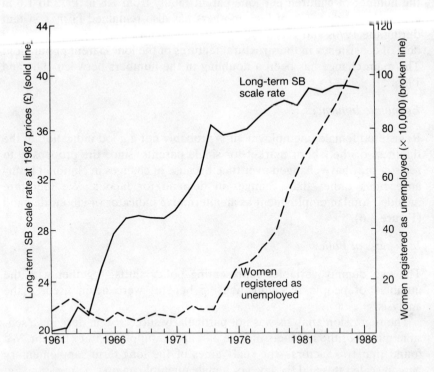

Figure 3.9   Female unemployment and long-term supplementary benefit scale rates, 1961–86

Table 3.5 A generalized least squares model of the number of lone parents on supplementary benefit

Number of lone parents on supplementary benefit
$$= B_0 + B_1 X_1 + B_2 X_2$$

Adjusted R^2 = 0.765	Rho = 0.883	DW = 1.14
s.e. regression = 13808.2	s.e. rho = 0.086	F(2,23) = 38.46

Variable	Estimated coefficient	t-statistic
Constant	−42.13	−0.80
X_1 Long-term supplementary benefit level (1987 prices)	6.21	3.65
X_2 Level of female unemployment	0.33	9.72

employment opportunities, lone parents have a limited capacity to respond. Child care responsibilities are an obvious constraint on single parents' freedom to respond to economic incentives.

6. Conclusion

In this historical and largely descriptive analysis, we have explored one of the most remarkable trends in Britain's post-war social security system, the massive increase in dependence on supplementary benefit. We have found that different types of factors have influenced trends in the dependence of the different groups examined. Social security dependence is a hand-maiden to many influences, and the attainment of the 'sheer delight of personal achievement' is not likely to be the prerogative of the Secretary of State for Social Services alone.

Appendix: Variables Used in Analysis

Number of pensioners (recipients and dependants) receiving supplementary benefit Source 1: The 1985 figure is our own estimate.

Total pensioner population Source 2: Mid-year estimates for men aged 65 and over and women aged 60 and over. The 1986 figure is our own estimate.

Female pensioners aged 75 and over Source 2: Mid-year estimates. The 1986 figure is our own estimate.

Flat-rate retirement pension Source 3: Standard retirement pension for a single person under 80 on own insurance at April 1987 prices.

Long-term supplementary benefit rate Source 3: Scale rate for a single householder at April 1987 prices. 1961 to 1965 is a single rate. 1966 to 1972 includes the long-term addition. 1973 to 1986 is the long-term rate. 1980 to 1986 includes an addition for fuel (Source 4). Where additions are made, these are adjusted to real terms using the pensioner price index (1987=100).

Pensioners in receipt of graduated pensions Source 1: From 1972.

Average amount of graduated pension and State Earnings-Related Pension Source 1: Average amounts recalculated as averages for *all* pensioners.

Average amount of occupational pension Source 5: Calculated from income from annuities and pensions (other than social security benefits) for one-adult households, men aged 65 and over and women aged 60 and over. These figures do not include SERPS or graduated pensions. Figures for 1961 to 1970 are extrapolated.

Numbers of people receiving housing benefit Sources 1 and 6: People in receipt of rate rebates, including rent allowance and rent rebate, from 1968.

Housing costs Source 3: The housing element of the retail price index is used to derive the amount of long-term supplementary benefit which it represents at 1987 prices. The amount for 1986 is our own estimate.

Total unemployment Source 7: 1961 to 1982 quarterly averages. 1983 to 1986 figures are adjusted by the unemployment unit index.

Supplementary benefit claimants classified as unemployed Source 1: Includes those with and without contributory benefit. 1985 figure is interpolated. 1961 figure from National Assistance Board Annual Report.

Number of recipients of unemployment benefit Source 2: Includes Great Britain and Northern Ireland. 1986 figure taken from Source 1 for Great Britain with an adjustment made for Northern Ireland.

Number of recipients of earnings-related unemployment benefit Source 1: 1966 to 1982.

Number of people unemployed for more than 2 years Source 7: Quarterly averages, wholly unemployed by duration.

Unemployment benefit rate Source 3: Standard rate of benefit for a single person on own insurance.

Short-term supplementary benefit rate Source 3: For a single householder. In calculating supplementary benefit as a percentage of unemployment benefit, the figures used for each are those which apply for the greater part of the year in question.

Benefit as percentage of net income Source 3: Rates used are those pertaining to a married couple with two children, one under age 5 and one aged 5 to 10 years.

Number of lone-parent recipients of supplementary benefit Source 1: One-parent families not included in other supplementary benefit groups receiving regular weekly payments in a week in November or December up to 1984, and in February 1986. The figure for 1985 is interpolated.

Number of one-parent families in Great Britain Source 8: 1961 to 1977 based on General Household Survey and census data and interpolated. Source 9: 1978 to 1984. Figures for 1985 and 1986 are extrapolated in consultation with the National Council for One Parent Families.

Females unemployed and females in the employed labour force Source 2: Mid-June estimates for each year.

Sources

1. *Social Security Statistics*. DHSS. HMSO.
2. *Annual Abstract of Statistics*. CSO. HMSO.
3. *Abstract of Statistics for Index of Retail Prices, Average Earnings, Social Security Benefits and Contributions*. DHSS Branch HQ SR8A.

4. *National Welfare Benefits Handbook*. CPAG.
5. *Family Expenditure Survey*. DE. HMSO.
6. *Housing and Construction Statistics*. DE. HMSO.
7. *Employment Gazette*. DE. HMSO.
8. National Council for One Parent Families, Information Sheet Number 5, January 1982.
9. *Population Trends*, **45**. OPCS, 1986.

4

Social Security and the Economics of Housing

RICHARD BERTHOUD*

1. Introduction

Central and local government have many different methods of influencing the costs of housing. These include regulation of the contract between landlord and tenant, planning controls, and the package of rates, rates support, and rates rebates. But there are three ways in which public finances provide direct support for people's housing costs:

- social security benefits (rent rebates and allowances, plus some income support covering mortgage interest; these cost nearly £4 billion in 1987–8);
- 'bricks and mortar' subsidies (the Department of the Environment records a public contribution of £1.3 billion to the current costs of local authorities and housing associations);
- tax relief to owner-occupiers (the exact nature of the subsidy is subject to debate; mortgage interest tax relief costs £4.8 billion).

The present government introduced one major overhaul of housing benefit in 1982, and another one in 1988. It has acted to increase rents and reduce subsidies to public sector housing, and has it in mind to eliminate direct subsidies altogether. On the other hand, it has eagerly promoted the sale of council houses at subsidized prices. The purpose of this paper is simply to get across two points:

- each change in policy has been considered in isolation, so that no government has ever examined the impact and interactions of all three programmes;
- two of the three sets of policy executed in the name of housing have been set up without regard to their impact on the supply of accommodation to people in need.

* Richard Berthoud is a Senior Research Fellow at the Policy Studies Institute.

This paper was presented at a conference on 'The Economics of Social Security', organized by the Institute for Fiscal Studies, held on 15 April 1988.

The paper draws on ideas developed in collaboration with John Ermisch during an earlier study supported by the Joseph Rowntree Memorial Trust. It has benefited from criticism and suggestions from Andrew Dilnot, John Hills, Alan Holmans, Peter Kemp, and Ian Walker.

The net effect is serious problems in the housing market, affecting millions of people; billions of pounds are circulating in the housing market with little identifiable advantage to anybody.

2. Social Security Benefits

When Beveridge laid down the social security system whose outline we still recognize, he had some difficulty with what he called 'the problem of rent'. Should National Assistance include a fixed amount with which claimants could bargain for housing in the market-place? Or should it pay people's actual rents? In the end he concluded that people could not bargain in the market-place in the short term, and that rents varied so much that a fixed rent allowance would be unfair—claimants with above-average rents would find themselves with less than the minimum scale rates with which to pay for food, fuel, clothing, and so on. So he recommended that housing costs should be met directly. He was assuming, of course, that the number of people having to claim National Assistance would be very small, and that for working-age families this would only be temporary; if both these assumptions were correct, the effects on the housing market would be minor.

One of the reasons why the number of National Assistance, then supplementary benefit, now income support, claimants remained so high was that no arrangements were made to cover the housing costs of claimants of National Insurance benefits. Whenever insurance benefits have been set at £x, social assistance benefits have usually been set at around £x plus housing costs. This, combined with the rise in long-term unemployment, has left the Government paying 4 million claimants' housing costs more or less directly. This is a housing policy only to the extent that it has prevented poor people from being evicted onto the streets. The design of the scheme was much more concerned with income maintenance objectives than with improving the general supply of housing for low-income families.

Rent rebates (for council housing) and rent allowances (for the private sector) became standard national schemes in 1972. While supplementary benefit claimants had the whole of their rent paid for them, many people just above the supplementary benefit line had previously had no help at all. Rent rebates and allowances were designed to fill this gap, for two reasons: first, to bring to fairly low-income households some of the protection available to very low-income households; second, to counter the work-disincentive effects created by the complete withdrawal of housing support when unemployed people found low-paid jobs. Both of these motives were strengthened by the policy of reducing council housing subsidies and increasing rents. But it will be seen that the objectives lay in the field of income maintenance, and were not designed to improve the supply of adequate accommodation.

The impetus for a reform of social security support for housing costs came from the Supplementary Benefits Commission, which was impatient with the administrative burden of recalculating supplementary benefit entitlements every time the council increased the rent, simply to pay out public money which tenants had to repay to the public purse a few days later. Then there was the 'better off' problem: the rent element of supplementary benefit was calculated according to a different formula from rent rebates, so claimants on the borderline could never be sure which they ought to be claiming.

Housing benefit was introduced in 1982, but never looked like living up to its advance billing as a 'comprehensive' solution. It was just the two old schemes tied together—with red tape. Although 'certification' of supplementary benefit claimants' rent rebates reduced the work-load of local DHSS offices, the complexities of the formulas for rent and rates rebates, not to mention housing benefit supplement, boggled the minds of local authority housing departments almost as much as of claimants. One of the new housing benefit's duties was to cope with the effects of a 50 per cent increase in local authority rents, and this introduced many more tenants to the Byzantine world of means-testing. The 'administrative reform' of housing benefit led to one of the worst problems in the history of bureaucracy.

It was ironic that housing benefit should have been an administrative failure. This was not a case of starry-eyed idealists failing to understand the practical implications of their theories. The design of housing benefit owed nothing to consideration of non-administrative issues. The two existing benefits were retained; the proper relationship between them was not examined; nor the relationship between them and the other two state influences on housing costs. No one wondered what the role of a benefit should be within a national housing policy. No one asked how support for the costs of housing might fit into an integrated taxes and benefits policy.

The disadvantages of this short-sighted course became apparent almost immediately, and the Secretary of State for Social Services, Norman Fowler, announced a complete review of the housing benefit scheme only 11 months after the first attempt had been implemented. The new housing benefit scheme introduced in April 1988 has a calculation formula for the rent and rates rebates of people not on income support which fits well with the equivalent calculation for income support claimants. Income support had to be rather drastically simplified—in some respects excessively simplified—in order to make this possible, but so far as the rent and rates calculation is concerned, the formula resolves many of the worst absurdities of the previous attempt. But, for the second time in the space of a few years, means-tested rent and rates support is being changed without any analysis of what it ought to be achieving. No one has wondered what the role of a benefit should be within a national housing policy. No one has asked how support for housing costs might fit into an integrated taxes and benefits policy.

The new housing benefit scheme appears to be based on the assumption that the supply of housing for rent is fixed and that rents are predetermined. The only role for social security, therefore, is to enable poor claimants to meet those costs without eating into the meagre amounts available for other items of expenditure. This was Beveridge's conclusion. And indeed those assumptions are a pretty accurate summary of the short-term choices facing individual claimants. Protecting the poor from the vagaries of the rest of the market is one of the criteria on which any social security benefit should be judged. But the new housing benefit formula insulates all tenants within its scope from the effects of any variations in their rent, extending 100 per cent protection from the vagaries of the market not only to income support claimants but also to tenants above the income support line. In combination with the inexorable increase in the number of income support claimants, this means that even more tenants—probably more than half the total—will not have to worry about the level of their rent. Good for them in the short term, perhaps, but bad for the other bidders in their market, if they make no effort to resist rent increases, pay over the odds when bargaining for a tenancy, or move into more expensive property than they ought to be able to afford.

It may fairly be argued that this description of a housing market in which people 'bid', 'bargain', or have access to 'expensive property' bears no relation to the forces acting on the level of rents in the real world—where council rents are set on the basis of a combination of historic costs and political decisions, and many private rents are subject to tight controls. In those circumstances, it does not matter that housing benefit claimants are insulated from the effects of the marginal pound in rent. On the other hand, the Government intends to move towards economic pricing subject to market forces throughout the rental sector. So its social security reforms seem likely to undermine the viability of its housing proposals.

Because of the insensitivity of tenants to the level of their rents, two further difficulties arise. One is that a bureaucratic control will have to be exercised over the level of rents accepted for benefit purposes in the private sector: the local authority's rent officer will be asked to certify that the charge is a 'fair market rent'. Second, the Government finds itself obliged to restrict the number of families entitled to the benefit, in order to limit the damage which might be done to the market for rented housing.

Once housing benefit has been designed along these lines, the only element over which Ministers retain control is the rate of 'taper': the steepness of the formula for withdrawing benefit as income rises. Since 1979, the costs of housing benefit have seemed to increase: because most of the housing elements of supplementary benefit were transferred to the housing benefit heading, as unemployment has risen; and as rents in the public sector have increased. None of these represents an extension of housing benefit. Indeed, the rise of rent rebates to meet increasing rents conceals a significant reduction in public expenditure in this area. It is therefore a mistake to think of housing benefit as having become 'more generous' over the years. The 'needs allowance' part of the formula has risen at about the same speed as supplementary benefit rates, but the taper formulas have been tightened again and again—from 17 per cent of gross earnings in 1981 to 43 per cent in 1988. The 1988 relaunch of housing benefit includes the latest cuts based on the idea that 'far too many people' have been turning to welfare for help with their housing; this is an idea which will produce echoes when we turn to consider the other two state influences on the price of housing.

3. 'Bricks and Mortar' Subsidies

Public subsidies to the providers of housing have always been analysed in terms of the effects on the supply and pricing of accommodation, to an extent that subsidies directed at the people who live in the housing have not. Council housing was initiated during the First World War at a time when 90 per cent of all households rented their accommodation, and when there was concern about the scarcity of the stock of homes in adequate condition. The great heyday of municipal construction between 1945 and 1975 also came at a period when there were fewer houses available than there were families wanting to live in them, when whole areas of many cities had fallen into neglect, and when some landlords were happy to exploit that scarcity at the expense of their tenants. Public building subsidies were therefore aimed at relieving the overall problems of scarcity and poor quality affecting large numbers of 'ordinary people' as well as the poorest. Rehabilitation of the inner cities was seen as a 'public good' in the technical sense, meaning things like roads or the police which benefit the public at large rather than particular individuals.

Two things happened in the 1970s. First, the building programme just about caught up with its objectives, to the extent that in most parts of the country there were enough houses in satisfactory condition to accommodate the people living there (although there was not necessarily enough rented accommodation in every market to meet local need). Second, both ideological and economic trends led to a more critical consideration of public expenditure. Recorded housing subsidies formed one of the fastest-rising elements in public expenditure up until 1975; and one of the fastest-falling ones ever since. Note that the turn-round came during the period of office of a Labour government, so the retreat from subsidized public housing should not be interpreted simply in political terms.

The end of the concerted public housing programme brought about a number of changes in the provision and cost of housing for low-income families. One was the general rise in rent levels, with the increasing emphasis on means-tested rent rebates already referred to. Another was an increasing polarization of the housing market, as more and more middle-income households bought their own homes, leaving more and more of the rented houses, especially in the public sector, to the poor. Public housing has become welfare housing. Third, local authorities have been unable to respond to increasing pressures on local markets, and to the rapid deterioration of the homes put up in such a hurry only a few years ago. So the pre-1975 use of subsidies to deal with conditions of overall scarcity is no longer available, and this has led to the overheating of housing markets in some areas, notably London. One of the results has been homelessness, with its high costs to councils as well as the distress to families.

Another set of changes in recent years has been the diversification in the targets for producer-subsidies. There has been growing, and often justified, disenchantment with local authorities as large-scale landlords: their rents, set according to historic costs without regard to the underlying value of properties; their bureaucratic queuing procedures; their often ineffective repair and maintenance services. Some of these problems have been caused at least as much by the scarcity of housing, and by the constraints of the regulatory framework, as by incompetence in town halls. The more pluralistic approach to the supply of housing will nevertheless be welcomed in many areas. But it should not be imagined that this is being achieved without recourse to subsidy. The Housing Corporation's support for housing associations has been one effective way of delivering resources to groups with particular needs. Other subsidies have included the discounts offered on the sale of council houses to sitting tenants, and the tax reliefs offered to private landlords, for instance through the Business Expansion Scheme. These incentives have not been recorded as housing subsidies, but that is what they are. Some commentators have argued that favouring the private sector in this way is at least as great an interference in the operation of a free market as the old frankly acknowledged public sector subsidies were.

Direct subsidies to the producers of housing should not, however, be thought of simply in terms of capital support for new building. The true subsidy lies in enabling the landlord to charge a lower rent (on new or old properties) than would otherwise be necessary to provide an economic return on the capital currently invested in the property. The thrust of the Government's current plans, however, is to allow rents to rise to their economic level, in order to allow private investors to compete on level terms with the public and voluntary sectors. So subsidies to 'bricks and mortar' will be phased out, and public support to tenants will be restricted to income-tested housing benefit for the poorest.

But this is one of the points at which it is crucial to examine the inter-actions between the two types of policy. One of the main objectives of end-ing subsidies in the public sector and of decontrolling the private sector is an increase in the supply of privately rented houses. If this happens, then the people enabled to live in the extra housing will benefit. Those within the scope of housing benefit would be largely protected from the direct financial effects of the increased rents. But housing benefit would then extend further up the income scale, so that large numbers of people earn-ing modest salaries would have to apply. Bureaucratic complications and unease about submitting to a means test would prevent many of them from getting their money. There would be a big increase in the number of fami-lies facing 100 per cent protection against rent increases, and this might have even more serious consequences for the market. People receiving the benefit would also be paying a marginal tax rate of 90 pence in the pound or higher, and this would affect their work incentives. People just above the threshold would have to devote a very large proportion of their income to housing costs; they would be little better off than if they were unem-ployed; people would think that this was damaging to their incentives (though there is little evidence that there would actually be any effect on the supply of labour). Other people, including Press and politicians, would look down on the families who were having to claim housing benefit and say that they were excessively dependent on welfare. There would be 'far too many people' relying on support intended for the poorest; there would soon be pressure to cut down on this debilitating use of public money. In short, the increased reliance on income-tested benefits would create pre-cisely the problems that the Government says it wants to avoid.

4. Tax Relief to Owner-Occupiers

All of the discussion so far has been concerned with rents—because public policy tends to be more concerned with families on low incomes, and because most families on low incomes are tenants. But the majority of the population, including large numbers of families with ordinary incomes, are owner-occupiers. It is therefore important to consider the role of public subsidies for owner-occupation.

There is little doubt that owner-occupation is usually a better form of tenure than renting. There is no doubt at all that the majority of British people prefer it. There is therefore every reason—in the public good as well as at election time—for governments to support and encourage owner-occupation. It can be argued, on the other hand, that the present arrangements do *not* encourage owner-occupation, and may have effects which actually discourage the extension of home-ownership. At the same time, the general preference for owner-occupation ought not to be so strong as to exclude a healthy market in rented housing, which needs to be stimulated in the interests of those households unable to purchase, or who would prefer a relatively short tenancy to meet their immediate needs.

Owner-occupiers pay no taxes on any of the resources transferred into or out of their home, other than on interest payments on mortgages above £30,000. This tax relief is a cost to the exchequer and a gain to the occupier, and therefore represents a subsidy. There is, however, room for argument and analysis as to exactly how the subsidy operates. To the general public and their representatives, the tax relief is thought to consist of the rebate of income tax on mortgage interest payments. This is visible to the taxpayer. All economists who have considered the question, however, seem to agree that the true subsidy lies in permitting the owner to enjoy the value of the property (i.e. live in it) without paying tax on the rent that the occupier would normally pay to the owner. Tenants pay rent out of taxed income; landlords pay tax on their rental income; owner-occupiers escape altogether.

There is definitely a subsidy; the only argument is about what precise form it takes. Indeed, it can be said that there are *two* subsidies. It may be helpful to compare the effects of reimposing tax on either of these elements. A tax on imputed rent would spread throughout the period of ownership, and would tend to fall on relatively better-off households, especially people who had done well out of a period of rising house prices. Abolishing tax relief on mortgage interest would affect the beginning of the period of ownership, and would fall on relatively worse-off households, especially those entering a high-price market. Thus the taxation of imputed rent would be more progressive, whereas the taxation of mortgage interest would tend to affect the first-time buyer.

Economic analysis therefore indicates that the most important subsidy to owner-occupation is the non-taxation of imputed rent. That does not necessarily mean that imputed rent should be taxed. Many commentators have reacted in horror to the very concept of a tax imposed on people's use of their 'own' property; but property taxes are levied in many other countries, and the idea seems no more outrageous than a tax on people's 'own' earnings. In fact, tax was assessed on imputed rent under 'Schedule A' until 1963, though the valuations were nearly 30 years out of date by the time it was abolished.

Leaving aside the exact definition, what effects does tax relief for owner-occupiers have? Part of the subsidy has almost certainly been capitalized in the form of house prices rising to a higher level. To the extent that this has happened, the gainers from the subsidy are the people who already owned property before prices rose. People trying to get into the market are not helped at all, so the subsidy does not encourage owner-occupation. The losers from the ending of the subsidy, however, would be the current set of owners, who would expect to see the value of their properties fall. This provides quite a convincing political argument against making any change.

Another result of artificially inflated house prices may have been the squeezing of private landlords out of the market, unable to compete with the bids from subsidized owner-occupiers. Alternatively, landlords would have had to charge higher rents to meet their costs, and it would be private tenants who would be contributing to the owner-occupiers' subsidy.

To the extent that the subsidies have not affected prices, they would affect owners' incomes. Whichever aspect of the subsidy is considered, it is clear that the effect is regressive: richer people gain most, though the £30,000 ceiling on mortgages qualifying for relief has improved matters. If the Government is keen to lower the taxes paid by high earners, it could do this more directly, and with better effects on marginal tax rates and incentives, by reducing tax rates even further, instead of by continuing the relief on property ownership. If, on the other hand, the Government is serious about targeting resources on those in greatest need, a completely different mechanism would be required.

One effect of the indiscriminate subsidy may be the encouragement of over-consumption of housing among middle- and upper-income groups. In particular, people may tend to remain in large houses after their children have left home, and so artificially inflate the value of the limited stock of accommodation.

The subsidies are, however, highly unlikely to have had any effect on the extent of owner-occupation. Most of the benefit goes to people who would have been able to buy their own property anyway, and very little of it goes to those on the borderline, to whom a more effective support might make all the difference.

The most important comparison is between the financial support available to owners and to renters. Both direct and indirect support for tenants is aimed as far as possible at those with low incomes; thus, in general, poor tenants can count on a significant subsidy, while rich tenants get none at all. For owner-occupiers it is the other way round: rich owners are heavily subsidized, while poor ones get very little. Thus, far from encouraging owner-occupation among those with moderate and low incomes, the combination of the two systems provides strong incentives for them to remain in the rented sector.

It is a common complaint that far too many tenants get help with their housing costs, and that some of them do not really need it. All owner-occupiers—two-thirds of all households—get help with their housing costs. Many of them do not need it at all. For those who do need it, the help is ineffective. Billions of pounds are being wasted. It is therefore appropriate to look for a better targeted and more effective way of supporting the housing expenditure of ordinary households and encouraging the further extension of owner-occupation.

5. Looking for a New Policy

The Government seems to have three broad objectives: encouragement of owner-occupation, revitalization of rented housing, and support for those in greatest need. Most people would probably welcome these objectives. But they cannot be achieved, as long as the three forms of financial support for housing are considered in blinkered isolation.

It will not be possible to change the whole of housing finance overnight. But the long-term aim should be equivalent treatment of all tenures. That might mean either that owner-occupiers should be brought into the tax net, or that renters should be let out of it. It might mean that 'bricks and mortar' subsidies should in certain circumstances be available to private landlords and to builders for owner-occupation, on similar terms to those available in the public and voluntary sectors. It might mean that a means-tested housing benefit should be available to low-income owner-occupiers as well as to tenants. It would probably mean a much more open market in rented property than exists at the moment, although it would probably still be necessary for the public authorities to intervene in areas of acute scarcity.

There have been two recent attempts to work out a more equitable and efficient system of housing support.

The Policy Studies Institute proposal: This was put to the Rowe housing benefit review team, though the committee felt unable to extend its remit to include a complete rethink of housing finance. Mortgage interest tax relief would have been retained, but owner-occupiers would have paid tax on the rental value of their property. All low-income households—tenants and owner-occupiers alike—would be able to claim a housing allowance based on the usual rental cost of accommodation suitable for their family size; they would pay (or save) the marginal pound of rent themselves. The proposal was designed to allow market signals to influence supply and demand, and rent levels. But a long lead-in period was required, during which tenants' benefit would be based at least partly on actual rents paid.

The Duke of Edinburgh proposal: This was recommended by an independent Committee of Inquiry into British Housing chaired by Prince Philip. Mortgage interest tax relief would be abolished. A 'needs-related housing allowance' would be available to low-income households in both sectors: for tenants, this would be based on actual rents and other charges up to a ceiling; for owner-occupiers, on actual mortgage interest payments and other charges subject to the same maximum. The maximum rate would vary by family structure and by region. Rents, which the Inquiry agreed should continue to be regulated, would be linked to the capital value of the property.

It is not the purpose of this paper to argue for or against the detail of either of these proposals, or to put forward another. But it is stupid for the Government to go on proposing changes to particular aspects of housing policy without addressing the distortions caused by the interactions between its three arms. This is at least as much a political problem as an economic one: no solution will work if it ignores the opposing policy interests of the Treasury, the Department of the Environment, and the Department of Health and Social Security, and also ignores the conflict between the long-term objectives of policy and the short-term concerns of millions of voters.

But something has to be done. Housing problems are getting worse. If present trends continue, London will eventually be inhabited by only two classes of people: very rich people owning expensive houses, and unemployed tenants, unable to take a job for fear of losing their housing benefit.

5

Poverty, Incentives, and Linear Income Taxation

RAVI KANBUR AND MICHAEL KEEN*

1. Introduction

The reform of social security and income maintenance programmes is now on the policy agenda of many OECD countries, there being a widespread view that these systems are rife with inefficiencies—that they involve excessive leakages of benefits to the non-poor and severe disincentive effects. The UK Government began a review of the system in 1985. This culminated in the legislation that came into effect in 1988, billed as the most radical reform of the social security system for 40 years. Summarizing its merits, the Secretary of State for Social Services claimed that 'This new, more coherent and better targeted structure will direct help more clearly where it is most needed and foster incentives to work' (John Moore, *Hansard*, cols. 121 and 179).

A social security and income maintenance system may serve many purposes. It might be used, for instance, to help households achieve a preferred allocation of resources over the life cycle, or to provide them with insurance of a kind that private markets are thought unable to offer. The central objective, however, is clear enough: it is the alleviation of poverty. This was certainly a major plank of the Beveridge proposals that launched the modern social security system in the UK; and the other main plank—the insurance principle—is arguably now little more than illusion (Dilnot, Kay, and Morris (1984)). Illusion aside, it is poverty alleviation that lies at the heart of the current debate. This is clear both from the claims made by John Moore and other advocates of the Fowler reforms and from many of the counter-claims made by their opponents. John Moore's defence of the

* Ravi Kanbur is a Professor at the University of Warwick and Michael Keen is a Reader at the University of Essex.
This paper and its companion piece, Kanbur and Keen (1988), were presented at a conference on 'The Economics of Social Security', organized by the Institute for Fiscal Studies, held on 15 April 1988 to mark the introduction of major social security and income maintenance reforms by the United Kingdom Government. The authors are grateful to participants at that conference for their comments, and to Tim Besley for helpful discussions.

reforms also raises the other recurrent theme: a concern with incentive effects. One may, of course, believe that social security is (or should be) about more than the relief of poverty (see, for instance, Stern (1987)); one might also take the view that labour supply responses—at least those of principal earners—are for practical purposes rather insignificant (though it would be difficult to believe that they place no ultimate constraint on the relief that can be provided). Nevertheless, it is the two issues of targeting and incentives that have come to dominate policy discussion in the UK; and it is these policy concerns that determine the focus of this paper.

On targeting, two aspects of the strategy associated with the Fowler reforms are especially noteworthy. The first is a tendency towards increased means-testing (income-testing). The second is a redirection of resources towards low-paid working families at the particular expense, many believe, of pensioners. Can these policies be justified in terms of their own stated objective of reducing poverty? The purpose of this paper and its companion piece, Kanbur and Keen (1988), is to develop a framework within which questions of this kind can be addressed. In the context of a theoretical model in which individuals can freely vary their labour supply, we attempt to make precise the trade-offs to be faced when the objective is to minimize poverty, and incentive effects on both poor and non-poor have to be taken into account. In subsequent work, we hope to apply this framework in greater empirical detail to the UK and to the US.

In the present paper, attention is confined to linear tax and benefit systems; that is, ones which are simply equivalent to the imposition of a poll tax or subsidy (demogrant) combined with the taxation of all other income at a constant marginal rate. This includes, of course, many of the most familiar proposals for radical social security reform: the simplest negative income tax, social dividend, and tax credit schemes, for instance, are all of precisely this form. Section 3 of the paper considers, from an explicit perspective of poverty alleviation, the design and evaluation of such schemes when a single linear tax structure is to be applied to a homogeneous population; the use of non-linear taxation for poverty alleviation is analysed in Kanbur and Keen (1988). Section 4 moves on to the case in which contingent information can be used to apply different linear tax structures to different groups of the population. This provides a simple setting within which many of the current issues of retargeting can be considered. By way of illustration, we provide some preliminary calculations bearing on the sort of retargeting from pensioners to working families that is currently emerging in the UK.

Before proceeding to a detailed consideration of poverty alleviation strategies, however, we need to consider how exactly poverty is to be measured once incentive effects are recognized. The next section begins the analysis by addressing this question.

2. Labour, Leisure, and the Measurement of Poverty

There is, of course, a vast literature on the concept and measurement of poverty (recently reviewed by Atkinson (1987)). The almost invariable strategy in applied work, however, is simple enough: someone is regarded as poor if and only if their income is below some specified poverty line, and measures of aggregate poverty are then constructed from the existence and (perhaps) extent of such income shortfalls. Measures of poverty thus rest, in practice, on measures of income. Empirical studies have indeed emphasized a variety of issues in the detailed construction of income variables, such as the nature of any adjustment for family composition and the relative merits of short- and longer-term income definitions. Their broad objective, nevertheless, remains that of measuring the income that a household actually receives. The larger question that this raises becomes especially evident when—as here—labour supply responses are at issue: for in attaching significance only to income, poverty measures of the usual kind attach no importance at all to the effort made to generate that income. They attach no value, that is, to leisure.

The difficulties that consequently arise in gauging poverty in terms of income received are obvious. A household or individual—terms we shall take as synonymous—could have enormous potential earnings and yet, in preferring instead to remain idle, be counted as poor. Conversely, such measures would treat as non-poor someone who managed to raise their income above the poverty line only by working inordinately hard. One response to such problems would be to assess poverty by reference not to the income that a household actually *does* receive but to that which it *could* receive by working some 'standard' number of hours. This of course opens up the question as to what should constitute standard hours. Nevertheless, such a formulation in terms of 'standard income' does have some appeal in capturing the commonplace view that by working a reasonable number of hours, a household ought to be able to secure a reasonable income, and locates the policy interest firmly in the low wage rates of the poor. This approach also corresponds to a notion of poverty as the absence of 'capabilities', advanced in a more general setting by Sen (1985).

From the usual welfare-theoretic perspective, however, neither received nor standard income is a satisfactory summary statistic: on either definition, it is perfectly possible for a change in the environment to lead, for instance, to a reduction in a household's income and yet leave that household, in its own view, better off than before. Consider, for instance, Figure 5.1, and suppose that the budget constraint is initially AA'; the household then works AL hours, which we can imagine to be exactly the amount deemed acceptable under the standard income approach. The tax and benefit system is now reformed, changing the budget constraint to ABB'.

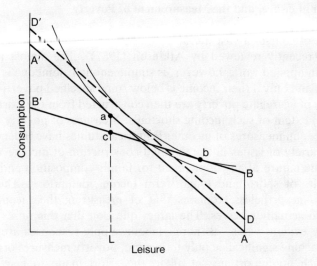

Figure 5.1

As a result, the household's received income falls (since b is below a) and so does its standard income (since c also lies below a). But the household also now attains a higher level of utility.

This points to a third and explicitly welfaristic approach to the treatment of leisure, focusing not on income gaps but on shortfalls between the utility levels households actually attain and some poverty level u_z. Denoting by $e(w,u)$ the virtual income needed to achieve utility u at a marginal wage w, choice of some reference wage w_r leads to

$$z(w_r) = e(w_r, u_z)$$

as a corresponding poverty line level of equivalent income (in the sense of King (1983)). The poverty of a household that achieves utility u could then be gauged by comparing its equivalent income $e(w_r,u)$ with this poverty line. In this way it would be straightforward to ensure that a reform which raised a household's welfare could not also increase its measured poverty. In Figure 5.1 for instance, and taking as the reference wage that corresponding to the initial budget constraint AA', the welfare improvement generated by the reform is reflected in an increase in equivalent income of AD (the line DD' being parallel to AA').

There are thus (at least) three distinct concepts of income that might be used to define and measure poverty: received, standard, and equivalent. These lead in turn to alternative criteria for the design and evaluation of policies for the alleviation of poverty, each of which has its merits. The equivalent income approach embodies the welfarism characteristic of the optimal tax literature. Indeed, it amounts to little more than imposing additional structure on a social welfare function of the usual kind. For this reason, we shall explore this approach no further. Those who view poverty purely in terms of household welfare may consequently be inclined to stop reading at this point. Yet the alternative approaches sketched out above do seem to capture concerns central to the discussion of policy in this area. The formulation in terms of standard income makes some concession, albeit a crude one, to Sen's influential critique of welfarism (1985). That in terms of received income corresponds directly to the procedures that dominate empirical work and underlie everyday debate. Whilst recognizing their limitations, and certainly without meaning to discard the lessons from existing welfaristic analyses, it therefore seems worth while exploring the implications of these alternative approaches for the construction of policies to relieve poverty. That is the purpose in the remainder of the paper.

To formalize issues of poverty alleviation, it is necessary to put more structure on the poverty index than we have yet had to do. Though it will be clear that some of the conclusions below are of more general relevance, attention will here be confined to the P_α-class of measures developed by Foster, Greer, and Thorbecke (1984). For a non-negative income variable y distributed with density $f(y)$, and with a poverty line of z, these take the form

$$P_\alpha = \int_0^z \left(\frac{z-y}{z}\right)^\alpha f(y)\mathrm{d}y, \ \alpha \geq 0. \tag{2.1}$$

Also used in related contexts by Besley and Kanbur (1987) and Kanbur (1986 and 1987), the P_α-class has the merit of combining analytical convenience and—through the parameter α—ethical flexibility. Taking $\alpha = 0, 1$, and 2, for instance, one has

$$P_0 = H \tag{2.2}$$

$$P_1 = H\left(\frac{z-\bar{y}_p}{z}\right) = HI \tag{2.3}$$

$$P_2 = H[I^2 + (1-I)^2 V_p^2], \tag{2.4}$$

where H is the simple headcount measure (the proportion of the population in poverty), $\bar{y}_p = E[y|y \leq z]$ is the mean income of the poor (so that I is just the income-gap ratio), and V_p is the coefficient of variation of income amongst the poor. More generally, as α increases, the P_α measure becomes increasingly sensitive to the incomes of the very poorest households; hence α is sometimes described as parameterizing 'poverty aversion'.

3. Linear Income Taxation with a Homogeneous Population

A linear income tax is one characterized by a constant marginal tax rate t and a poll subsidy G. As noted in the introduction, schemes of this kind have—in various guises—occupied a central position in discussions of social security reform. But while linear taxes have been widely studied in the context of social welfare maximization (see for instance Dixit and Sandmo (1977)), the poverty-orientated literature has gone little beyond the simple arithmetic of the trade-off between providing a decent basic benefit and maintaining reasonably low marginal tax rates. This leaves unanswered the obvious question: when labour supply effects are explicitly recognized, how would one design a linear income tax to achieve the maximal reduction of poverty? This section addresses that question in the setting of a homogeneous population, with a single tax schedule to be applied to all households.

Suppose then that households have identical preferences $u(c,1-h)$ defined on consumption c of a composite good and on leisure, the latter being the time endowment (normalized at unity) less hours worked, h. Households differ only in their (non-negative) wage rates, which are denoted by w and distributed with a density $f(w)$ that is unaffected by the tax system. Given its wage rate, each household chooses the hours that it works to maximize its utility, subject to the budget constraint

$$c = G + (1-t)wh$$

implied by the linear tax structure, leading to a labour supply function of the form $h[(1-t)w,G]$.

As discussed in the preceding section, the objective of poverty alleviation might be formulated either in terms of the income that a household actually receives, now given by

$$y(w) = G + (1-t)wh[(1-t)w,G], \qquad (3.1)$$

or in terms of that it would receive if it worked some standard number of hours L (assumed to be constant across households), which is given by

$$y_L(w) = G + (1-t)wL. \qquad (3.2)$$

We begin with the first of these approaches.

Denoting by h_w the derivative of labour supply with respect to the net wage, the assumption that

$$h + (1-t)wh_w > 0 \qquad (3.3)$$

(equivalently, that the wage elasticity be no less than -1) implies that net income strictly increases with the wage rate. There then exists some poverty line wage ω, defined by

$$y(\omega) = z, \qquad (3.4)$$

such that a household is poor if and only if it faces a wage lower than ω. This enables the poverty index corresponding to the received income approach to be written as

$$P_\alpha = \int_0^\omega \left(\frac{z-G-(1-t)wh[(1-t)w,G]}{z}\right)^\alpha f(w)dw \qquad (3.5)$$

(and we henceforth assume $\alpha > 0$). The problem of poverty alleviation thus becomes that of choosing the tax parameters t and G to minimize P_α in (3.5), subject to the constraint that

$$t\int_0^\infty wh[(1-t)w,G]\,f(w)dw - G = R, \qquad (3.6)$$

where R denotes the revenue (per caput) required by the government. The first-order conditions for this program are easily derived. It is more instructive, however, to cast the problem explicitly as one of reform: starting from an arbitrary initial tax structure, how would poverty be affected by a revenue-neutral increase in the marginal tax rate?

The bench-mark case is that in which labour supply is completely inelastic, say at h^*. From the revenue constraint (3.6), an increase in the marginal rate then enables the poll subsidy to be increased by

$$\frac{dG}{dt} = \overline{w}h^*, \qquad (3.7)$$

where $\overline{w}$ denotes the mean wage in the population. Differentiating (3.5), the effects through ω vanish (as a consequence of (3.4)) to leave

$$\frac{dP_\alpha}{dt} = \int_0^\omega J[z,y(w)]\left(\frac{dG}{dt} - wh^*\right)f(w)dw \qquad (3.8)$$

where

$$J[z,y(w)] \equiv \frac{-\alpha}{z}\left(\frac{z-y(w)}{z}\right)^{\alpha-1} \qquad (3.9)$$

is strictly negative for $w < \omega$. Combining (3.7) and (3.8) gives

$$\frac{dP_\alpha}{dt} = \int_0^\omega J[z,y(w)]\{\overline{w} - w\}h^*f(w)dw. \qquad (3.10)$$

So long as the poverty line wage is less than the mean wage, one thus has the expected conclusion: in the absence of incentive effects, a revenue-neutral increase in the marginal tax rate unambiguously reduces poverty (unless there are no poor households to begin with), with the increase in the basic benefit that it allows more than offsetting a directly adverse effect. One is thus led to continue increasing the marginal rate until either it reaches 100 per cent, or the basic benefit is raised to the poverty line, or at least some of those with above-average wages are impoverished.

No such simple prescriptions are available when labour supply responses are admitted. Denoting by h_G the derivative of hours worked with respect to the poll subsidy, the analogue to (3.8) is then

$$\frac{dP_\alpha}{dt} = \int_0^\omega J[z,y(w)]\left(\frac{dG}{dt}[1 + (1-t)wh_G] - w[h + (1-t)wh_w]\right)f(w)dw,$$
(3.11)

where dG/dt is again derived from the revenue constraint (3.6) but now also depends on supply responses. Comparing (3.11) with (3.8), the assumption in (3.3) implies that the direct effect of increasing the marginal tax rate is still to worsen poverty. Against this, a higher marginal rate may again generate increased revenue and so finance a more generous poll subsidy; but since $h_G \leq 0$ (so long as leisure is normal), the beneficial effects of this on measured income may now be dampened by an induced reduction in labour supply. At this level of generality, there is little more to be said: few enlightening and perfectly general formulas seem to be available.

Consider then the special case in which preferences are of the Cobb–Douglas form

$$u(c,1-h) = (1-\delta)\ln[c] + \delta\ln[1-h], \ \delta\in[0,1],$$

generating the labour supply function

$$h[(1-t)w,G] = (1-\delta) - \frac{\delta G}{(1-t)w}$$
(3.12)

and hence net income

$$y(w) = (1-\delta)\{(1-t)w + G\}.$$
(3.13)

Higher values of δ thus imply more sensitive labour supply behaviour; and $1-\delta$ is simply the proportion of full income that each household allocates to the consumption good. Suppose also that $R = 0$, so that the government merely requires the tax and benefit system to break even. Using these simplifications in (3.11) and the revenue constraint (3.6), and recalling too the definitions of $J(z,y)$ and P_α, one finds after lengthy manipulations that the effect of a balanced-budget increase in the marginal rate is given by

$$\left\{\frac{(1-t)z}{\alpha}\right\}\frac{dP_\alpha}{dt} = (P_{\alpha-1} - P_\alpha)z - \sigma(\delta,t)\left\{\frac{GP_{\alpha-1}}{t}\right\}$$
(3.14)

where

$$\sigma(\delta,t) = \frac{(1-\delta)(1-t)}{1-t(1-\delta)} \in [0,1]$$
(3.15)

Table 5.1 The critical marginal tax rate t^*

δ	Ratio of mean received income of poor to poll subsidy (K)		
	1.1	1.5	2.0
0.2	.57	.46	.36
0.4	.42	.33	.26
0.6	.26	.23	.18

Note: Equations (3.15) and (3.17) in the text lead to a quadratic equation with solutions, in obvious notation,

$$t^+, t^- = \{K + 1 - \delta \pm [(K + 1 - \delta)^2 - 4K(1-\delta)^2]^{\frac{1}{2}}\}/2(1-\delta)K.$$

With $K > 0$ and $\delta \in (0,1)$, it is readily shown that $t^+ > 1$. The critical value t^* is therefore t^-, and this is the figure reported.

(and we are assuming $t \in (0,1)$). The first term on the right-hand side of (3.14) is unambiguously positive (by the definition of P_α), and can be thought of as capturing the harmful direct effect of increasing the marginal rate. (This interpretation, and more generally the significance here of $P_{\alpha-1}$, will become clearer in the next section.) The second term captures both the opposing effect of an increased poll subsidy and the mitigating consequences of labour supply adjustments. Note that one simple implication follows immediately from (3.12): since $\sigma(\delta,t)$ is decreasing in δ, a revenue-neutral decrease in the marginal rate is more likely to reduce poverty, *ceteris paribus*, the more responsive is labour supply. Perhaps surprisingly, however, the implications of alternative degrees of poverty aversion seem to be ambiguous: both $P_{\alpha-1}$ and the difference $P_{\alpha-1} - P_\alpha$ are readily shown to be decreasing in α.

The formula (3.14) provides a convenient framework for illustrative calculations. Take for instance the case $\alpha = 1$. Denoting by $K \equiv \bar{y}_p/G \, (> 1)$ the ratio of the mean (received net) income of the poor to the poll subsidy, (3.14) then becomes

$$\left\{\frac{t(1-t)z}{HG}\right\}\frac{dP_1}{dt} = tK - \sigma(\delta,t). \tag{3.16}$$

Note from the definition in (3.15) that $\sigma(\delta,t)$ is strictly decreasing in t, with $\sigma(\delta,0) > 0$ and $\sigma(\delta,1) = 0$. Applied to (3.16), these observations imply the existence of a critical marginal tax rate $t^* \in (0,1)$, defined by

$$t^*K = \sigma(\delta,t^*), \tag{3.17}$$

such that a small revenue-neutral increase in the marginal rate will reduce poverty (conversely, increase it) if and only if the rate is initially less (greater) than t^*. Table 5.1 reports this critical marginal rate for a range of values of δ and K. The observation following (3.14) above implies that t^* must decrease with δ, and this emerges strongly from the calculations. Rather less obviously, it also emerges that t^* decreases with K; that is, increasing the marginal rate is less likely to reduce poverty the higher is the average income of the poor relative to the basic benefit. The intuition here is that when K is low, the pre-tax earnings of the poor are so insubstantial that reducing the marginal rate has little impact on their net incomes while raising the poll subsidy has a considerable one. Clearly the critical tax rate varies widely across the circumstances shown in the table. Bearing in mind, however, that the tax system is not being required to raise any revenue, the rates that emerge tend perhaps to be rather higher than might have been anticipated: even when the poor receive, on average, twice the basic benefit and δ is as high as 0.6, poverty alleviation points to a marginal tax rate of nearly 20 per cent. Of course, it must be emphasized that these numbers— and others to follow—are no more than suggestive, relating as they do to a particular choice of α and a very special preference structure.

It remains to consider the second approach, in which poverty is defined not in terms of the income that households *do* receive but that which they *could* receive by working standard hours. The relevant income concept is then that of (3.2) above, and the object of policy becomes that of minimizing

$$P_\alpha^L = \int_0^\omega \left(\frac{z - G - (1-t)wL}{z} \right)^\alpha f(w)dw, \qquad (3.18)$$

subject again to the revenue constraint (3.6). (Typically of course both the poverty line wage ω and the poverty line income z will now differ from their counterparts in (3.5); to save notation, this is not made explicit.) Differentiating (3.18) for the effect of increasing the marginal rate, one now finds

$$\frac{dP_\alpha^L}{dt} = \int_0^\omega J[z, y_L(w)] \left(\frac{dG}{dt} - wL \right) f(w)dw. \qquad (3.19)$$

Table 5.2 The critical marginal tax rate t^L

δ	Ratio of mean standard income of poor to poll subsidy (K^L)		
	1.1	1.5	2.0
0.2	.66	.54	.43
0.4	.58	.48	.40
0.6	.54	.45	.37

Note: By the same arguments as in the note to Table 5.1, t^L is calculated by using $(1-\delta)K^L$ instead of K in the formula given there.

This is identical in form to the corresponding expression (3.8) for the received income approach with inelastic labour supply; the number of hours that the government considers 'reasonable', L, appears in the same way as did the actual hours, h^*. What is different, of course, is that dG/dt is here typically not a constant; labour supply responses, while no longer directly affecting the minimand, retain importance through their implications for revenue.

Taking again the special case of Cobb–Douglas preferences, further manipulations now yield

$$\left\{\frac{(1-t)z}{\alpha}\right\}\frac{dP_\alpha^L}{dt} = (P_{\alpha-1}^L - P_\alpha^L)z - \frac{\sigma(\delta,t)}{(1-\delta)}\left\{\frac{GP_{\alpha-1}^L}{t}\right\}. \tag{3.20}$$

Comparing this with the analogous expression (3.14) for the received income approach, it is clear that—other things being equal (including the initial values of the poverty indices for α and $\alpha-1$)—a revenue-neutral increase in the marginal tax rate is now more likely to reduce poverty. For that under the received income approach, labour supply responses are likely to diminish the attractions of financing a higher poll subsidy by rais- ing the marginal tax rate: so long as leisure is normal in demand and hours worked increasing in the marginal wage (as in the Cobb–Douglas case), both of these tax changes reduce labour supply, tending on that account to reduce the incomes received by the poor and so to increase their measured poverty. When poverty is gauged in terms of standard income, however, these considerations are absent: since the revenue implications are unchanged, increasing the marginal tax rate is therefore more likely to prove beneficial.

Further simplification can again be achieved for the case $\alpha = 1$. Arguing as before, and denoting by K^L the ratio of the mean standard income of the poor to the poll subsidy, the condition

$$t^L(1-\delta)K^L = \sigma(\delta,t^L) \tag{3.21}$$

then defines a critical marginal tax rate $t^L \in (0,1)$ such that a small revenue- neutral increase in the marginal rate reduces (increases) poverty if and only if t is initially below (above) t^L. Some calculations are reported in Table 5.2. Interestingly, the numbers that emerge are not only uniformly higher than those in Table 5.1 but also considerably less sensitive to the strength of labour supply responses.

4. Taxation and Targeting by Contingencies

It is now widely recognized that one way of easing the tension between the provision of a decent level of support and the avoidance of high marginal tax rates may be by using non-income ('contingent' or 'categorical') information to impose different tax and benefit schedules on different groups of the population. This idea underlies, for instance, both the modified Social Dividend scheme of the Meade Committee (1978) and the more thoroughgoing proposals of Dilnot, Kay, and Morris (1984). At a more formal level, the potential advantages of 'tagging' have also been emphasized by Akerlof (1978). And indeed it is obvious that the British social security system has long made considerable use of contingent information. No less obvious is the general principle that the enlightened use of such information can only improve matters (assuming, heroically, that its collection and exploitation are costless). What is not clear, however, is the precise form that, from the perspective of poverty alleviation, an enlightened usage would take. How might one decide, for instance, whether poverty in the UK will be reduced by the policy of retargeting resources away from the elderly and towards low-paid families with children? More generally, how should one design the tax structures to be imposed on distinct groups in order to have the maximum impact on aggregate poverty? That is the issue explored in this section.

Suppose then that the population can be divided into two mutually exclusive and exhaustive groups, A and B, to which distinct linear tax systems may be applied. The underlying contingencies are assumed to be absolute, so that households are unable to switch between groups. Denoting by $\theta \in (0,1)$ the proportion of the population in group A, the results of Foster, Greer, and Thorbecke (1984) imply that the P_α measure of aggregate poverty now decomposes as

$$P_\alpha = \theta P_\alpha^A + (1-\theta)P_\alpha^B, \tag{4.1}$$

where P_α^i is the corresponding index of poverty within group i. For brevity, attention will be restricted in this section to the case in which poverty is defined in terms of received income and preferences are Cobb–Douglas. Assuming these preferences to be identical within groups but perhaps different between them, the relevant contingency-specific poverty indices are then, in obvious notation,

$$P_\alpha^i = \int_0^{\omega_i} \left(\frac{z_i - G_i - (1-t_i)wh^i[(1-t_i)w,G_i]}{z_i} \right)^\alpha f_i(w)\mathrm{d}w, \ i = A,B \tag{4.2}$$

where

$$h^i[(1-t)w,G] = (1-\delta_i) - \frac{\delta_i G}{(1-t)w}, \ \delta_i \in [0,1] \tag{4.3}$$

(and note that the poverty lines of the two groups may differ). Using (4.2) and (4.3) in (4.1) gives the minimand for a policy of poverty alleviation; the revenue constraint now takes the form

$$\theta\left\{t_A\int_0^\infty wh^A f_A(w)dw - G_A\right\} + (1-\theta)\left\{t_B\int_0^\infty wh^B f_B(w)dw - G_B\right\} = R, \quad (4.4)$$

with the h^i given by (4.3).

The trade-offs to be faced are clearly now much more complex than in the homogeneous population case. It is helpful to begin by considering just one: that between the poll subsidies paid to the two groups. Holding marginal tax rates constant at their initial (arbitrary) levels, under what circumstances would aggregate poverty be reduced by cutting the poll subsidy given to one group in order to finance an increase in that paid to the other? From (4.1)–(4.3), perturbing the poll subsidies in such a way causes aggregate poverty to change by

$$dP_\alpha = -\theta\left(\frac{\alpha(1-\delta_A)}{z_A}\right)P^A_{\alpha-1}dG_A - (1-\theta)\left(\frac{\alpha(1-\delta_B)}{z_B}\right)P^B_{\alpha-1}dG_B, \quad (4.5)$$

while revenue-neutrality requires, from (4.4) and (4.2), that

$$-\theta\left\{\frac{(1-\delta_A)}{\sigma(\delta_A,t_A)}\right\}dG_A - (1-\theta)\left\{\frac{(1-\delta_B)}{\sigma(\delta_B,t_B)}\right\}dG_B = 0, \quad (4.6)$$

where $\sigma(\delta,t)$ is as in (3.15) above. Combining (4.5) and (4.6) gives

$$dP_\alpha = -\left\{\frac{\alpha\theta(1-\delta_A)}{\sigma(\delta_A,t_A)}\right\}\left[\frac{\sigma(\delta_A,t_A)P^A_{\alpha-1}}{z_A} - \frac{\sigma(\delta_B,t_B)P^B_{\alpha-1}}{z_B}\right]G_A. \quad (4.7)$$

Thus a retargeting of resources away from group B and towards group A— in the sense of a small reduction in the poll subsidy to the former accompanied by a balanced-budget increase in that to the latter—will reduce aggregate poverty if and only if

$$\frac{\sigma(\delta_A,t_A)P^A_{\alpha-1}}{z_A} > \frac{\sigma(\delta_B,t_B)P^B_{\alpha-1}}{z_B}. \quad (4.8)$$

This reduces to the simple condition

$$P^A_{\alpha-1} > P^B_{\alpha-1} \quad (4.9)$$

if the two groups have the same poverty line and either $\delta_A = \delta_B = 0$, so that labour supply is perfectly inelastic (as in Kanbur (1986)), or $\delta_A = \delta_B$ and $t_A = t_B$, so that the two groups have the same preferences and face the same marginal tax rate (in which case differential treatment may nevertheless be desirable as a response to different wage distributions).

The appearance in these conditions of the terms $P^i_{\alpha l}$ emphasizes that the reduction of aggregate poverty measured in some particular way is typically *not* best pursued by redirecting resources towards whichever group is poorest in terms of that same measure. What matters, of course, is the *marginal* effect on the measure of interest. The structure of the P_α index is such that the implied rule takes an especially simple form to minimize the aggregate index for some specific choice of α, look first at the within-group indices for $\alpha-1$. Suppose for instance that we have chosen $\alpha = 1$ and that the poverty lines of the two groups are the same. Recalling (2.3), our objective is then simply to maximize the net income of the poor. Imagine now that we have some fixed sum to spend on increasing the poll subsidy to one group or the other, and assume for simplicity both that labour supply is inelastic and that the groups are of the same size. Which group should we favour? The disadvantage of having to spend this money as a poll subsidy is that some of it will be wasted on the non-poor; giving it to group i, the proportion of our fixed sum that will reach the poor is just the proportion of that group which is in poverty. To achieve the largest possible increase in the total income of the poor, we should therefore allocate the funds to whichever group has the higher headcount ratio. Recalling (2.2), we thus arrive at the comparison implied by (4.9): that between P_o^A and P_o^B.

Returning to the general case in which labour supply may vary and poverty lines differ, it is immediate from (4.8) that retargeting towards group A is more likely to be desirable, *ceteris paribus*, the higher is $\sigma(\delta_A, t_A)$ and the lower is z_A. As already noted, $\sigma(\delta, t)$ is decreasing in both δ and t. Thus group A is more likely to be favoured the less responsive is its labour supply behaviour and the lower is the marginal tax rate it faces. The intuition here is straightforward. When δ_A is relatively low, the income effect of increasing the poll subsidy to group A—which points towards a reduction in net income, dampening the beneficial impact on poverty—is relatively weak; conversely, a high δ_B indicates a relatively powerful income effect acting to mitigate the impact of reducing the poll subsidy to group B. And when t_A is relatively low, so too is the revenue cost of the reduction in the hours worked by members of group A as a result of their receiving a higher poll subsidy; conversely, a high t_B is helpful in recouping revenue from the increased labour supply in group B. The reason why group A is more likely to be favoured the lower its poverty line is simpler still: the smaller is z_A, the larger is the effect of a unit increase of income on the proportionate poverty gaps used to calculate P_α.

Consider, by way of example, the inferences that might be drawn from the UK statistics shown in Table 5.3. Suppose first that labour supply is completely inelastic in both groups and the two poverty lines the same, so that the condition in (4.9) applies. Then, since both P_o^i and P_1^i are higher for pensioner couples, reduction of aggregate poverty measured with either $\alpha = 1$ or $\alpha = 2$ calls for a retargeting of lump-sum payments *towards* this group and away from the non-pensioner families. Nor is this conclusion plausibly overturned by allowing for different poverty lines or the operation of incentive effects. Since the supplementary benefit levels

Table 5.3 Poverty indices for 1983

	P^i_α	
	$\alpha = 0$	$\alpha = 1$
Pensioner couples	.111	.010
Non-pensioner couples with two children	.029	.006

Source: Taken from Table 3.2 in Morris and Preston (1986), where further details may be found. Calculated from Family Expenditure Survey data, in terms of 'normal net income', and with poverty lines set at supplementary benefit levels.

underlying the figures in Table 5.3 were higher for the non-pensioners than the pensioners, (4.8) implies that the first of these considerations unambiguously favours retargeting towards the pensioner group. And it is equally clear that, under the natural approximation of $\delta_i = 0$ for the pensioners, any responsiveness of labour supply amongst the non-retired—however small—only strengthens still further the case for retargeting away from them. Suppose, for example, that the two groups both face a marginal tax rate of 0.4, that $\delta_i = 0$ for the pensioners and $\delta_i = .25$ for the non-pensioners; measuring aggregate poverty with $\alpha = 1$ (and even ignoring the difference in poverty lines), the headcount ratio of 11.1 per cent for the pensioners implies that retargeting away from this group would only be justified if the proportion of the non-pensioners in poverty were not 2.9 per cent but more than 17.3 per cent.

So far we have looked only at the balance between the poll subsidies paid to the two groups, taking as given the marginal tax rates that they face. Turning now to the full optimization problem, the necessary conditions for poverty minimization (with $t_i \neq 1, i = $ A,B) can be written

G_i:
$$P^i_{\alpha-1} - \left(\frac{\lambda z_i}{\alpha}\right)\frac{1}{\sigma(\delta_i,t_i)} = 0, i = A,B \tag{4.10}$$

t_i:
$$(P^i_{\alpha-1} - P^i_\alpha)z_i - (1-\delta_i)G_iP^i_{\alpha-1}$$
$$-\left(\frac{\lambda z_i}{\alpha}\right)\left\{(1-t_i)(1-\delta_i)\overline{w}_i - \frac{\delta_iG_i}{(1-t_i)}\right\} = 0, i = A,B \tag{4.11}$$

where λ is the Lagrange multiplier attached to the revenue constraint (4.4) and $\overline{w}_i$ denotes the mean wage of group i. From (4.10) one finds at an optimum

$$\frac{P^A_{\alpha-1}}{P^B_{\alpha-1}} = \frac{\sigma(\delta_B,t_B)z_A}{\sigma(\delta_A,t_A)z_B}, \tag{4.12}$$

as indeed was evident from (4.7) above. Substituting from (4.10) into the second term of (4.11) and recalling (3.13), optimal deployment of both sets of instruments yields the further simple rule:

$$\frac{P_{\alpha-1}^A - P_\alpha^A}{P_{\alpha-1}^B - P_\alpha^B} = \frac{y^A(w_A)}{y^B(w_B)}, \tag{4.13}$$

where $y^i(w)$ denotes the net income of a household in group i facing gross wage w. And since Cobb–Douglas preferences imply that net income is linear in the wage rate (again recalling (3.13)), the right-hand side of (4.13) is just the ratio of the mean net incomes of the two groups. Suppose for instance that we have chosen $\alpha = 1$, and consider once more the figures in Table 5.3: (4.13) implies that, in a world of linear taxes, the situation they reveal could be optimal only if the net incomes of pensioner couples were on average more than four times larger than those of the non-pensioners. Pursuing the case $\alpha = 1$, the condition in (4.13) reduces further to

$$\frac{S^A}{S^B} = \frac{z_A}{z_B} \tag{4.14}$$

where

$$S^i = \int_0^{\omega_i} y^i(w) f_i(w) dw \left(\int_0^\infty y^i(w) f_i(w) dw \right)^{-1}. \tag{4.15}$$

The minimization of aggregate poverty P_1 thus requires that the within-group income shares of the poor stand in the same ratio as their poverty lines. Such information is typically *not* produced in empirical work. Yet it is crucial for ascertaining the optimality or otherwise of current retargeting strategies. It is our intention to conduct such detailed empirical analysis in future work.

5. Concluding Remarks

The object of this paper has been to develop a framework for analysing the efficacy of alternative tax and benefit structures in terms of the commonly stated objective of poverty reduction. The analysis has led to some appealingly simple rules. In addition, preliminary and illustrative calculations have been given that suggest a prima-facie case against the kind of retargeting currently being attempted in the UK, away from the old and towards the young. Of course, even if one puts aside both the restrictiveness of the assumptions from which they derive and the narrowness of the single objective—that of poverty minimization—to which they relate, rules of this kind cannot be expected to eliminate all controversy. What they can do, however, is identify the critical issues of disagreement or doubt. It may be, for instance, that a policy of retargeting away from the retired and towards low-paid working families appears desirable in terms of aggregate poverty alleviation only at high degrees of poverty aversion or when using equivalence scales very different from those implicit in official benefit rates. As in other areas of optimal tax theory, the essential purpose is not to close debate but to inform it.

While they may offer administrative advantages, there is no compelling reason to confine attention to the linear tax structures studied here. The use of non-linear income taxation for poverty relief is considered in Kanbur and Keen (1988), where it is shown that minimization of a poverty index defined in terms of received income requires that the poorest of the poor (assuming that they work) face a strictly *negative* marginal tax rate. One implication of this is worth noting here. For it is well known that maximization of any orthodox social welfare function requires that the marginal rate of tax be everywhere non-negative (Mirrlees (1971)), so that such a situation would then be precluded. The consequences of pursuing a non-welfaristic programme of poverty alleviation are thus not merely quantitative; the policy implications may be qualitatively different from any that could be generated by a welfaristic approach.

6

The Effect of Transfer Programmes on Work Effort and Human Capital Formation: Evidence from the US

ROBERT MOFFITT AND ANURADHA
RANGARAJAN*

1. Introduction

Research in the United States on the effects of welfare programmes—programmes providing benefits to those with low income, mostly the poor—has accumulated for over twenty years. The primary impetus for the US research came in the 1960s from two different sources. First, among economists and those interested in reform of the welfare system, the notion of a negative income tax, or guaranteed annual income with work-incentive features built in, emerged as a major policy alternative and was heavily studied. Second, the existing transfer system in the US underwent a major transformation in the late 1960s and early 1970s, changes which resulted in both an expansion of the case-load of the system and increases in the types of benefits available. These events set up another round of research among economists, but also fundamentally changed the atmosphere of public discussion by focusing attention on how the case-load in the system might be reduced instead of expanded.

In this paper we shall review the findings from the research in the US, emphasizing those findings' bearing on the work-incentive effects of changes in the benefit-reduction rate. This is a major issue in the UK at the time of writing, for the Fowler reforms are explicitly intended, in part, to increase work incentives. Our summary will reveal that the US community has moved away from the use of the benefit-reduction rate as a tool to pro-

* Robert Moffitt is Professor of Economics at Brown University and Anuradha Rangarajan is also at Brown University.

This paper is a revised version of one presented at a conference on 'The Economics of Social Security' sponsored by the Institute for Fiscal Studies, London, on 15 April 1988. The authors would like to thank Andrew Dilnot, Ian Walker, and the other participants of the conference for their comments. The research reported here was partially supported by the US Department of Health and Human Services through a grant to the Institute for Research on Poverty at the University of Wisconsin. All opinions and errors are those of the authors and not of the sponsoring agency.

Table 6.1 Average monthly case-loads of the major income-tested transfer programmes (millions)

	1960	1965	1970	1975	1980	1985
AFDC[a]						
Families	.8	1.0	2.2	3.5	3.7	3.7
Recipients	3.0	4.3	8.5	11.3	10.8	10.8
AFDC-UP						
Families	–	.06	.08	.10	.14	.26
Recipients	–	.36	.42	.45	.61	1.13
Number of states with programme	–	18	23	27	26	25
Food Stamp recipients	–	.4	4.3	17.1	21.1	21.3
Medicaid recipients						
Total	–	–	15.5	22.0	21.6	22.2
Adults with dependent children	–	–	3.4	4.5	4.9	5.5
Dependent children	–	–	7.3	9.6	9.3	9.4

[a] Includes AFDC-UP.

vide work incentives, and has turned instead to other issues, one of which is the effects of human capital formation on the poverty rate and welfare dependence, as well as the effects of the transfer system on human capital formation. We shall then report new evidence on the latter of these effects.

2. Research on the US Transfer System

The implications of the research in the US on transfer systems cannot be fully understood without an understanding of the context in which the research has taken place. Therefore, we shall first review the trends in the US transfer system and in the work levels of the poor over the last twenty or so years.[1]

Table 6.1 shows the trends in the case-loads of the major US transfer programmes for the low-income population. The table shows clearly the two major changes in the system that have occurred over the period. First, the case-load in the major cash transfer programme in the US, the Aid to Families with Dependent Children (AFDC) programme, exploded in the late 1960s and early 1970s. The AFDC programme provides monthly cash benefits to families which are headed by a female and which contain

[1] This section is based largely upon the review in Moffitt (1987a).

children under the age of 18, but which contain no able-bodied male who is providing for their support. As the table shows the number of these 'female headed' families receiving benefits doubled from 1965 to 1970 and then increased by another 50 per cent or so from 1970 to 1975, leaving the case-load in 1975 more than triple what it had been in 1965. Although the case-load has since levelled off, the continuing high case-load in the programme is one of the major policy issues in the US.

The table also shows the case-loads in the AFDC-UP programme, which provides cash benefits to families in some states where there is an able-bodied male present. The programme has been available in only about half of the states and eligibility has been highly restricted, with the result that the case-load has been insignificant relative to that of the main component of the AFDC system.

The second major change in the system has been the introduction of in-kind transfers, such as those for food and medical care.[2] The Food Stamp programme provides food coupons to low-income families, and the Medicaid programme provides subsidized medical care services to the poor. The Medicaid programme is closely tied to the AFDC programme, for AFDC eligibility essentially guarantees Medicaid eligibility. Those not on AFDC are covered by Medicaid in only some states and only then under severe eligibility restrictions. Food Stamps are available to all families regardless of family type, but AFDC recipients constitute the largest single category of recipients in the programme.

As Table 6.1 shows, the Food Stamp programme was not present prior to 1965 but has grown so rapidly since then as to provide benefits now to double the number of recipients as does the AFDC programme. Medicaid receipt is even larger than in the Food Stamp programme. The reasons for this new dominance of in-kind transfers over cash transfers is not completely clear, but it does appear that such transfers are more popular among taxpayers than are cash transfers. It is also the case that suppliers of agricultural products and of medical services are strong supporters of such programmes, whereas there is no corresponding support group for cash transfers.

US government policy toward the programme has varied over this period, partly in response to these changes. Table 6.2 shows the trend in the level of benefits in the various programmes. The AFDC benefit grew in real terms over the 1960s but has since declined drastically. However, the introduction of the Food Stamp and Medicaid programmes has kept total benefits higher than they have been historically. The fall in AFDC benefits and increase in in-kind benefits are probably not coincidental, and it has

---

[2] Another significant in-kind transfer programme is that which provides housing benefits. It is not discussed here.

Table 6.2 Benefits in the US welfare system and characteristics of female heads

	1960	1964	1968	1971	1975	1979	1984
Real monthly benefits[a]							
AFDC[b]	483	471	506	513	490	448	387
Food Stamps[b]	0	0	n.a.	214	247	233	234
Medicaid[c]	0	0	n.a.	n.a.	152	148	111
Sum[d]	483	471	–	–	742	695	616
Other AFDC parameters[e]							
BRR (%)	100	100	100	67	67	67	100
Monthly BE ($)	483	471	506	766	731	669	387
Labour market characteristics of female heads							
Percentage working	n.a.	n.a.	52	49	48	56	53
Hours worked per week	n.a.	n.a.	19	18	17	21	19
Annual earnings[a,f]	n.a.	n.a.	4,745	5,022	5,314	6,364	6,282

[a] In real 1982 dollars.
[b] Maximum amount paid for a family of four.
[c] Average of adult and children payments per adult.
[d] Medicaid plus Food Stamps plus 70% of AFDC.
[e] BRR = benefit reduction rate; BE = break-even level = AFDC benefit divided by BRR.
[f] Includes non-workers.
n.a. = not available.

been argued elsewhere (Moffitt (1987b)) that the fall in AFDC benefits was in response to the increase in in-kind transfers.[3] In addition, the reduction in AFDC benefits was partially a response to the case-load explosion described earlier.[4]

The growth in both AFDC and the in-kind transfers has also resulted in a larger share of gross national product (GNP) committed to means-tested transfers. Whereas in 1960 only 1.3 per cent of GNP was so devoted, the figure rose to almost 3 per cent around 1980, since which time it has been

[3] That this could happen is a result of the complex federal structure of the US transfer system. AFDC benefit levels are set by the states whereas Food Stamps and, to a great extent, Medicaid benefit levels are set by the US Congress. This made it possible for states to lower AFDC benefit levels after the Congress introduced Food Stamps and Medicaid.
[4] Although there is a prima-facie case that the case-load increase was a result of the jump in the benefit sum, there is some contradictory evidence. One is that reductions in the stigma of welfare receipt and relaxation of several eligibility conditions in the late 1960s increased case-loads independently of the benefit. Another is that earnings in the labour market grew even faster than benefits over the period.

declining slowly. Of course, these percentages are much smaller than comparable ones for the UK.

These trends in case-loads and benefits in the US transfer system help explain the continuing research interest in the work-incentive effects of transfer programmes. However, interest in work incentives in welfare programmes was also generated by the discussion of a negative income tax in the 1960s, a programme endorsed by both Friedman (1962) and Tobin (1965). But the continued interest over the 1970s and 1980s in work incentives, even after the failure of enactment of a negative income tax, has been a result of the high case-loads in the programmes.

The major work-incentive issue upon which US economists have conducted research is whether a lowering in the benefit-reduction rate, or 'tax rate', in a transfer programme in general—and in the AFDC programme in particular—could be expected to increase work effort. By lowering such a rate, recipients are allowed to 'keep' a higher percentage of their earnings; that is, their benefit is not reduced by as great an amount if they earn more. Thus a direct financial inducement to work is provided. Such a lowering was a key feature of negative income tax plans proposed in the 1960s and early 1970s, and was the chief reason for the popularity of such plans among economists. In addition, Congress lowered the benefit-reduction rate in the AFDC programme from 100 per cent to 67 per cent in 1969, as shown in Table 6.2, for this reason. However, in 1981 the newly elected Reagan Administration increased the rate back to 100 per cent.

After considerable research on this issue, the consensus at the present time among both economists and policy-makers in the US is that changes in the benefit-reduction rate have no significant effect on work effort, if not a perverse effect in the opposite direction to that intended. This applies in both directions: a lowering of the rate will not significantly increase work effort and may even reduce it, and an increase in the rate will not significantly reduce work effort and may even increase it.

This consensus has a firm theoretical and empirical basis. The theoretical basis is clear when it is recognized that a lowering of the benefit-reduction rate, for example, increases the 'break-even' level of income—that is, the maximum income level for which benefit eligibility can be retained. This must be so because the work incentives of the change are provided precisely by allowing many recipients with moderate-to-high levels of earnings to be eligible now for some level of benefits, whereas they had not been previously. Unfortunately, allowing families with moderate-to-high earnings levels to be eligible for the programme brings onto the rolls many families who had not been recipients before, and this is a clear work disincentive. Whether overall work effort rises or falls is ambiguous theoretically and depends upon the relative numbers of individuals initially on the programme (whose work effort will increase) and of individuals newly brought into the programme (whose work effort will fall). Likewise, an increase in the benefit-reduction rate will reduce work incentives for those who remain on the programme but will reduce the break-even level of income, thereby eliminating families from the rolls and inducing an increase in work effort. Note that this ambiguity has nothing to do with the traditional ambiguity generated by opposing income and substitution effects.[5]

The empirical basis for the consensus is provided by three different sorts of evidence. First, cross-sectional econometric studies of the AFDC programme across the US states have shown that higher benefit-reduction rates are associated with either no change in work effort or higher work effort. Second, simulations of changes in the benefit-reduction rate on representative cross-section samples of the US population—samples containing both existing recipients and those who would be newly eligible if the rate were lowered—show that the two opposing effects virtually cancel each other out for female heads and that there is no significant change in work effort from either lowering or increasing the benefit-reduction rate.

It may be noted that these simulation results are likely to be similar for the UK. Econometrically estimated elasticities of male labour supply (Pencavel (1986)) and female labour supply (Killingsworth and Heckman (1986)) in the UK are similar to those in the US. In addition, the earnings distributions in the two countries are of a similar overall shape. Of course, whether the US results would in fact apply can be determined only by an actual UK simulation.

Third, the time-series evidence on the effects of the lowering of the rate in 1969 and the increase in the rate in 1981 supports the cross-sectional results. As Table 6.2 shows, the employment rate and hours of work of female heads not only did not rise after 1969, they actually fell. Real earnings of female heads did rise, but at no faster rate, if not a slower rate, than in the later 1970s. Note that the table also shows the dramatic increase in the break-even level that resulted. Furthermore, after 1981 there was no major reduction in work effort by female heads, for employment rates and hours of work appear to have been fairly stable. The only evidence in support of work-incentive effects is the pattern of real earnings after 1981, which demonstrate a marked slow-down in growth.[6] In fact, the most remarkable finding is that the work effort of female heads is almost completely inelastic in the face of major changes in benefit-reduction rates, benefit levels, and drastic changes in the macro-economic environment.

It should be pointed out that a lowering of the benefit-reduction rate is still advocated by some on equity grounds. In the US, it is still possible to

[5] See Levy (1979) and Moffitt (1985).
[6] Elsewhere it has been argued (Moffitt (1986)) that there was a disincentive effect of the 1981 changes, but it was so slight as to be unimportant for policy purposes.

work full-time for 52 weeks a year at the minimum wage but still be below the poverty line, yet remain ineligible for benefits of any type. Families in such situations may be deserving of coverage regardless of the work-incentive issue.

In any case, attention in the US has turned decisively away from manipulation of the benefit-reduction rate as a means to increase work incentives. The most widely discussed policy alternative now is the implementation of 'workfare' programmes or programmes which go under a similar name. Such programmes come in many different varieties. A few are primarily punitive in nature and are intended to request of recipients a 'reciprocal' relationship; that is, one in which the benefits provided by society are reciprocated by work on the part of the recipient. On the other hand, most of these programmes are intended more constructively to increase the human capital levels of recipients by providing them with job training and thereby increasing their labour market opportunities. A number of states have tested such programmes to date, with results indicating some significant earnings gains when meaningful training is provided (Moffitt (1987a)). Legislation currently before the US Congress has as a major goal the nation-wide implementation of such programmes.

Research by economists has taken similar directions, including an increased interest in the effects of human capital formation on transfer receipt. Most directly relevant to work and training programmes are questions concerning the manner in which human capital formation among potential welfare recipients takes place. For example, it is of interest to determine why, if job training of recipients 'pays off', it has not also done so in the private labour market. It may be that there is a failure in the private market for training, but this has not been established. In fact, elementary empirical questions, such as whether experience in the labour market does or does not result in higher future earnings of welfare recipients (as it does for other members of the population), have not been examined. Indeed, virtually nothing is known about the life cycle profiles of labour supply and earnings of female heads of family, or even their life cycle patterns of welfare receipt.[7] If the human capital and labour supply of female heads are to be increased and their welfare receipt decreased, it now seems important to determine the existing profiles of these variables.[8]

---

[7] Since marital status is a key eligibility criterion, the manner in which its life cycle pattern develops along with those of labour supply and earnings is also important.

[8] A related development in the US is an increased interest in education. If job training does pay off, it may be that formal education should as well. In fact, many of the job training programmes for welfare recipients provide basic educational skills rather than occupational or specific job training. This naturally raises the question of whether the existing educational system has failed to provide those skills, or whether welfare recipients simply failed to stay in school long enough. Alternatively, there is the possibility that education does not 'pay off' for female heads as it seems to for other members of the population.

The empirical study in the next section of the paper is related to this issue. First, life cycle profiles of earnings, labour supply, wage rates, and welfare participation are examined for female heads in the US. Second, a specific hypothesis related to the effects of the AFDC programme on human capital formation is examined. It has been argued by some that the low levels of human capital of female heads in the US are, in part, a result of the provision of transfer benefits itself. According to this hypothesis, the provision of benefits results in withdrawal from the labour market or some other form of work disincentive, leading to a reduction in private labour market experience and hence lower future potential wages. In fact, it is often hypothesized that recipients fall into a 'welfare trap', whereby the reduction in job experience resulting from welfare receipt leads to a gradual deterioration in job skills and a consequent worsening ability to obtain a viable wage in the labour market. This leads to continued receipt in the future. There are many issues raised by these conjectures which we shall not address, but we shall provide at least a first set of evidence on some of them.

3. Evidence on Human Capital Effects of the US AFDC Programme

To examine the human capital profiles of female heads of family in the US, we employ a set of data on women from 1968 to 1983. Using the data, we provide both graphical evidence and econometric evidence on those human capital profiles and on the consequences of transfer receipt.

Data

The data we use are drawn from the Michigan Panel Study of Income Dynamics (PSID). The PSID began a series of annual interviews of 5,000 families in 1968 and is still ongoing. We employ data that end in 1983, giving us 16 years of data for each individual. We select from this sample of the US population those women who were female heads with a child under the age of 18 in at least one year.[9] Also, because we wish to measure the effect of lagged AFDC participation on current wages, we select for analysis only those individuals who are observed late enough in the observation period for us to have one or more years of data on their AFDC participation history. We also impose a number of miscellaneous sample exclusion

---

[9] We only utilize those years that the woman was a female head, of course, excluding those years she was married or without children under 18.

restrictions.[10] Our resulting sample contains information on 1,042 women for an average of about 5 years, giving us 5,262 person-year observations altogether.

Table 6.3 shows the means of the major variables used in our analysis. Mean hourly wages are fairly low, though not extremely so compared with the rest of the US population for this period. About 33 per cent of the sample are on AFDC per period (about the same as national figures from other sources) and 45 per cent have been on the programme sometime in the previous 5 years. The table also shows means of AFDC participation lagged for more than 5 years, but these means are constructed on a smaller sample inasmuch as we can use only observations after 1975 to construct the variable. The other means in the sample are self-explanatory.

Graphical Evidence

Figure 6.1 shows the profiles of log wages, annual hours of work, annual earnings (including zeros), and AFDC participation (percentage on AFDC) by age. Log wage profiles show a typically concave shape, though peaking relatively early in life, at about 35 years of age. Hours of work rise gradually, though with a dip in the middle years no doubt resulting from the presence of young children, and fall off in later ages. Earnings profiles, which are roughly a product of those for wages and hours, also show a concave shape. Finally, the profile of AFDC participation shows a steady decline with age. In fact, the AFDC programme is disproportionately a programme for young women with children. AFDC participation rates decline in later years because eventually some children age past 18 or leave the home, which lowers the potential benefit, and because wage rates grow and therefore increase work in the labour market.

Figure 6.2 shows separate log wage, hours, and earnings profiles for benefit recipients and non-recipients. For purposes of the figure, a person-year observation was included in the recipient subsample if the woman was on AFDC in that year and in the non-recipient subsample if not. As the figure indicates, the log wage profile for non-recipients shows the conventional concave shape but that for recipients is virtually flat and shows almost no wage growth over the life cycle. The hours profiles are much closer for the two groups, as are the earnings profiles, though in both cases there is a discernible, though sometimes faint, slower growth rate among benefit recipients.

[10] Women were included in the sample if in any year of the survey they were the head of the household with no spouse present and had a child under 18; were less than 66 years old; were in a family with fewer than ten children and with fewer than thirteen family members; were not a student or self-employed; and if all variables used in the analysis were present in the data and not missing. Some exclusions for outlying hours and wage data were also imposed.

Table 6.3 Means and standard errors of the variables

	Total sample		Lagged participants[a]		Lagged non-participants	
	Mean	Standard error	Mean	Standard error	Mean	Standard error
Log hourly wage[b]	0.95	0.59	0.73	0.50	1.07	0.61
Current AFDC participation dummy	0.33	0.48	0.68	0.41	0.05	0.25
Lagged AFDC participation dummies:						
1–5 years	0.45	0.51	–	–	–	–
1–10 years[c]	0.46	0.52	–	–	–	–
1 year	0.33	0.48	0.74	0.38	–	–
2–5 years	0.40	0.50	0.90	0.26	–	–
6–10 years[c]	0.31	0.48	0.67	0.41	–	–
Age	38.39	10.26	32.52	8.84	39.91	11.78
Experience[d]	11.51	9.06	8.92	7.13	13.61	10.74
Years of education	11.31	2.60	10.41	2.17	12.05	2.85
Race dummy (= 1 if white)	0.64	0.49	0.47	0.44	0.77	0.50
Cohort dummies:[e]						
1925–35	0.04	0.20	0.02	0.13	0.05	0.26
1936–46	0.16	0.38	0.14	0.31	0.18	0.46
1947–57	0.30	0.47	0.28	0.39	0.32	0.56
1958–68	0.35	0.49	0.35	0.42	0.35	0.58
1969–79	0.15	0.36	0.22	0.36	0.09	0.35
Region dummy (= 1 if south)	0.32	0.48	0.25	0.38	0.37	0.58
No. of family members	3.43	1.49	3.83	1.46	3.09	1.41
Age of youngest child	8.69	4.97	7.35	4.12	9.77	5.71
No. of children	1.99	1.22	2.37	1.22	1.68	1.09
AFDC guarantee family of four	316.27	122.98	327.17	103.04	307.34	147.34

n = 5,262 in total sample

[a] Lagged participants are those on AFDC in the prior 1–5 years.

[b] *n* = 3,445 (workers only); in 1972 dollars. Computed as a ratio of previous year earnings and hours worked.

[c] *n* = 3,369 in total sample.

[d] No. of years worked since age 18.

[e] Year at which individual attained age of 17.

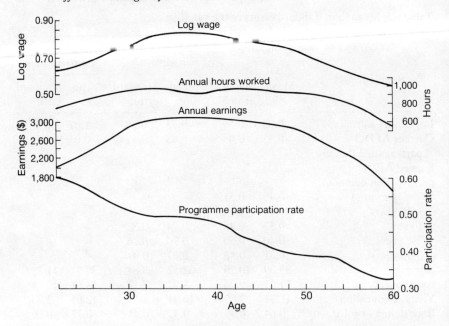

Figure 6.1   Log wage, hours, earnings, and programme participation profiles for
US female heads

Unfortunately, these figures are not reliable because they are certainly
strongly affected by the self-selection process that determines receipt.
Since receipt requires low earnings, hours, and log wages by definition, the
recipient profiles in Figure 6.2 must remain relatively flat by construction.
For example, a woman whose wage grows sufficiently to allow her to
depart the programme will no longer be counted in the recipient profile but
will move to the non-recipient profile.

To circumvent this problem to some extent, profiles can be constructed
to include identical women over the life cycle. Figure 6.3 shows such log
wage profiles (hours and earnings profiles are ignored) separately by
cohort. The cohort separation, it will be seen, will be important in accurately portraying the life cycle patterns of wages. The profiles in Figure 6.3
were constructed separately for 'usual recipients' and 'usual non-
recipients', where the state of usual recipiency is defined as having participated in the programme for over 50 per cent of the sample period and that
of usual non-recipiency is defined as the converse. Thus a given woman
remains in the same category over her life cycle.

The figure indicates that the wage profiles of usual non-recipients are
generally increasing until age 40–45, after which they appear to remain
constant until age 50–55 or so, after which they decline. The importance of

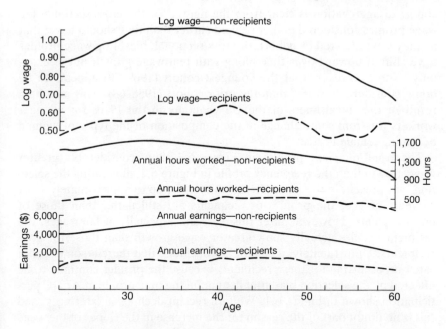

Figure 6.2   Log wage, hours, and earnings profiles by recipiency status

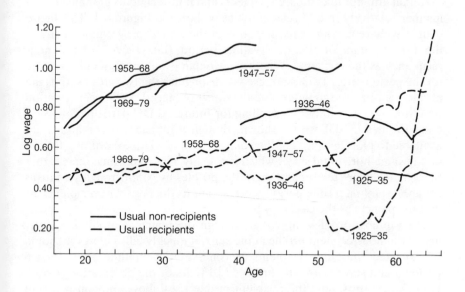

Figure 6.3   Log wage profiles by usual recipiency and cohort

cohort disaggregation is clear from the figure, for the cross-sectional log wage profiles considered earlier peaked earlier than they should have; that is, they were affected by cohort, or cross-sectional, bias. Log wage profiles have shifted upward over time along with real wage growth in the economy. Note, however, that the youngest cohort (1969–79) appears to be doing considerably worse than the prior cohort (1958–68). This may be a result of the sluggishness of the US economy in the 1970s for younger workers, or from some change in the composition of the types of women becoming female heads.

The usual-recipient profiles in Figure 6.3 show considerably greater wage growth than the recipiency profile in Figure 6.2, illustrating the selection bias present in the latter. In the early ages, up to approximately 40 or so years of age, the profiles of recipients are still flatter than those of non-recipients. However, after this age, and especially at later ages, the recipient profiles actually show greater wage growth than those for non-recipients. Unfortunately, it cannot be concluded that there is some sort of catch-up occurring for these recipients because the profiles continue to be affected by the selection bias attendant upon the time profile of AFDC participation shown in Figure 6.1. Welfare receipt declines in later ages, and this is no doubt part of the reason for the increase in the slopes of the wage profiles for usual recipients in the later ages. That is, the time they are on the programme occurs disproportionately in the earlier portions of their lifetimes.

A final attempt to compare recipients and non-recipients graphically in a manner relatively free of selection bias is shown in Figure 6.4. This figure defines welfare receipt as participation in the AFDC programme in any of the first 5 years of the observation period (i.e. 1969–73), and non-recipiency as the converse. Whether a woman is on or off the programme for the periods after 1973 is not used to distinguish the two groups; thus the profiles can be used to determine the effect of lagged AFDC participation on future wages, without controlling for future AFDC participation. Separate profiles by cohort are shown, though insufficient observations are available to plot the wages of the youngest cohort. The cohorts are aligned on the same horizontal scale, which is roughly a calendar time scale rather than an age scale; the separation of the profiles by cohort roughly controls for age. The first 5 time periods correspond to the period of recipiency or non-recipiency, as the case may be.

The topmost profiles show that, though the recipient profile is slightly above the non-recipient profile at the start, it quickly falls below (as should be expected since the recipients are on AFDC sometime in the first 5 periods) and stays so for the first 9 or 10 years of the observation period. However, surprisingly, the recipient profile rises above the non-recipient profile in later years and rises sharply toward the end. The final upward

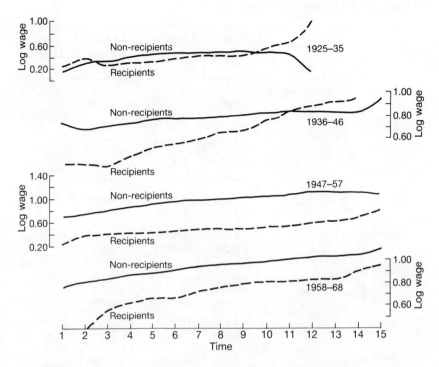

Figure 6.4 Log wage profiles by cohort recipiency status in first five years

movement may be a result of small sample size, but there is no doubt that evidence of catch-up is present. The subsequent cohort (1936–46) shows the same pattern of catch-up over the life cycle, and once again a surpassing at the later ages. The profiles of the two younger cohorts do not show as dramatic a difference, but there is evidence for convergence even for them toward the end of the period. It is quite likely that the slower rate of convergence for the two younger cohorts arises from a higher rate of continued programme participation into the middle ages than that of the older cohorts at their older ages. If this is correct, the combined evidence of the figures suggests strongly that wages do in fact recover not too many years after programme participation effectively ends.

Econometric Evidence

Table 6.4 shows regression evidence that corresponds conceptually to Figure 6.4. In column 1, log wages are regressed upon a lagged AFDC participation dummy for receipt in the 5 years preceding the date of the wage observation. Conventional human capital variables for age and education

130   *Moffitt and Rangarajan*

Table 6.4 OLS wage regressions

	Total sample (1)	Lagged participants (2)	Lagged non-participants (3)
Lagged participation dummy	−0.203* (0.018)	–	–
Education	0.094* (0.004)	0.057* (0.006)	0.111* (0.005)
Age	0.027* (0.010)	0.022 (0.015)	0.030* (0.013)
Age squared/100	−0.025* (0.013)	−0.004 (0.020)	−0.033* (0.016)
Race dummy	−0.054* (0.018)	−0.075* (0.025)	−0.047 (0.026)
Cohort dummies:[a]			
1936–46	−0.066 (0.066)	0.510* (0.150)	−0.193* (0.079)
1947–57	0.134 (0.079)	0.764* (0.165)	−0.002 (0.096)
1958–68	0.117 (0.087)	0.964* (0.177)	−0.088 (0.106)
1969–79	0.071 (0.091)	0.922* (0.182)	−0.121 (0.114)
Intercept	−0.786* (0.189)	−1.405* (0.305)	−0.836* (0.251)

Note: Standard errors are given in parentheses beneath the coefficients.
* Significant at 5% level.
[a] Omitted dummy is 1925–35.

are also included, as are dummy variables for cohort membership and racial status. Not surprisingly given Figure 6.4, the AFDC participation dummy is negative and significant, and implies about a 20 per cent reduction in future wages accompanying AFDC participation. Columns 2 and 3 show separate estimates by lagged AFDC receipt. Interestingly, and somewhat in confirmation of Figure 6.4, the age profiles of recipients are steeper than those of non-recipients after about age 30, because of a smaller quadratic term, though not significantly so ($F_{2,3433} = 1.36$). It is also interesting to note that the rate of return to education amongst recipients appears to be only half that of non-recipients. Of course, education may appear to not 'pay off' for transfer recipients to the same degree as for non-recipients only because of selectivity effects—that is, those who have below-average wages for independent reasons are more likely to be recipients—but the effect may also be genuine, for benefit recipients may be more difficult to educate for some other reason. The extent to which there is heterogeneity in the rate of return to education, and whether this is connected to benefit receipt, would be an interesting topic for future research.

The ordinary least squares (OLS) regressions in Table 6.4 are nevertheless subject to at least two sorts of selectivity biases. First, there is the conventional bias arising from the availability of wages for workers only (Heckman (1974)). Second, there is the potential endogeneity of lagged AFDC participation itself. The strongly negative participation coefficient in column 1 of the table is clearly observable in Figure 6.4 from the relative positions of the profiles for recipients and non-recipients, but it is likely that recipients are drawn from the lower tail of the wage distribution in the first place. Whether welfare receipt has an added negative effect on wages remains to be seen, and requires the estimation of a model which controls for the endogeneity and self-selection of recipiency. In the Appendix we outline a simple three-equation model containing the wage equation, a selection equation for whether the woman works, and an equation for lagged AFDC receipt. Allowing the error terms across the equations to be correlated and estimating the model by maximum likelihood, any selection bias that is present is eliminated.

The results are shown in Table 6.5, where column 1 shows the wage-equation coefficients and columns 2 and 3 show probit coefficients for the determination of employment status (i.e. whether employed or not) and lagged AFDC participation, respectively. The estimates of the covariance matrix (not shown) indicate that there is a strong negative correlation between the unobserved components of employment and AFDC participation ($\pi = -.468$, s.e. $= .025$) but that the correlations between the unobserved component of the wage equation and those of the employment and AFDC participation equations are small and insignificant ($\pi = -.003$, s.e. $= .053$; $\pi = .127$, s.e. $= .088$). Therefore, it appears that there is no significant selection bias either in the selection of workers or in the inclusion of lagged AFDC participation as an exogenous regressor in the wage equation.

The results of the wage equation confirm this result, for the estimated coefficients are quite close to those obtained with OLS. In particular, the coefficient on the lagged AFDC participation variable remains negative and significant, and of the same magnitude. Thus it appears as though programme participation does exert a true, not a spurious, negative effect on human capital formation.

The probit coefficients in the employment and AFDC participation equations are, for the most part, as expected. Interestingly, the cohort

Table 6.5 Maximum likelihood estimates of full model

	Log wage equation (1)	Lagged participants (2)	Lagged participation equation (3)
Lagged participation dummy	−.236* (.044)	–	–
Education	.097* (.004)	.182* (.006)	−.168* (.006)
Age	.028* (.007)	.084* (.017)	−.129* (.017)
Age squared/100	−.026* (.008)	−.148* (.021)	.132* (.021)
Race dummy	−.054* (.015)	.327* (.035)	−.789* (.030)
Cohort dummies:			
1936–46	−.055 (.039)	−.375* (.101)	.520* (.108)
1947–57	.143* (.049)	−.661* (.126)	.469* (.130)
1958–68	.129* (.055)	−.930* (.140)	.340* (.148)
1969–79	.082 (.057)	−.982* (.150)	.468* (.158)
Region dummy	–	.446* (.037)	−.665* (.045)
No. in family	–	.005 (.021)	–
Age of youngest child	–	.038* (.004)	–
No. of children	–	−.122* (.026)	–
Real AFDC guarantee/100	–	–	−.049* (.027)
Lagged family variables:			
No. in family	–	–	−.216* (.017)

Table 6.5—*continued*

	Log wage equation (1)	Lagged participants (2)	Lagged participation equation (3)
Age of youngest child	–	–	−.033* (.004)
Presence-of-spouse dummy	–	–	.006 (.160)
No. of children	–	–	.434* (.020)
Intercept	−.840* (.147)	−1.844* (0.338)	5.043* (0.350)
σ	.464* (.005)	–	–

Log likelihood = −7,566.2

Note: Standard errors are given in parentheses beneath coefficients.
  * Significant at 5% level.

dummies in the employment equation imply steadily falling employment rates for successive cohorts of female heads. Whether this is a result of an increased availability of transfer benefits, or a reflection of a change in the composition of female heads over time, cannot be determined.

Table 6.6 shows several additional estimates of interest. Column 1 shows the effect of interacting education with AFDC participation.[11] The interaction term is negative and significant, indicating that the wage profiles of more educated women are lowered more than those of less educated women (in fact, the coefficient on the uninteracted AFDC participation variable is positive and significant). One speculative possibility is that those women with the lowest skills have available to them jobs with very little human capital content in any case and for which there would be little wage growth even if they were continuously working and not participating in the transfer programme. Those women with relatively high skills may be the only female heads who have available to them jobs with significant wage growth.

Columns 2 and 3 show the results of a more detailed examination of the time pattern of lagged AFDC participation effects. Column 2 indicates that

[11] AFDC participation was also interacted with age and age squared but the coefficients were insignificant individually and jointly.

Table 6.6 Additional estimates of the log wage equation (maximum likelihood)

	(1)	(2)	(3)	(4)
Lagged participation dummies:				
1–5 years	.342* (.083)	–	−.191* (.029)	−.078* (.029)
1 year	–	−.166* (.017)	–	–
2–5 years	–	−.081* (.022)	–	–
6–10 years	–	–	−.039* (.019)	.028 (.039)
(1–5) × (6–10)	–	–	–	−.103* (.047)
Education	.113* (.004)	.099* (.003)	.095* (.005)	.010* (.005)
Education × lagged participation dummy (1–5 years)	−.050* (.005)	–	–	–
Age	.024* (.007)	.027* (.006)	.057* (.010)	.061* (.010)
Age squared/100	−.020* (.008)	−.026* (.008)	−.065* (.012)	−.069* (.012)
Race dummy	−.071* (.015)	−.039* (.014)	−.069* (.019)	−.039* (.019)
Cohort dummies:				
1936–46	−.045 (.039)	−.071 (.038)	−.374* (.054)	−.397* (.054)
1947–57	.169* (.049)	.122* (.048)	−.260* (.071)	−.289* (.071)
1958–68	.167* (.055)	.097 (.053)	−.292* (.078)	−.312* (.078)
1969–79	.130 (.057)	.045 (.056)	−.262* (.081)	−.293* (.081)
Intercept	−.992* (.146)	−.849* (.142)	−.922* (.211)	−1.118* (.212)
σ	.459* (.004)	.462* (.005)	.442* (.006)	.442* (.006)
Log likelihood	−7,542.8	−7,549.8	−4,663.9[a]	−4,666.6[a]

Note: Standard errors are given in parentheses beneath coefficients.

 * Significant at 5% level.

 [a] $n = 3,369$. Smaller sample required for availability of 10 years of AFDC history data.

the effect of very recent AFDC participation (in the most recent year) is twice as large ($-.166$) as participation in the prior 4 years ($-.08$). This by itself indicates that the negative effects of participation decline relatively rapidly, consistent with the graphical evidence in Figure 6.4. Column 3 shows the relative effects of having participated in the programme in the last 5 years and in the 5 years prior to that, estimates obtained by necessity on a smaller sample. These estimates indicate that the effects in the most recent 5 years ($-.19$) are almost 5 times larger than those in the prior 5 years ($-.039$).

Finally, in column 4 we interact the 1–5 and 6–10 participation lags. The results imply that a woman who has been on AFDC for 10 years has a 15 per cent lower wage ($-.153 = -.078 + .028 - .103$) but that a woman who has been on AFDC for 5 years but left the programme at least 5 years ago has no significant wage reduction ($.028$, s.e. $= .039$). Thus, while continued AFDC participation has a cumulative impact on potential wages, a woman who departs AFDC experiences no negative wage impact after 6 years or so of being off the programme.

6. Summary and Conclusions

In this paper we have reviewed the US research on the work incentives of changing the benefit-reduction rate. The research has led US economists and policy-makers to conclude that there is no significant change in work effort to be found from either raising or lowering the rate. Research in the US has turned toward more direct means of increasing work effort and employability by studying and testing the effects of work and training programmes for recipients of welfare benefits.

We have also conducted an empirical and exploratory examination of the effect of a major US transfer programme, the Aid to Families with Dependent Children (AFDC) programme, on the human capital formation of female heads of family, the major recipient group of the programme. Both graphical and econometric evidence from a panel of women interviewed from 1968 to 1983 were obtained, and log wage equations were estimated as a function of conventional human capital determinants (age, education) as well as lagged AFDC participation. The results indicate a negative effect of recent AFDC participation on current wages of about 20 per cent, but one which drops off rapidly over time. Beyond 5 years the effect is no more than 4 per cent, and it drops to zero somewhere in a 6–10 year range. The results also indicate that the wage-depressing effects of programme participation are greater for the more educated female heads in the population, who may have better wage opportunities in the labour market.

Appendix

To account for the two selection biases referred to in the text, we formulate a simple three-equation model which includes a log wage equation, an employment equation, and a lagged AFDC participation equation:

$$\ln W_i = X_i\beta + \varepsilon_i, \text{ observed if } E_i = 1$$

$$E_i^* = V_i'\psi + v_i$$

$$E_i = 1 \text{ if } E_i^* \geq 0; \ E_i = 0 \text{ if not}$$

$$P_i^* = Z_i'\theta + \omega_i$$

$$P_i = 1 \text{ if } P_i^* \geq 0; \ P_i = 0 \text{ if not}$$

where $\ln W_i$ is the log wage, E_i is an employment-status dummy (1 if working, 0 if not), and P_i is a lagged AFDC participation dummy (1 if on, 0 if not); X_i, V_i, and Z_i are vectors of variables in the wage, employment, and participation equations respectively; β, ψ, and θ are their respective coefficient vectors; and ε_i, v_i, and ω_i are their respective error terms. The log wage equation is observed only for workers, and the employment and AFDC participation equations are formulated as binary-choice index functions. The errors will be assumed to follow a trivariate normal distribution:

$$\begin{vmatrix} \varepsilon_i \\ v_i \\ \omega_i \end{vmatrix} \sim N(0, \Omega)$$

where

$$\Omega = \begin{vmatrix} \sigma_\varepsilon^2 & \varrho_3\sigma & \varrho_2\sigma \\ & 1 & \varrho_1 \\ & & 1 \end{vmatrix}.$$

The log likelihood function for the model will not be given, for brevity, but is available upon request from the authors, as is the computer program to compute the maximum likelihood estimates of the parameters. The BHHH (Berndt, Hall, Hall, and Hausman (1974)) optimization algorithm is used.

7

Income Risk and Income Maintenance: Implications for Incentives to Work

STEPHEN JENKINS AND JANE MILLAR*

1. Introduction

The view that the income maintenance system may have a significant effect on labour force participation decisions is one of the most enduring in history (Garraty (1978)). Most recent discussion has been in terms of an individual's 'replacement rate'—the ratio of total income received while continuing unemployed to that received if in work—and it is commonly argued that if this is high, there is a financial disincentive to work: the 'unemployment trap'.[1] By the same logic, incentives may be improved by placing an upper limit on benefits for the unemployed (as proposed by, for example, Minford (1983)), or alternatively, and recognizing the income maintenance role of unemployment benefits, by increasing the incomes of those in work. And doing this via increases in non-means-tested benefits, especially child benefit, rather than relying on means-tested benefits such as family credit, has the advantage that marginal tax rates for those in work are unaffected (see, for example, Treasury and Civil Service Sub-Committee (1983, Ch. 11)).

In this paper we shall also be discussing work incentives, but our aim is to draw attention to a different feature of the income maintenance system. We argue this may be particularly relevant to the labour force participation

* Stephen Jenkins and Jane Millar are both lecturers at the School of Social Sciences, University of Bath.

This paper was presented at a conference on 'The Economics of Social Security', organized by the Institute for Fiscal Studies, held on 15 April 1988.

Ken Cooke and Eithne McLaughlin made a substantial indirect contribution to this paper, for it is their recent interviews with unemployed families in West Yorkshire and Northern Ireland, undertaken jointly with Jane Millar (see McLaughlin, Millar, and Cooke (1988)), which suggest the importance of the 'income risk' concept. The authors are also grateful to the editors and Robert Moffitt for their comments. Nevertheless, responsibility for the views expressed lies with the authors alone.

[1] This sentence conflates much. For a superb extended analysis of the appropriate definition of replacement rates, and their relationship to disincentives, see Atkinson and Micklewright (1985). In principle, high replacement rates may provide a disincentive to work, but the relationship is more complex than is commonly assumed. Most econometric work suggests the disincentive effect is relatively small.

decisions of one group in particular, namely unemployed men of families with children.[2] The underlying idea is quite simple.

Making the transition from unemployment to employment implies changes not just in potential income levels, but also in the degree of income risk. An unemployed person's income in the near future (from unemployment benefit and/or income support, and housing benefit) is relatively certain if they stay out of work. But on return to work, total family income can come from earnings, child benefit, family credit, and housing benefit, and at the time of the participation decision, the amount to be received from these various sources is relatively uncertain, primarily because the transition into work implies reassessment for means-tested benefits. Although the benefits available for those out of work may, nominally, be just as complex as the benefits for those in work, the *change* in status leads to differences in risk. Thus taking a job may not only increase expected income levels (stimulating work incentives), but also increase uncertainty about future income flows (a disincentive to work to risk-averse individuals). In other words, even if replacement rates are relatively low, risk-averse individuals may not participate because of the offsetting effects of the income risk. If the policy goal is to increase participation, the implications are clear. In so far as means-testing is the primary source of the income risk, the means-tested component of income support for those in work should be simplified and/or reduced.

The remainder of the paper expands this argument. In Section 2 we clarify the definition of income risk and incorporate it in a simple model of the participation decision. Section 3 discusses alternative policy strategies for increasing participation with reference to the model. Section 4 provides concluding comments. We concentrate on a single leading case in the main text but discuss some variations on the basic model in the Appendix.

2. The Model

We are concerned with families with dependent children and with the participation decision of the man in the family. Although 'unemployed families' usually have neither parent in employment (Cooke (1987)), it is mostly the man who is registered unemployed, and unless the woman can earn a substantial wage (more difficult for a woman), or work very long hours, her return to work is unlikely to lift the family off supplementary

[2] Approximately half of the men aged 16 to 64 recorded as unemployed in the 1985 General Household Survey were married and had dependent children (Office of Population Censuses and Surveys (1986, Table 6.25)).

benefit. We assume the woman is not employed.[3] Furthermore, the majority of unemployed families receive supplementary benefit instead of, or in addition to, unemployment benefit (Atkinson and Micklewright (Ch. 1, this volume)), and so we take supplementary benefit/income support as the main source of out-of-work income.

We assume the preferences of the unemployed man we are considering can be represented by the utility function $u(c,L)$, where c is total family income and L leisure. Before discussing the form of this in more detail below, we consider the relevant constraints on c and L.

For the representative man from a family of some given size, income when unemployed is

$$c_0 = I, \tag{1}$$

where I is income from income support (and/or unemployment benefit). Remember child benefit is considered part of assessable income for income support and so is offset. And for the vast majority of families, the level of assistance with housing costs does not enter the equation either, being paid not to the householder but directly to local authorities under the certificated housing benefit scheme.

To facilitate our presentation, we suppose throughout that a job is actually available at some given wage, though it should be remembered that this may not be at all realistic in practice. If the man in question were to take a job, income may come from several sources: first, earnings net of direct taxes (income tax and National Insurance contributions)

$$v(wh-A) + A, \tag{2}$$

where for simplicity a linear tax system has been assumed, and v equals 1 minus the marginal tax rate, w is the wage rate, h the number of hours worked, and A the tax threshold. This linear approximation may be justified by the argument that the men are considering full-time work and that the earnings from this are likely to take them beyond the lower National Insurance (NI) contribution rates and over the tax threshold. (For those with gross earnings below the tax threshold, $v = 1$ and $A = 0$.)

In practice, there may be uncertainty about the wage available: the standard 'job search' problem. We feel that this aspect is (relatively) not very significant for the group being considered, that most have a good idea of what the 'going rate' is, and that there is little variation in this. Neverthe-

[3] Women married to unemployed men probably face even more of a financial disincentive to work than their husbands (Dilnot and Kell (Ch. 8, this volume)). Because of their lower expected wages and the fact that benefit is reduced pound for pound for any earnings above £5 per week (£15 for a long-term unemployed couple), such women are very unlikely to return to work *before* their husbands. There is some evidence, though, suggesting that they are likely to return to work *after* their husbands have left unemployment (Moylan, Millar, and Davies (1984)).

less, *net* take-home pay may not be known precisely beforehand. There may, for example, be unforeseen tax adjustments, or work expenses, or uncertainties about deductions for National Insurance. We shall be abstracting from these uncertainties here, on the argument that they are small relative to the others detailed below. This simplification should be remembered when considering the conclusions drawn below.

The second income source is child benefit, nB, where n is the number of children and B the payment per child.

The remaining sources are the means-tested benefits, principally family credit and housing benefit, and it is these, we argue, which lead to the most uncertainty about future income at the time of deciding whether or not to participate. There are three reasons why this may be so.

First, the individuals may have imperfect information and misconceptions about how the schemes operate. Each of the benefits referred to is notoriously complex in its own right, and an individual's estimation of the net outcome is potentially complicated by interactions between the two (for example, family credit is to count as assessable income for housing benefit), and between them and other benefits (for example, higher incomes can lead to the loss of 'passported' benefits).

To keep the model simple, we shall assume that there are just two possible outcomes: a relatively good one and a relatively poor one, i.e. net income from means-tested benefits is given by

either: F_1, with probability $1-p$

$$(3)$$

or: $F_2 = F_1 - d$, with probability p.

Thus the individual attaches a probability p to the occurrence of the bad outcome, and $(1-p)$ to the good one, and d represents the (absolute) difference between the two outcomes. We shall assume that p and d are the same for all heads of families of the same composition, and that neither of the parameters varies with unemployment income (this latter assumption is relaxed in the Appendix).[4]

This specification assumes that every individual claims the means-tested benefits if in work, that all claims are successful, and that there are no costs associated with claiming. Relaxing these assumptions leads to different interpretations of (3). For example, suppose the level of benefits available is known for sure, but the act of claiming involves 'transactions costs' or 'hassle', arising from the 'obstacles presented by the administration of the

[4] It has been suggested to us that p might be a function of w (or indeed wh or $(1-v)A + vwh$). If potential wages are positively correlated with attributes such as education, communication skills, social class, etc., then one might expect those with higher w to have a better knowledge of the system. However, it is not clear to us whether this would be associated with a lower p or a lower $1-p$.

income support system itself' (Cowell (1986, p. 1)). In this case, p would represent the probability that a claim will be unsuccessful.

Alternatively, costs may arise from 'stigma'—the 'disadvantages which a person perceives to arise from others' awareness of his using the system, or from his own perception of his claim in the light of the prevailing climate of opinion about receiving benefit' (Cowell (1986, p. 1))—in which case p should be interpreted as a probability of being observed claiming.

In practice, misconception, hassle, and stigma are all likely to contribute to income risk to different degrees, but in this paper we shall be emphasizing the first. Interviews with unemployed families in West Yorkshire and Northern Ireland that one of us has recently carried out (McLaughlin, Millar, and Cooke (1988)) strongly suggest that this is the most significant source, at least for this group.[5]

To summarize, total income if in work is given by

either: $\quad c_1 = vwh + (1-v)A + nB + F_1$, with probability $1-p$

$$(4)$$

or: $\quad\quad\quad\quad c_2 = c_1 - d$, with probability p.

The Participation Decision[6,7]

Assuming individuals are expected-utility-maximizers, then they will each participate as long as the expected utility from working is greater than that from continuing unemployed, i.e.

$$(1-p)\, u(c_1, L_w) + p\, u(c_2, L_w) > u(c_0, L_u) \tag{5}$$

---

[5] On the difficulties of apportioning importance using data sets such as the Family Expenditure Survey, see for example Blundell, Fry, and Walker (1988). For a review of previous work on ignorance or misconception, hassle, stigma, and the take-up of means-tested benefits, see Deacon and Bradshaw (1983, Ch. 7).

[6] The model used below is closely related to Moffitt's (1983) 'general model'. We are in effect giving renewed emphasis to his point that 'it is not true that "income is income" from whatever source derived' (p. 1024). The principal differences are, first, that he emphasizes not complexity, as here, but stigma or, on a different interpretation, hassle (see Cowell (1986, p. 23 n.)). Second, the current paper uses a (different) parameterization of preferences to analyse reasons for non-participation and the implications of various policy changes, rather than to do empirical work. Two other papers examining risk in the context of the (US) benefit system, though with a different emphasis, are Betson and van der Gaag (1985) and Halpern and Hausman (1986).

[7] Although we concentrate on the participation decision, the income risk idea could also be applied to the analysis of incentives for benefit recipients in work to work additional hours. The usual discussion, under the heading of the 'poverty trap', focuses on changes in certain income levels (summarized in terms of marginal tax rates), but by similar arguments, the change in hours may also have uncertain consequences for the means-tested component of future income.

where L_w and L_u are the leisure enjoyed if working and if unemployed respectively. This expression can be rewritten approximately as

$$u(c_1,L_w)/(\partial u/\partial c) - pd > u(c_0,L_u)/(\partial u/\partial c), \qquad (6)$$

taking $\qquad [u(c_1,L_w) - u(c_2,L_w)]/d \approx \partial u/\partial c.$

The right-hand side of (6) gives the reservation utility level in monetary terms, while the left-hand side is the maximum possible utility in work less the expected 'loss', in the same units.

The equation shows participation depends on the interaction of four main factors in addition to the purely financial ones, c_0 and c_1. The first two, and most obvious, are the size of p and d. The higher the probability attached to the bad outcome, and the worse the outcome actually is, the less likely participation is, *ceteris paribus*. Third, there is the difference between the amount of leisure enjoyed in and out of work: even if c_0 is substantially below c_1 (the 'minimum replacement rate' is low), this may not induce participation if the advantages of increased income are offset by a sufficiently large decrease in available leisure. And of course, fourth, the net effect will depend on the nature of preferences: individuals' marginal rates of substitution between income and leisure, and their marginal utility functions for income and leisure, and hence attitudes to risk.[8]

To analyse the interaction of these factors in more detail, it is useful to use a particular parameterization of preferences, and the one we use is:[9]

$$u = (-1/\beta\varepsilon)(cL^\beta)^{-\varepsilon}, \varepsilon > -1, \varepsilon \neq 0$$
$$u = (1/\beta) \ln(cL^\beta), \varepsilon = 0. \qquad (7)$$

This implies a marginal rate of substitution between income and leisure of $-\beta c/L$ (where $0 < \beta \leq 1$); the higher the β, the greater the degree of 'leisure preference'. The parameter ε succinctly describes individuals' attitudes to income risk, for this utility function implies a constant degree of relative risk aversion, $R_R = 1+\varepsilon$, and decreasing absolute risk aversion, $R_A = (1+\varepsilon)/c$.

We must also now be more explicit about the difference between L_w and L_u. Taking the total number of hours available as ι, then clearly $L_w = \iota - h$. The definition of L_u is more controversial. At one extreme, it could be argued that since $h=0$, L_u is simply ι (Case a), but this 'has the rather unattractive implication that time when one is laid off is pure leisure, thus destroying the distinction between voluntary and involuntary unemployment' (Cowell (1981, p. 695)). We could suppose instead that unemployed individuals spend a certain amount of time in non-leisure activities and that

---

[8] A corollary of all this is that it is only under strong assumptions that participation decisions will be influenced by c_0 and c_1 in ratio form (see below), and by these variables only.

[9] This is a special case of the function used by Cowell (1981).

Table 7.1 Summary of the participation condition

Risk aversion	An individual participates if . . .	
	Case a: $L_u = \iota$	Case b: $L_u = \iota - h$
$\varepsilon > 0$	$\alpha^\varepsilon(1-p+p\delta^\varepsilon) < [(\iota-h)/\iota]^{\beta\varepsilon} < 1$	$\alpha^\varepsilon(1-p+p\delta^\varepsilon) < 1$
$\varepsilon = 0$	$\alpha\delta p < (\iota-h)/\iota < 1$	$\alpha\delta p < 1$
$\varepsilon < 0$	$\alpha^\varepsilon(1-p+p\delta^\varepsilon) > [(\iota-h)/\iota]^{\beta\varepsilon} > 1$	$\alpha^\varepsilon(1-p+p\delta^\varepsilon) > 1$

where $\alpha \equiv c_0/c_1$;
$\delta \equiv c_1/c_2 = c_1/(c_1-d)$;
c_0 is income when unemployed;
c_1 is income when employed (good outcome);
c_2 is income when employed (bad outcome).

these hours have the same disutility as working hours. This may include time in voluntary job search as well as in activities required as a condition of benefit receipt. We take Case b, $L_u = \iota - h$, as our leading case below,[10] but also report some results for Case a.

These assumptions taken together imply a neat characterization of the more general expression set out in (5). This is summarized in Table 7.1. Note first that if there were no income risk ($\delta = 1$) and if $L_u = L_w$, then regardless of the degree of (relative) risk aversion, the participation decision hinges solely upon whether the replacement rate is less than unity. Not surprisingly, the bound is somewhat stricter in Case a, reflecting the need to take account of the extra leisure forgone by taking a job.

Consider Case b in more detail now. With income risk ($\delta > 1$), the decision depends on the interplay between a 'certainty component' and an 'uncertainty component'.[11] The former is a function of the 'minimum replacement rate', α, and assuming, realistically, that $\alpha < 1$, this factor provides a stimulus to participation. The size of this is larger, the larger the degree of risk aversion, since if the good outcome were available for sure, then (from the utility function) it would be valued more by those who were the more risk-averse (i.e. had a larger ε).

However, against this factor must be set the offsetting influence of the second term. Clearly, *ceteris paribus*, the more risk-averse people are, the more likely the bad outcome is thought to be (the higher the p), or

[10] Cf. Sjoquist (1976, p. 930): 'The notion of supplying hours of effort [which are not worked] is something different from being on the golf course. We assume that it is the same as working. This assumption is no more unrealistic than to assume that such hours are considered leisure'.

[11] These terms are borrowed from Cowell (1981).

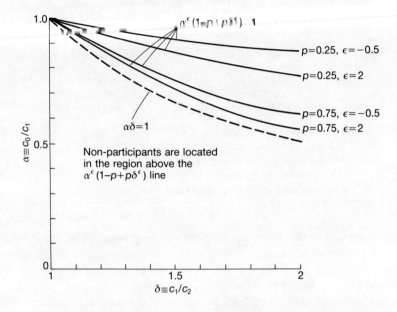

Figure 7.1 Graphical representation of the participation decision (Case a)

the worse the bad outcome actually is (the larger the d, and hence δ), the less likely participation is.

For an alternative perspective, let us define the certainty-equivalent income, c_3, to be that which, if received for sure by the individual, would provide exactly the same utility level as the risky income prospect $(1-p)c_1 + pc_2$. In fact

$$c_3 = c_0[\alpha^\varepsilon(1-p+p\delta^\varepsilon)]^{-1/\varepsilon}, \tag{8}$$

and this implies a 'certainty-equivalent replacement rate':

$$c_0/c_3 = [\alpha^\varepsilon(1-p+p\delta^\varepsilon)]^{1/\varepsilon}, \tag{9}$$

But we know from Table 7.1 that individuals participate as long as the right-hand side of (9) is less than 1. In other words, the participation condition is that the certainty-equivalent replacement rate be less than 1.

The overall situation is summarized in Figure 7.1. The contour lines represent combinations of parameters such that individuals are just indifferent between taking a job and staying unemployed. The region above the line represents situations where the uncertainty component dominates and individuals do not participate. Below the line, the converse occurs. Also it turns out that for plausible values of the parameters, the higher the degree of risk aversion, the larger the 'non-participation' region (i.e. increasing ε has a greater effect on the uncertainty component than the certainty one).[12] Note, finally, that income risk plays a role only if d is large enough to ensure that the worst possible income from working is less than that available when unemployed. If not, then individuals must be in the region below the dashed line in Figure 7.1 (where $\alpha\delta = c_0/c_2 < 1$), and hence participating.

Much the same story can be told for Case a. In terms of Figure 7.1, the non-participation region is larger here when $\varepsilon > 0$, as the contour lines all now pass through not $(\delta,\alpha) = (1,1)$, but the lower point $(1,[(\iota-h)/\iota]^{\beta\varepsilon})$. In this case there can be situations where individuals do not take jobs even if $\alpha\delta < 1$.

Although the degree of risk aversion plays a key role in determining non-participation, we should stress that we are *not* saying that the policy problem is that unemployed family heads are somehow different from other people and are not willing to take risks *per se*. Indeed, our specification of preferences—a standard one—assumes that rich and poor alike (in families of the same composition) have the same underlying attitudes to risk. But because, broadly speaking, a given amount of uncertainty is more significant for those at low incomes, income risk has a relatively larger influence on behaviour for this group.

We have demonstrated the potential disincentive effects of income risk. The next section considers alternative policies for increasing participation.

3. Policies for Increasing Participation Propensities

The analysis has shown that participation propensities can be increased by reducing certainty-equivalent replacement rates. With reference to Figure 7.1, either or both of α and δ must fall sufficiently to move the individual below the contour line: for any income parameter z, then $\partial\alpha/\partial z$, $\partial\delta/\partial z < 0$ ensures

$$\partial[\alpha^{\varepsilon}(1-p+p\delta^{\varepsilon})]/\partial z = \varepsilon\alpha^{\varepsilon-1}[(1-p+p\delta^{\varepsilon})\partial\alpha/\partial z + \alpha p\delta^{\varepsilon-1}\partial\delta/\partial z] < (>) 0$$
$$\text{when } \varepsilon > (<) 0. \qquad (10)$$

Assuming for the moment that the level (or indeed variance) of c_0 is not

---

[12] In Case b, all the contours go through the point $(\delta,\alpha) = (1,1)$, and so they can each be characterized by their slope. Letting s be the absolute value of this, then it may be calculated that $\partial s/\partial\varepsilon \equiv \varepsilon \ln(\delta) [\varepsilon(1+p)-p\delta^{\varepsilon}] + (1-p+p\delta^{\varepsilon}) \ln(1-p+p\delta^{\varepsilon}) > (<) 0$ in general, reflecting the two roles for ε cited earlier. The result cited in the text is based on graphs of the line $\alpha^{\varepsilon}(1-p+p\delta^{\varepsilon})$ for $\varepsilon = -0.5, 0, 2, 10$ and $p = 0.25, 0.5, 0.75$.

changed,[13] the policy instruments are restricted to elements of the stochastic budget constraint given in (4).

There are two main types of policy available. The first includes measures reducing income risk directly by changing means-tested benefits. This could be done in a number of ways. One of the most straightforward of these would be to reduce d by introducing lump-sum payments into family credit. One could have a child benefit 'supplement' restricted to family credit recipients. Income would determine eligibility but not the basic guarantee. Because it is the transition into work that gives rise to problems, this suggests paying the supplement for a limited time period. (This restriction would also help avert potential problems arising from the introduction of a 'notch' into budget constraints at the point where family credit eligibility is lost.) Another possibility would be to try to reduce the general ignorance and misconception about means-tested benefits by using one with a simpler means test, for example by an extension of the current Jobstart scheme under which workers receive a flat-rate subsidy for 26 weeks if they take a job with a wage below a certain level. This would also reduce the risk arising from perceived delays in benefit receipt. A strategy with the same effect as this would be continuing to provide assistance with high housing costs under the certificated housing benefit scheme for a limited period, rather than requiring an immediate new claim to be made and assessed when a job is taken.

The other main type of policy instrument affects income risk by increasing the share of income in work provided by the relatively certain sources of income. The principal method available for this is an increase in child benefit. Less directly, a cut in marginal tax rates (a rise in v), or a rise in the tax threshold (A), would increase income from earnings and hence reduce the need for benefit supplements.

Comparing Policy Strategies

We turn now to examine the incentive effects of each of these reforms, concentrating on Case b, and, following the discussion above, we focus attention on the implications of such changes for the size of α and δ.

A complication arising in the analysis is that these parameter changes may in turn alter the optimal number of hours of work (h^*) that would be chosen if the individual did participate. But if h^* and hence earnings change, this may have further knock-on effects for two reasons. First, the net payment received from means-tested benefits will change and, second, the perceived potential income difference d may itself be a function of h.

---

[13] We assume it will not be reduced for income maintenance reasons. In the Appendix we show that in certain cases there are grounds for raising I, even though this would increase nominal replacement rates.

Table 7.2 Effects on $\alpha \equiv c_0/c_1$ and $\delta \equiv c_1/c_2$ of *ceteris paribus* changes in each parameter (z) (assuming no second-round influences)

Parameter (z)	Elasticities	
	$(z/\alpha)\partial\alpha/\partial z$	$(z/\delta)\partial\delta/\partial z$
d	0	$[(\delta-1)/c_1]\{c_2\}$
v	$-[(1-r)/c_1]\{vwh-vA\}$	$-[(\delta-1)/c_1]\{(1-r)vwh\}$
w	$-[(1-r)/c_1]\{vwh\}$	$-[(\delta-1)/c_1]\{(1-r)vwh\}$
A	$-[(1-r)/c_1]\{(1-v)A\}$	$-[(\delta-1)/c_1]\{(1-r)(1-v)A\}$
B	$-[(1-r)/c_1]\{nB/(1-r)\}$	$-[(\delta-1)/c_1]\{nB\}$

With regard to the latter, it might be argued that the greater the number of hours chosen ('the further the step into the unknown'), the larger d might be. Alternatively, the transition *per se* may be of most relevance (making d a fixed amount), though this may be smaller the more hours that are worked (with higher earnings, the influence of means-tested benefits is less).

To the contrary, it might well be argued that in practice individuals have little choice over the number of hours they can work—the options are $h = 0$ or some $h = h°$ only—in which case neither of these 'second-round' influences will be of practical relevance. The fixed hours assumption is that adopted in most previous analyses of unemployment-trap reduction policies. The case certainly provides the most clear-cut results and is the one we concentrate on here, with the more general case considered in the Appendix.

The implications for α and δ of (infinitesimal) increases in v, w, A, and B, and decrease in d are summarized in elasticity terms in Table 7.2, where the calculations have assumed that the amount of means-tested benefits paid depends on earnings net of tax, i.e. $F_1 = F[v(wh-A) + A]$, and that the marginal rate of benefit withdrawal $F' = r < 1$. The table confirms that each of the policies would have the desired effects on participation propensities, though there is a clear difference in effects between the direct reductions of income risk which lead to westerly movements in Figure 7.1, and the other policies which lead to south-westerly ones. This does not mean that the latter are necessarily more efficient in increasing incentives: note that the effect on δ of a 1 per cent fall in d is much larger than a 1 per cent rise in any of the other parameters.

If one restricts attention to just v, w, A, and B, there is still no unambiguous ranking in the size of the elasticities, but comparing the relative magnitudes of the terms in curly brackets shows that the main 'contest' is between the B and w elasticities. The former is greater (smaller) than the latter as long as $nB/(1-r) > (<) (1-r)vwh$ so that, not surprisingly, child benefit is more effective the larger the number of children to be supported. Substituting the not implausible values $B = 7.25$, $r = v = \frac{2}{9}$ and $n = 2$ in the inequality, it becomes $196 \succ (\prec) wh$. And to put this into perspective, note that £196 is around 80 per cent of average weekly earnings (relatively high for the group we are considering); in other words, child benefit is likely to have the greater elasticity in this case.

We would emphasize, however, that all this is not conclusive evidence for one policy measure or another. After all, as (10) shows, it is not just the elasticities that are important, but also the individual's original location in Figure 7.1, and the position and shape of the contour. Furthermore, in comparing elasticities we are not really comparing like with like, for the total cost of engineering a 1 per cent increase in w, say, could be quite different from that of a 1 per cent increase in B.

What determines these costs? Several different elements might be distinguished. The first is the cost of the income maintenance payments themselves, and perhaps the most relevant factor in the current context is the extent to which payments can be targeted on the client group.[14]

Universal child benefit clearly scores worse than changes to d or targeted wage subsidies in expenditure terms. But there are other cost dimensions and in particular the costs of administering schemes, where these costs include not only those to the State in administration, but also those borne by claimants (including hassle and stigma). Here, child benefit would come into its own. It is a highly visible benefit with no take-up problems, and the extra administrative costs of raising benefit levels are surely minor. And if, plausibly, the degree of risk aversion tends to be larger for men with more children to support, then the benefit is well-targeted.

In contrast, Jobstart-like wage subsidy schemes, or the short-term continuation of certificated housing benefit for those moving into work, are much less visible, and the former at least would be likely to require a large investment in administrative apparatus. And their operation would be complicated by having to take account of the well-known instability of job attachments for a significant proportion of the unemployed. On the other hand, the time-limit feature of them does allow better targeting on the transition into work *per se*.

A potential compromise combining the advantages of child benefit but with better targeting would be to make time-limited child-related lump-sum payments under family credit as discussed above—in effect a move towards a 'social dividend' for low-income working families.

---

[14] Another important element is the incidence of the additional taxes (or reduced benefits) necessary to finance these changes—say by the complete abolition of the married man's allowance—and thence potential knock-on effects for labour supply.

4. Concluding Comments

We should stress that our analysis of policy options is speculative rather than conclusive (though at the very least our proposals, for example on child benefit, are not inconsistent with some previous suggestions for reducing the unemployment trap). Our main aim, however, has been to draw attention to income risk, a concept we think deserves greater consideration in the future.

To reiterate, our principal message is that financial incentives for the unemployed to take a job should not be summarized solely in terms of the nominal levels of income available in and out of work. Also of potential significance is the income risk which arises from making the transition into work, and which provides a disincentive to labour force participation for risk-averse individuals. There is a possible 'employment lottery', not just an 'unemployment trap'!

We have argued that income risk arises primarily from the complexity of the means-tested benefit system.[15] As it is the composition of income, not just its level, which is important, we suggest adding the proportion of a working family's income provided by the principal means-tested sources to the output of tax and benefit simulation models, and recommend this be discussed alongside the replacement rates now routinely produced. This additional summary statistic is obviously a very crude indicator of income risk, but in the short term may prove useful. In the longer term, the tax and benefit models will need to be adapted to account for the incentive effects of different income packages along the lines of, say, Blundell, Meghir, Symons, and Walker (1984) but using a labour supply model more like that estimated by Moffitt (1983).

Needless to say, only further research will reveal more precisely the degree of risk aversion and its variation across different family types, as well as the relative contributions of ignorance or misconception, hassle, and stigma to income risk. The latter issue will become increasingly important as pressure for greater computerization and integration of the personal taxation and social security systems grows. For example, a delivery system based around 'smart cards' might reduce hassle and stigma but have little effect on misconception if there is little simplification in tax and benefit structure. The success of the system thus depends on which factor plays the key role.

On the theoretical side, the basic participation model needs to be

---

[15] We are not arguing that means-testing is synonymous with complexity. In principle, a highly integrated tax-transfer system might be able to be summarized using a small number of parameters, and hence be quite 'simple'. The current system is not like this.

modified to allow for more than one potential worker per family. For example, if a wife were working, her earnings could provide a steady and sure source of income to the family which can mitigate against the income risk arising if the husband were to take a job. But this tends not to happen under the current system, as earnings-disregard levels provide a disincentive for women to stay in work when their husbands are unemployed.

More generally we have assumed in effect that increasing the participation of a particular unemployed group is the primary policy goal. A more sophisticated approach would consider the implications for society as a whole, as for example the optimal tax literature does. The analysis here gives added weight to suggestions that the optimal tax approach needs to be extended to take explicit account of the costs associated with the operation of different benefit delivery systems.

Appendix: The Model with Some Alternative Assumptions

In this Appendix we consider two main variations on the basic model presented in the main text. First, we relax the assumption that the individuals work a fixed number of hours if they participate, and thence allow for second-round effects of policy changes. Second, we relax the assumption that d does not depend on unemployment income.

Allowing for Second-Round Effects

Suppose now that individuals can choose the number of hours they work and that $\partial d/\partial h = 0$, and re-examine the implications for α and δ of changes in model parameters under Case a. In this situation the relevant elasticities become those in Table 7A.1 (cf. Table 7.2).

In general each of these elasticities may be positive or negative, though if (1) $\partial h/\partial z > 0$ and $\partial d/\partial h < 0$, then all the elasticities will be negative (positive for d), as in Table 7.2. On the other hand, if (2) $\partial h/\partial z < 0$ and $\partial d/\partial h > 0$, the elasticities will be positive (negative for d), and the second-round effects more than offset the initial ones, so that policy will have the reverse effect from that intended. If (3) $\partial d/\partial h = 0$, then, as long as $\partial h/\partial z$ is not 'too negative', the qualitative predictions summarized in Table 7.2 are unaffected.

As argued in the text, intuitive arguments suggest $\partial d/\partial h$ can take on any sign, but suppose for the sake of argument that $\partial d/\partial h \approx 0$, so that Case 3 is the relevant one. What then is the sign of $\partial h/\partial z$? To determine this, we need to solve for the optimal h (conditional on $h > 0$), i.e. find the h^* that

Table 7.A1

z	$(z/\alpha)\partial\alpha/\partial z$
d	$-(d/c_1)(1-r)vw. \ \partial h/\partial d$
v	$-(v/c_1)(1-r)[wh[1 + (v/h).\partial h/\partial v] - A]$
w	$-(w/c_1)(1-r)vh[1 + (w/h).\partial h/\partial w]$
A	$-(A/c_1)(1-r)[1-v + vw.\partial h/\partial A]$
B	$-(nB/c_1)[1 + n[(1-r)vw.\partial h/\partial B - (\partial d/\partial h)(\partial h/\partial B)]]$
z	$(z/\delta)\partial\delta/\partial z$
d	$-(d/c_1)[(\delta-1)(1-r)vw, \partial h/\partial d - \delta]$
v	$-(v/c_1)[(\delta-1)(1-r)wh[1 + (v/h).\partial h/\partial v] - \delta(\partial d/\partial h)(\partial h/\partial v)]$
w	$-(w/c_1)[(\delta-1)(1-r)vh[1 + (w/h).\partial h/\partial w] - \delta(\partial d/\partial h)(\partial h/\partial w)]$
A	$-(A/c_1)[(\delta-1)(1-r)[1-v + vw.\partial h/\partial A] - \delta(\partial d/\partial h)(\partial h/\partial A)]$
B	$-(nB/c_1)[(\delta-1)[1 + n[(1-r)vw.\partial h/\partial B] - n\delta(\partial d/\partial h)(\partial h/\partial B)]$

maximizes the left-hand side of (5) in the text. The required expression is in fact

$$h^* = [\iota vw(1-r)\lambda - \beta\theta]/[vw((1-r)\lambda + \beta)], \tag{A1}$$

where

$$\lambda \equiv 1 - [p\delta^\varepsilon(1-\delta) + \delta(\partial d/\partial h)/[vw(1-r)]]/[1-p+p\delta^\varepsilon]$$

and

$$\theta \equiv (1-v)A + F_1 + nB,$$

but its complexity has meant that we have been unable to derive any unambiguous conclusions about the sign(s) of $\partial h/\partial z$.

What then if the sign of each elasticity were the same as the corresponding one when there is no income risk? It may be checked that with certainty (A1) would simplify to

$$h^* = [\iota vw(1-r) - \beta\theta]/[vw(1-r+\beta)], \tag{A2}$$

implying $\partial h/\partial B$, $\partial h/\partial A < 0$ (standard income effects) and $\partial h/\partial v$, $\partial h/\partial w > 0$ (the substitution effect dominates for sure with the simple specification of preferences used). The qualitative predictions in Table 7.2 would thus go through, as long as the effects on h of changes in B or A were not too large. We should, however, stress that it is not at all clear that the premiss—corresponding signs the same—is correct, as demonstrated by Cowell (1981) in a related context.

The analysis so far has been in terms of Case b. Note that in Case a, unambiguous results are even more difficult to derive because the right-hand side of the inequalities in Table 7.1 is a function of h.

Implications of Variations in d with Unemployment Income

It could be argued that a family's ability to cope with the bad outcome if it occurred will depend on its unemployment income, i.e. the higher c_0 is for each family of a given size, the greater the possibility of it meeting the fixed costs of taking a job (having to buy work clothing, etc.) from its own resources. This argument suggests taking $d = d(c_0)$ with $\partial d/\partial c_0 < 0$, and can provide a rationale for a policy of increasing income support payments for incentive reasons, even though it increases nominal replacement rates.

Let the left-hand side of the participation condition in Table 7.1, $\alpha^\varepsilon(1-p+p\delta^\varepsilon) \equiv T$, so δ as well as α depends on c_0 now. Differentiation with respect to c_0 yields

$$\partial T/\partial c_0 = \varepsilon\alpha^{\varepsilon-1}[(1-p+p\delta^\varepsilon)/c_1 + p\alpha\delta^\varepsilon(\partial d/\partial c_0)/c_2] \qquad (A3)$$

which is negative—implying increases in I raise participation propensities—as long as the individual is sufficiently risk-averse ($\varepsilon > 0$) and the resource effect large ($\partial d/\partial c_0$ sufficiently negative).

8

Male Unemployment and Women's Work

ANDREW DILNOT AND MICHAEL KELL*

1. Introduction

Is there a link between male unemployment and women's work? Received wisdom has it that if a husband becomes unemployed, his wife will want to find a job, or work harder in her existing job, to replace lost household income. On the other hand, the wife may be discouraged from working as she realizes that the household's entitlement to social security benefits is sharply reduced when she earns any income. It is this latter possibility that forms the focus of this article.

The idea that the level and structure of social security benefits may create disincentives to work is not a new one; for much of the last decade there has been an active debate on this issue. Although the controversy continues, most results suggest that disincentive effects are not substantial.[1] However, the great bulk of this research has concentrated solely on men, and there is no reason to presuppose that these findings apply equally to women. Indeed, such work as there is explicitly on female labour supply suggests that, in general, married women are far more responsive to tax- and benefit-induced incentives and disincentives than are their husbands. In this article we present evidence showing that women married to unemployed men have observed work behaviour consistent with the incentives implied by the tax and benefit system.

We are at pains to emphasize that other factors may lie behind our results. In particular, it seems highly plausible that women married to unemployed men will be less likely to work because they have low education and skill levels (like their husbands) and because they live in areas of the country where there is low demand for all types of labour, male and

* Andrew Dilnot is a Programme Director and Michael Kell is a Research Officer at the Institute for Fiscal Studies.

This paper was first published in *Fiscal Studies*, August 1987.

The work is part of the IFS project on the distributional implications of fiscal policy, which is supported by the Economic and Social Research Council and the Gatsby Foundation. The authors would like to thank Richard Blundell and Costas Meghir for helpful comments on an earlier draft.

[1] See Atkinson and Micklewright (1985) for a survey, and Minford (1983) for an alternative view.

female. Sorting out the relative importance of these and other explanations for the observed work behaviour of married women requires a detailed and carefully estimated econometric model of female labour supply,[2] which is a longer-run aim of our research. In the mean time, we present results which we believe may indicate a problem of incentives created by the benefit system, while stressing the preliminary nature of our work.

In Section 2 we describe the UK benefit system as it affects the unemployed and their wives, and consider the work behaviour we would expect to observe. In Section 3 we present results from Family Expenditure Survey (FES) data. Finally, in Section 4, we consider briefly the implications for policy and further research.

2. The Benefit System Described

There are three principal benefits available to the unemployed in the UK. Some of the unemployed receive all three. The benefit that comes most readily to mind is unemployment benefit, which is the least commonly received, despite its name. Unemployment benefit is topped up or entirely replaced by supplementary benefit and/or housing benefit (either certificated or standard).

Unemployment benefit is a contributory National Insurance benefit, payable for a maximum of a year to an individual with a complete contribution record. The full rate for an individual is currently £31.45 per week, and is increased by £19.40 per week for an adult dependant such as a wife or husband. An unemployed man will receive the addition in full unless his wife earns more than £19.40 per week, in which case he receives none of it. This is the only way in which unemployment benefit entitlement is related to wife's income.

Since unemployment benefit is only paid for a year, and only then to those with full contribution records, the growth of youth and long-term unemployment has reduced the proportion of the unemployed who receive it. In 1987, only 950,000 of around 3.1 million unemployed individuals in the UK will receive unemployment benefit; the remainder are dependent on other sources of income within their family or, in the great majority of cases, on supplementary benefit and housing benefit.

Supplementary benefit (SB) exists to prevent any family in the UK from falling below a given level of income.[3] The basic requirements of each claimant are calculated according to their marital status, age, and number of dependants. Supplementary benefit entitlement is calculated by sub-

---

[2] Along the lines developed by, for example, Blundell, Ham, and Meghir (1987).

[3] Note, however, that it is possible for people without children who are working, but on very low incomes, to fall below the 'SB line'.

tracting from these basic requirements any income received by the family, subject to the first £4 per week of earned income being disregarded. In addition to the basic requirements, certain weekly additions are available for specific needs such as heating or special diets, and one-off payments that cannot be met from the normal weekly benefit may be covered by a special 'single payment'.

The main weekly rates of supplementary benefit as they apply to the unemployed are:

Single householder	£30.40
Married householder	£49.35
Single non-householder	£24.35
Children 0–10	£10.40
Children 11 and over	£15.60
Earnings disregard	£4.00

Of the 3.1 million unemployed, some $2\frac{1}{4}$ million receive supplementary benefit at a cost of around £5 billion per annum.

The third benefit commonly received by the unemployed is housing benefit. Since 1983, there have been two principal forms of housing benefit, 'certificated' and 'standard'. Certificated housing benefit is paid to those in receipt of supplementary benefit, and essentially pays all housing costs. Until 1983, this was part of the supplementary benefit system itself. Standard housing benefit is paid to any household other than those on supplementary benefit. Under this system, up to 100 per cent of housing costs are paid for, but the amount of benefit received is reduced once income exceeds a given level, by amounts ranging from 8 pence to 46 pence, or 70 pence for pensioners, for each £1 by which income exceeds the specified level. Most of the unemployed receiving housing benefit are receiving certificated housing benefit.

Thus far we have merely described the benefits. Perhaps the best way of explaining their impact on the incentives for women to work is to present hypothetical examples of families receiving the different benefits. Table 8.1 illustrates the net income that would be received by a married couple with two children aged 11–15, paying £20 per week rent and £5 per week rates. The husband is unemployed, the wife can work at a wage rate of £2.50 per hour.

If the wife works not at all, the family's net income is £105.55, made up of certificated housing benefit, supplementary benefit, and child benefit. If the wife works for 10 hours, the first £4 of her income is ignored; thereafter, supplementary benefit is reduced by £1 for each £1 earned, so net income rises by just £4 as a result of the £25 rise in gross income. A further 10 hours of work have no effect on net income, with supplementary benefit falling by the same amount as net income from work rises. The same is true

Table 8.1 Net incomes at different hours worked by wife: two children, head on supplementary benefit

Wife's hours	0	10	20	30	40	50
Wage	–	25.00	50.00	75.00	100.00	125.00
Income tax[a]	–	–	–0.91	–7.66	–14.41	–21.16
National Insurance	–	–	–2.50	–5.25	–9.00	–11.25
Housing benefit	25.00	25.00	25.00	25.00	13.66	5.55
Family income supplement	–	–	–	–	7.35	–
Child benefit	14.50	14.50	14.50	14.50	14.50	14.50
Supplementary benefit	66.05	45.05	23.46	7.96	–	–
Net income	105.55	109.55	109.55	109.55	112.10	112.64

[a] We have assumed the wife does not opt for the married man's allowance. If she did, her take-home pay would be higher, but SB would be reduced by a corresponding amount.

of a further 10 hours, taking the working week to 30 hours. An increase to a 40-hour week does bring some benefit: supplementary benefit is exhausted and the family moves on to family income supplement and standard housing benefit. The increase in gross wages from £75 per week to £100 per week brings a gain in net income of £2.55. The final jump from 40 to 50 hours per week increases net income by only £0.54. Having come off supplementary benefit and on to family income supplement and standard housing benefit, the family promptly falls into the poverty trap, paying £0.27 of income tax and £0.09 of National Insurance (NI) and losing £0.50 of family income supplement and £0.23 of housing benefit for each extra £1 earned, a total of £1.09. Even at 50 hours, having lost entitlement to family income supplement, the overall marginal tax rate is 82 per cent (27 per cent income tax, 9 per cent NI, and 46 per cent housing benefit). The incentive for a woman to participate in the labour market faced by such circumstances is clearly rather slight. However, this is a fairly extreme case, since we have assumed no entitlement to unemployment benefit, that there are children, and that the family lives in rented accommodation; all three assumptions tend to intensify the disincentive effect.

Table 8.2 presents similar figures for a childless couple where the head is entitled to unemployment benefit. The couple have no entitlement to supplementary benefit since their unemployment benefit of £50.85 is above the level at which supplementary benefit is exhausted. If the wife works for 10 hours, the dependent spouse addition to unemployment benefit, of £19.40 per week, is lost completely. This is offset to some extent by the earnings disregard for housing benefit (HB) reducing the income taken into account when assessing HB, which thus rises to the full £25 per week. But overall, an increase in wages from zero to £25 per week produces a gain of just £8.57. From 10 to 20 hours per week, the gain is £14.23; housing benefit

Table 8.2 Net incomes at different hours worked by wife: childless couple, head on unemployment benefit

Wife's hours	0	10	20	30	40	50
Wage	–	25.00	50.00	75.00	100.00	125.00
Unemployment benefit	50.85	31.45	31.45	31.45	31.45	31.45
Income tax	–	–	–0.91	–7.66	–14.41	–21.16
National Insurance	–	–	–2.50	–5.25	–9.00	–11.25
Housing benefit	22.03	25.00	17.64	7.18	–	–
Net income	72.88	81.45	95.68	100.72	108.04	124.04

remains at its maximum over some of this range. From 20 to 30 hours, the gain in net income is only £5.04, as income tax, National Insurance, and housing benefit withdrawal all operate in this region. At 40 and 50 hours, no housing benefit entitlement exists: at 40 hours per week, with gross earnings of £100, the net benefit from the wife's work is £35.16; at 50 hours, with earnings of £125, it is £51.16. Thus for this type of family, the wife's incentive to work is greater than in the first example, especially if she is considering full-time work. On the other hand, part-time work is still not financially attractive. The reason for this is the loss of dependant's allowance once the wife works more than 7 hours a week (in our particular example). We can see this as a 'fixed cost' of working more than 7 hours a week, which reinforces the fixed costs that are more usually incurred in working, such as travel or child care costs. These 'traditional' fixed costs are usually seen as sufficient to deter most wives from working just a handful of hours a week, but not so large as to deter part-time work involving 15 or 20 hours a week. The additional fixed cost when the husband is on unemployment benefit (UB) may well discourage a woman such as the one in our example from taking any job with fewer than perhaps 20 hours work a week.

Table 8.3 illustrates the impact of the tax system on the net income gained through work by the wife of a man in work, in a family with no entitlement to means-tested benefits. The final two rows of the table show the gains accruing to the families of Tables 8.1 and 8.2 from the woman's working. The clearest contrast is between the 'supplementary benefit family' and the family with the working head; the first gains £7.09 from 50 hours of the woman's work, the second £92.59. The 'unemployment benefit family' gains £51.16, substantially more than that with entitlement to supplementary benefit, but still less than the family in which the head is employed. The relative divergence in net income between the SB household and the 'no benefit household' (a rough measure of work

Table 8.3 Additional net income at different hours worked by wife: husband in work, no means-tested benefit entitlement

Wife's hours	0	10	20	30	40	50
Wage	–	25.00	50.00	75.00	100.00	125.00
Income tax	–	–	–0.91	–7.66	–14.41	–21.16
National Insurance	–	–	–2.50	–5.25	–9.00	–11.25
Net income	–	25.00	46.59	62.09	76.59	92.59
Additional income as a result of wife working						
SB household	–	4.00	4.00	4.00	6.55	7.09
UB household	–	8.57	22.80	27.84	35.16	51.16

disincentive) is large at all hours of work, but widest for full-time work. For the UB household, the relative divergence is largest at a few hours of work a week. The way in which net incomes change as the number of hours worked increases for these three examples is drawn in Figure 8.1, which assumes for simplicity that the net income of all three families is the same if the women do not work. The diagram shows how the 'fixed cost' of the loss of the dependant's addition for the UB household creates a kink in the wife's net income schedule which makes working 8 to 15 hours a week extremely unattractive.

Such hypothetical households can indicate only approximately the diver-

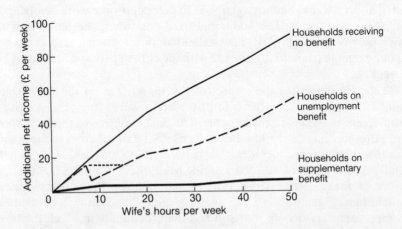

Figure 8.1　Additional net income from wife's work by household's benefit receipt

sity of experience of real households, to which we turn in the next section. However, they may serve to focus our attention on the type of behaviour we can expect to observe. The most important point is that we would expect to find a smaller proportion of women married to unemployed men in work than we find in the population at large, since the financial return from work is much lower for this group. A number of more specific points may also be made:

1. We would not expect to find women working in families that were receiving supplementary benefit, since benefit entitlement is reduced pound for pound in line with net earnings, removing all financial benefit from work (except for the £4 per week disregard).
2. Among those married to unemployed men who do work, we would expect to find longer average hours of work than for the population at large. As noted above, to 'escape' from the means-tested benefit system will generally mean working more than a small number of hours in a part-time job. The number of hours needed will obviously vary; in the case of our 'supplementary benefit family', a moderately well-paid full-time job would be required; for our 'unemployment benefit family', a part-time job might suffice.
3. Looking at the group of non-working women in households receiving supplementary benefit, we would expect the number of hours they would need to work to exhaust supplementary benefit entitlement and begin to gain from work to be quite high, indicating the pointlessness of part-time work for many of them. We must also recall that, as shown in Table 8.1 and Figure 8.1, even after supplementary benefit has been exhausted, further means-tested benefits, such as family income supplement and housing benefit, can continue to impose very high withdrawal rates on earned income.

We turn in Section 3 to an examination of data from the Family Expenditure Survey (FES) for the years 1980, 1982, and 1984, with which we hope to test our suppositions.

3. Empirical Results

In the last section we raised several questions which we hope to answer with reference to empirical data. The first, and most important, is whether male unemployment does, or does not, have a significant impact on women's work.

The few previous studies that have looked at this issue (albeit indirectly) have usually found that male unemployment does seem to exert a

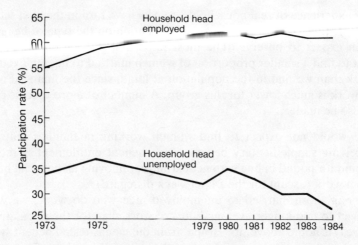

Figure 8.2   Wives' participation rates from GHS by employment status of
household head

downward influence on female employment. For example, a study by
Layard, Barton, and Zabalza (1980) found that 'wives with unemployed
husbands are 31 percentage points less likely to work than otherwise similar wives with husbands at work'. Layard et al. used the 1974 General
Household Survey (GHS) for their data; we have looked at survey data
from more recent years and found equally striking results.

Figure 8.2 presents evidence on the participation rates (i.e. the proportion of a sample of women who are observed working at least 1 hour a
week) of two groups of women over the period 1973–84. It is clear that the
participation rate of women married to unemployed men is consistently
and significantly lower than that of women with husbands in work. Moreover, the difference between the participation rates is growing over time;
the proportion of women married to employed men who work grew steadily through the 1970s, stabilizing since 1979 at around 61 per cent; mean-
while, the participation rate of women with unemployed husbands has
fallen steadily during the 1980s, to the point where in 1984 a woman with a
husband in employment is more than twice as likely to be working as a
woman with an unemployed husband.

Figure 8.2 is drawn from the 1984 GHS, which provides quick access to a
time series of reliable aggregate data. However, for more detailed investigation of the group we are interested in, we turn to the Family Expenditure
Survey. Both the GHS and the FES are continuous surveys of randomly
selected households in Britain, and while the GHS has a larger sample size,
the FES provides more information on household income and labour force
participation. It is also more consistent in its format from year to year, and

thus we can repeat our cross-sectional analysis over several years' data, which should permit a greater degree of confidence in our results.[4]

As Figure 8.3 shows, the evidence on women's participation rates derived from the FES completely confirms the striking picture painted by the GHS results: namely, that women married to unemployed men are far less likely to be in work than women married to employed men, and that this trend is increasing over time.[5]

Having presented powerful evidence to confirm that male unemployment does have a significant negative effect on female participation rates, we now consider the number of hours worked by women, so that we may address the next question: is it the case that, in order to 'escape' from the means-tested benefit systems, women married to unemployed men work longer hours than we would otherwise expect?

Figure 8.4 compares the distribution of hours worked by women married to unemployed men with the distribution of hours worked by women with employed husbands in 1984. We see again how three-quarters of women with unemployed husbands are not working at all; of those who are working, we see that, as we expect, a smaller proportion of the women with

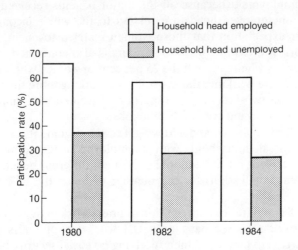

Figure 8.3 Wives' participation rates from FES by employment status of household head

[4] One of the main conclusions of a recent study of the employment of married women in the UK over the period 1970–83 by Gomulka and Stern (1986) was that 'the changes in coefficients which we find using a well-tried model and a standard, and apparently reliable, data set lead one to suggest great caution in either forecasting or numerical explanation of past events using estimates from a single cross-section'.

[5] The small differences in the participation rates derived from the two sets of survey evidence are the result of slight differences in definitions and random sampling fluctuations.

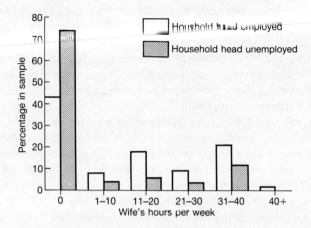

Figure 8.4   Wife's hours by employment status of household head (FES, 1984)

unemployed husbands are working part-time than women married to employed men. There is an unambiguous disincentive to the wife taking part-time employment because all the major benefits received by house-holds with unemployed heads are related to the wife's income to some extent. Our expectation that those women married to unemployed men who do work will tend to work long hours is also confirmed, though not categorically, by Figure 8.4. Of the 25 per cent of women with unemployed husbands who are working, the majority are working more than 30 hours a week; less than two-fifths of the subgroup of women with employed hus-bands who are working are in full-time jobs.

We can clarify matters, and add weight to our argument, by subdividing our sample of all households with unemployed heads according to the benefit(s) received; for as Section 2 explained, different benefits can have very different implications for the number of hours the wife is likely to work.

Figure 8.5 compares the distribution of hours worked by women married to unemployed men receiving only UB with that of hours worked by women married to employed men receiving no social security benefits (the latter is our yardstick or 'control' group). It now becomes apparent that where UB is the applicable benefit, wives are more likely to be observed working full-time than in the control group. They are also less likely to work part-time: in our 1984 sample, no women married to men on UB are working 1 to 10 hours a week, compared with 8 per cent of the women in the control group. This pattern of hours worked conforms to our expec-tations; because of the loss of the dependant's allowance once the wife earns more than £19.40, there is little reason for her to work only a few hours a week. The 'fixed cost' of the loss of the dependant's allowance, especially when combined with other fixed costs of working, appears to be sufficient to deter part-time work. At the same time, because the main part of UB received is not contingent on the wife's income, there is no disincentive to the wife finding or keeping a full-time job to replace lost household income. It is also the case that many of these households would be entitled to SB, if the wife did not work; to escape the 100 per cent withdrawal rate of SB, long hours of work may have been necessary. The point we are making here is that entitlement to social security benefits can be as important to work incentives as the actual receipt of benefits.

When we looked closely at the women in the UB group who are working part-time, we found all of them to be in secure, well-paid jobs, earning substantially more than the dependant's allowance they were forgoing by choosing to work. In other words, all the women in the UB group appear to be responding to the incentive structure of UB (and SB) precisely as we expect.

However, we should stress that these findings are based on a rather small sample (just 40 in the 1984 FES data), and that the results are less conclusive for earlier years' data. As Table 8.4 shows, the disincentive to part-time work and incentive to full-time work implicit in the structure of benefits are much less manifest in the observed hours-worked distributions in 1980 and 1982. It is possible to discern a definite and consistent trend towards the 1984 hours-worked distribution within the UB group over time, which could be interpreted as evidence of some form of 'learning'

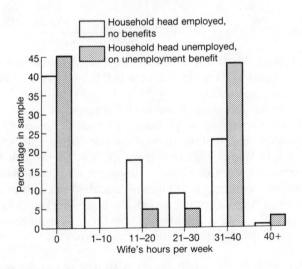

Figure 8.5 Wife's hours: UB and control groups (FES, 1984)

Table 8.4 Wives' hours worked by employment status and benefit receipt of husband

| Wives' hours worked (per week) | Husband unemployed | | | | Husband employed | |
| | UB | | SB | | No benefits | |
	No.	Percentage in sample	No.	Percentage in sample	No.	Percentage in sample
1984						
0	18	45	139	89	1,207	40
0–15	2	5	11	7	457	15
15–30	2	5	4	3	597	20
30+	18	45	3	2	729	24
Total	40	100	157	100	2,990	100
1982						
0	28	47	112	89	1,386	43
0–15	4	7	6	5	458	14
15–30	10	17	7	6	618	19
30+	17	29	1	1	747	23
Total	59	100	126	100	3,209	100
1980						
0	40	65	40	91	1,431	41
0–15	5	8	3	7	437	12
15–30	9	15	0	0	753	21
30+	8	13	1	2	905	26
Total	62	100	44	100	3,526	100

process as households slowly adapt to the incentive structure of UB (as unemployment grows). It is also possible that the results are influenced by random sampling fluctuations.

We now turn our attention to the work behaviour of women married to unemployed men receiving supplementary benefit.[6] Figure 8.6 compares the hours-worked distribution of women married to unemployed men receiving SB with that of the control group. It is not difficult to spot the extreme contrast in work behaviour: almost 90 per cent of women in the SB group are not working, as opposed to about 40 per cent of the control group. Moreover, unlike the UB group, the hours-worked distribution for women in the SB group is remarkably consistent over all the years' data studied, as Table 8.4 shows. It seems fair to say that the evidence confirms

[6] Remember that from 1983 onwards, almost all SB recipients are also paid certificated housing benefit.

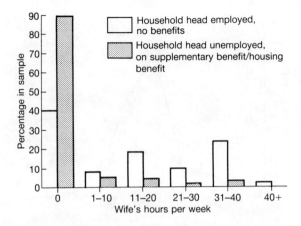

Figure 8.6 Wife's hours: SB and control groups (FES, 1984)

our expectation that receipt of SB is fundamentally incompatible with women's work; when on SB and all earnings over £4 are withdrawn pound for pound, the financial benefit of earning an amount which does not exhaust SB is effectively nil.

Given this, why do we observe that in 1980, 1982, and 1984, around 10 per cent of those women receiving SB are continuing to work? We know that the first £4 of any earnings are not lost, so there is some financial incentive to work while receiving SB—but why work more than 2 or 3 hours a week? Clearly we cannot explain all observed behaviour within the terms of our purely financial, and rather naïve, framework. There are, of course, reasons why women choose to work other than immediate financial reward. There may, for example, be 'human capital' considerations: if the wife of a man who becomes unemployed and eligible for SB is herself in a skilled, secure job (nursing, teaching, etc.), she may not want to let her skills deteriorate by leaving her job. (Note, however, that we found that those 10 per cent of women receiving SB and still working in our sample were, almost without exception, classified as unskilled or semi-skilled manual workers.) Similarly, the wife may believe that the husband will be out of work for only a short period, and it is thus sensible for her to keep her job for the time the household is receiving SB. But this explanation becomes less plausible in a period when the scale and duration of male unemployment has increased so dramatically. A more plausible explanation is that these women view part-time work as the best way into full-time work, which might then remove any dependency on SB. Alternatively, some of the wives of the unemployed may simply prefer working to staying at home, for any number of reasons. Finally, we cannot discount the

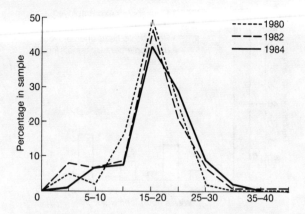

Figure 8.7   'Break-even' hours for women in SB group

possibility that these women are not declaring their earnings to the benefit authorities, though it is hard to believe they would do that while revealing the same income to the interviewers conducting the Family Expenditure Survey.

The fact remains that Figure 8.6 confirms that the vast majority of women in households receiving SB are behaving as we predict, i.e. not working. Figure 8.6 cannot, however, give any indication of the number of hours such women would have to work to 'escape' the disincentive inherent in SB, because those women who were eligible for SB but have chosen to work will, almost by definition, not receive any SB and therefore not be included in the SB group. We therefore calculate for all those households where the head is unemployed and receiving SB the number of hours the wife would have to work in order to exhaust SB receipt, and become marginally better off by working. Figure 8.7 shows the distribution of these 'break-even' hours across the SB groups in 1980, 1982, and 1984.

The distribution of 'break-even' hours is stable over the three years' samples, and shows that around three-quarters of the women in the SB group would have to work at least 15 hours a week to become marginally better off. This suggests that there is little doubt that SB receipt is a significant disincentive to part-time work for women married to unemployed men. On the other hand, Figure 8.7 does not provide conclusive evidence that SB is a disincentive to full-time work—in fact, it appears that almost all households on SB would be (marginally) better off if the wife worked 30 or more hours a week. However, before concluding that SB is therefore not a disincentive to full-time work, we should bear in mind the following points. First, in calculating the break-even hours shown in Figure 8.7, we assumed the women could earn the average part-time wage of female workers (£2.70 per hour in 1984); in practice, we would not expect women who are presently on SB to command the going wage rate—and the lower the wage rate, the more hours' work required to break even. Second, and more important, for simplicity of computation we have calculated the 'break-even' hours point to be at the number of hours of work where SB entitlement is exhausted, where the marginal tax rate falls below 100 per cent. But, as the hypothetical example in Section 2 made clear, the combination of other benefits (housing benefit, family income supplement) being withdrawn, with income tax and National Insurance payments, means that many women will face extremely high effective marginal tax rates on their earned income beyond the point at which SB is exhausted. So it is possible that while SB receipt in itself is not necessarily an absolute disincentive to full-time work (as it undoubtedly is to part-time work), other aspects of the tax and benefit system can interact after SB is exhausted to make the net financial gain from full-time work extremely slight for these women.

To conclude this section, we briefly summarize our findings. We have presented evidence which confirms that male unemployment does have a significant impact on the participation and hours-worked decisions of wives. We have further presented evidence consistent with our hypothesis that the benefit system imposes significant disincentives to work for women married to unemployed men. The precise nature and importance of this disincentive varies according to individual circumstances, but it seems fair to say that all the major social security benefits create a disincentive to part-time work for women. As far as full-time work is concerned, unemployment benefit by itself does not seem to act as a disincentive; for households entitled to supplementary benefit where the wife does not work, there is potentially more of a problem.

4. Conclusions

There is thus evidence to confirm our supposition that the benefit system does lead to significant work disincentives for women married to unemployed men. Of course, such disincentives are only a problem if the jobs that women are being discouraged from taking actually exist. It is possible that those women married to unemployed men who are at present out of work could never find a job, whatever the structure of the benefit system, either because their personal characteristics are such that no one would ever want to employ them, or because there are simply no jobs in the area. Once again, we stress that we have made no attempt to control for these other influences on the work behaviour of women married to unemployed men. Nevertheless, it seems clear to us that, potentially at least, a problem of incentives exists—and this could become more acute as the other factors restricting female employment become less of a problem, as a result of such measures as better job training and education. On the demand side, it seems likely that much of any growth in women's employment will occur in part-time employment—precisely where the present benefit system causes the greatest problem.

The incentive problem, in so far as it exists, is clearly worse for those entitled to means-tested benefits if the wife does not work, and worst of all for those entitled to supplementary benefit, which has an earnings disregard of only £4 per week. One solution might be simply to increase the level of the earnings disregard, but this merely shifts upwards the range of weekly hours that it is not worth working. The incentive problem for the wives of unemployed men is more accurately seen as a problem of the unit of assessment for benefit payments. When a married woman with two children, in a family where her husband is unemployed and they receive supplementary benefit, takes a job, it is not merely the supplementary benefit that is to support her, but also that for her husband and their children, which is withdrawn. It is the withdrawal of all the benefit which imposes the wide range of 100 per cent marginal rates. If the benefit unit were the individual, the benefit withdrawn would be less, allowing either a short range with 100 per cent withdrawal, or a long range with a lower withdrawal rate. However, moving to the individual as the unit of benefit assessment would be extremely expensive, since it would entitle many individual wives in quite well-off circumstances to apply for and receive benefit. Such a system seems unlikely to succeed when funds for social security are already hard pressed.

There are no easy solutions. Even reasonably generous levels of benefit to the unemployed necessarily require high withdrawal rates if expenditure is to be held at current levels. However, it would be difficult to believe that the current system is optimal. Under the Fowler reforms, the earnings disregard for the long-term unemployed or their wives will be increased to £15 per week, which may make some part-time jobs more attractive. We plan to engage in further research to examine methods of reforming the benefit system in ways which maintain its support for the poor, while reducing its disincentive effects. Such work will require a more complex model of female labour supply behaviour, but is vital if we are to succeed in designing a system which is less of a disincentive to women's work.

9

The Poverty Trap, Tax Cuts, and the Reform of Social Security

ANDREW DILNOT AND GRAHAM STARK[*]

1. Introduction

The poverty trap is probably the most frequently cited problem of the UK tax and benefit systems. It is probably also the least well understood. There is confusion about what it is, who it affects, whether it matters, and what might be done to alleviate it. Perhaps the most obvious manifestation of this is the frequent suggestion that raising tax allowances is a sensible way of solving the problem. To add to the confusion, the recent Social Security White Paper (DHSS (1985b)) proposes reforms which will radically alter both the nature of the poverty trap and the effect on it of changes in the direct tax system. In Section 2 of this article, we explain the effect of the poverty trap on an individual family. Section 3 examines the extent of the problem, using IFS models of the UK tax and benefit systems, and emphasizes the rather small number of people currently affected. Section 4 discusses possible ways of alleviating the problem, concentrating on the popular but ineffective suggestion of raising income tax allowances. Section 5 describes the impact of the proposed reform of social security on the poverty trap, and Section 6 returns to the issue of the effect of direct tax changes.

2. An Example of the Poverty Trap

The poverty trap in its most extreme form affects families in work who would find themselves worse off if they earned an extra £1. In this form it can only affect families with children who pay income tax and National Insurance, and receive family income supplement (FIS) and housing benefit. An extra £1 of earnings can lead to a 30p increase in income tax, a 9p

* At the time of writing this article, Andrew Dilnot was a Senior Research Officer and Graham Stark a Research Officer at the Institute for Fiscal Studies.

This paper was first published in *Fiscal Studies*, February 1986.

The work is part of the IFS project on the distributional implications of fiscal policy, which is supported by the Economic and Social Research Council and the Gatsby Foundation.

Table 9.1 The poverty trap for a hypothetical household,[a] November 1985 tax and benefit system

	Pounds per week					
Wage	70.00	85.00	100.00	115.00	130.00	145.00
less Tax	1.07	5.57	10.07	14.57	19.07	23.57
National Insurance	4.90	5.95	9.00	10.35	11.70	13.05
plus Family income supplement	19.50	12.00	4.50	–	–	–
Child benefit	14.00	14.00	14.00	14.00	14.00	14.00
Housing benefit	19.89	17.42	14.76	10.36	4.03	–
Net income	117.42	116.90	114.19	114.44	117.26	122.38

[a] Married man and his non-working wife, with two children of primary school age, living in rented accommodation for which they pay rent of £20 p.w. and rates of £6 p.w.

increase in National Insurance contributions, a 50p reduction in entitlement to family income supplement, and a 21p reduction in entitlement to housing benefit—a total of £1.10. Table 9.1 shows how net income changes as gross earnings rise from £70 per week to £145 per week for a married man and his non-working wife, with two children of primary school age, living in rented accommodation for which they pay rent of £20 per week and rates of £6 per week.

Net income falls as wages rise from £70 per week to £100 per week[1] and both FIS and housing benefit are received, and rises fairly slowly until housing benefit is exhausted at just below £145 per week. If such a family earning £70 per week were to compare its net income with that of a family earning £130 per week, it would find itself 16p per week better off than its better-paid counterpart. Such a position is clearly absurd.

3. The Extent of the Poverty Trap

While examples of the sort given above are useful for the purposes of illustrating the workings of the poverty trap, they offer no insight into its importance. If very few families are likely to be affected, we might be prepared to ignore the problem; if the numbers involved are large, it demands a good deal of attention and possibly resources. It is therefore important to know how many people are affected.

The extreme form of the poverty trap is where marginal tax rates (the amount of any increase in gross income that is lost in tax and reduced bene-

[1] In fact, to £109 per week, at which point FIS entitlement is exhausted.

fit) exceed 100 per cent. The principal culprit in this form is FIS, which was received in 1984 by only 200,000 families. Milder versions of the poverty trap, with marginal tax rates of slightly more than 80 per cent, can be experienced by recipients of housing benefit paying income tax and National Insurance contributions. Table 9.2 shows how many families of different types would face marginal tax rates in excess of 60 per cent if they received all the benefits to which they were entitled and paid all the taxes to which they were liable.

More than one-third of those facing marginal rates in excess of 100 per cent are single-parent families, 4.2 per cent of whom are in this position. There are as many couples with one or two children facing these very high marginal rates, but they form a much smaller fraction of their group, only 0.7 per cent. The frequency of very high marginal rates increases again for couples with three or more children. No pensioners or childless units face marginal rates in excess of 100 per cent. There are slightly more people in the 80–100 per cent range, and substantially more in the 60–80 per cent range although some of these are pensioners. Taken together, slightly more than 500,000 people could face marginal tax rates in excess of 60 per cent as a result of the combination of taxation and social security. This is less than 2 per cent of the $27\frac{1}{2}$ million tax units in the UK, and assumes full take-up of benefit entitlement. FIS has a take-up rate of only 50 per cent

Table 9.2 Number of tax units in the poverty trap[a] (in thousands, with percentages in parentheses)

	Marginal tax rate		
	60–80%	80–100%	Over 100%
Single-parent families	35	35	40
	(3.7)	(3.7)	(4.2)
Couples with 1 or 2 children	105	35	40
	(1.9)	(0.6)	(0.7)
Couples with 3 or more children	35	35	35
	(2.8)	(2.8)	(2.8)
Pensioners	25	10	0
	(0.4)	(0.2)	(0.0)
Childless units	110	35	0
	(0.9)	(0.3)	(0.0)
	310	150	115

[a] Figures in brackets give percentage of relevant population.
Source: IFS tax and benefit model. See Davis and Dilnot (1985) for full details.

and housing benefit of 70 per cent, so the numbers presented here overestimate the problem, although we should perhaps not use the ineffectiveness
of our social security system as an excuse for not tackling its structural
faults. Two further caveats should be added. First, it is not the case that a
change in an individual's earnings will lead to an immediate change in
benefit receipt. While housing benefit is in principle reassessed as soon as
circumstances change, this is not true of FIS, which is paid at the same level
for a year regardless of any change. Second, it may be that the poverty trap
reduces the economic welfare of families who are not directly affected by
it. People may work more or less hard than they would choose to, precisely
to avoid the high marginal tax rates of the poverty trap;[2] the figures given
in Table 9.2 and above would in this case underestimate the significance of
the problem.

4. Possible Solutions

Although the poverty trap does not affect a particularly large part of the
population, it is in its extreme form certainly absurd, and perhaps immoral.
That government policy should encourage people to earn less rather than
more is undesirable, however few people are affected. Nevertheless, it is
important to bear in mind that the general problem of a band of income
over which high marginal rates operate is inevitable if we wish to provide a
social security system that gives net incomes which substantially exceed
earnings for low-paid families with children. We cannot give everybody a
higher net income than they earn. At some point we must switch from net
incomes that exceed gross incomes to net incomes that are lower than gross
incomes.

Consider Figure 9.1. If there were no tax and benefit system, net income
and gross income would be equal, and would lie on the 45 degree line OE.
Imagine a system which gives OA to people with no earnings and to those
with earnings less than OB', and finances this by a lump-sum tax so that
people with incomes above OC' face a zero marginal tax rate but have
lower net income than gross, which puts them on the 45 degree line CD. To
get from AB to CD there must be a range of income OB' to OC' over
which the benefit OA is withdrawn. The line BC is horizontal, indicating a
marginal tax rate of 100 per cent. Were the marginal tax rate less high, as in
BF, there would be many more people affected, the cost of paying the
benefit would rise enormously, and thus the size of the lump-sum tax
required would also increase. It is important to note that in the UK, the
density of income distribution increases very rapidly as income rises, so any

---

[2] See Blundell, Meghir, Symons, and Walker (1984) for further discussion of this point and
possible ways of measuring its significance.

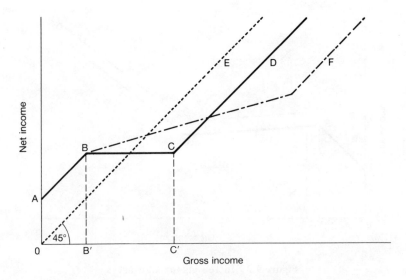

Figure 9.1 The poverty trap

increase in the range of income over which the poverty trap operates increases dramatically the number of people affected. Lump-sum taxes are of course impractical. The trade-off actually faced is between very high marginal rates on a small number of people with the current level of income tax rates on the rest of the population, and slightly lower, but still high, marginal tax rates on a larger group of the population and substantially higher direct tax rates on the rest of the population to finance increased benefit expenditure.

If changing the slope of the line is problematical, is there a way of reducing the band of income over which the poverty trap operates? That is the aim of those who suggest increasing income tax allowances as a solution to the problem. Raising tax allowances works by taking out of tax altogether those with earnings just above the current tax allowance, and thus reducing the marginal tax rate they face by 30 percentage points.

In Figure 9.2, ABCD is a simplified representation of the income schedule for a working family with children in the UK, with the range BC being the poverty trap. Raising allowances shifts the schedule to AB'C'D', reducing the marginal tax rates of anyone in the income range OY_1 to OY_2 by 30 percentage points.

Raising allowances to relieve the poverty trap is an extraordinarily wasteful and ineffective policy for a number of reasons. The married man's tax allowance in the UK is currently £66.44 per week. Family income supplement is paid to a two-child family at incomes of up to £109 per week. To

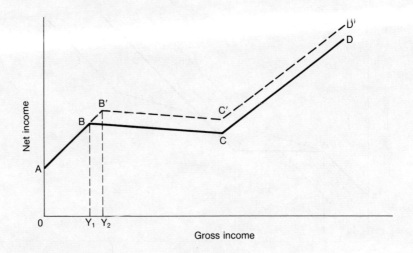

Figure 9.2   Increasing tax allowances

raise tax allowances even to this level would cost some £13 billion, requiring an increase in the basic rate of income tax to 43 per cent, and would still fail to remove families with three or more children from the poverty trap. Of those taken out of tax by an increase in tax allowances, only a very small fraction are families who could possibly be affected by the poverty trap, as shown in Table 9.3. Finally, there are far more families with earnings at the top end of the poverty trap income range than at the bottom end, so reforms aimed at the lower end of the range are bound to be less effective.

The increase in allowances in the 1984 Budget took 450,000 people out of tax; 10,000 of these were FIS recipients and therefore at risk from the poverty trap.

Table 9.3 Individuals relieved of tax by a 30 per cent increase in tax allowances

	Per cent
Wives	39
Pensioners	34
Single people	9
Childless couples	9
Couples with children	6
Single parents	3

Table 9.4 The poverty trap for a hypothetical household:[a] Social Security White Paper

	Pounds per week					
Wage	70.00	85.00	100.00	115.00	130.00	145.00
less Tax	1.07	5.57	10.07	14.57	19.07	23.57
National Insurance	4.90	5.95	9.00	10.35	11.70	13.05
plus Family credit	29.23	22.61	17.40	10.99	4.59	–
Child benefit	14.00	14.00	14.00	14.00	14.00	14.00
Housing benefit	6.01	4.32	2.98	1.33	–	–
Net income	113.27	114.41	115.31	116.40	117.82	122.38
Net income, current system	117.42	116.90	114.19	114.44	117.26	122.38

[a] As in Table 9.1. i.e. married man and his non-working wife, with two children of primary school age, living in rented accommodation for which they pay rent of £20 p.w. and rates of £6 p.w.

5. The Impact of Social Security Reform

The Social Security White Paper proposals substantially rationalize the interaction between direct taxes and means-tested benefits. FIS and housing benefit are to be recast. FIS is to be replaced by family credit. Entitlement to family credit is to be based on net income after the deduction of income tax and National Insurance. The withdrawal rate for family credit is to be 70 per cent. Thus for someone paying income tax and National Insurance, an increase of £1 in earnings will lead to 30p more income tax, 9p more National Insurance, and 42.7p less family credit $[(1.00-0.39) \times .70]$—a total of 81.7p. Housing benefit is to be simplified, and the withdrawal rates increased to 60 per cent for rent and 20 per cent for rates. Entitlement will be based on income after tax and National Insurance, and including family credit and child benefit. For someone on housing benefit as well as family credit, income tax, and National Insurance, an additional 14.6p of benefit entitlement will be lost from an extra £1 of earnings $[(1.00-0.817) \times 0.80]$, giving a total of 96.3p.

Thus benefit entitlements are now to be calculated sequentially, with entitlement at each stage being calculated on the basis of net income up to that stage. The implication of this is that it will now be logically impossible to face a marginal tax rate of 100 per cent or more, provided only that the withdrawal rates are less than 100 per cent. However, as we shall see below, many more people than before will now face marginal tax rates only slightly below this level.

Table 9.4 shows how benefit entitlement and net income would change

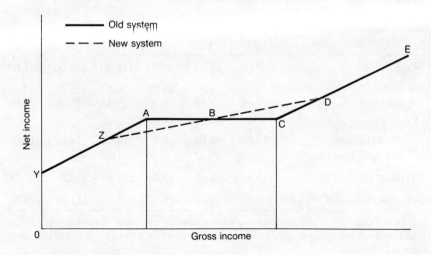

Figure 9.3   The poverty trap after the reform of social security

for the hypothetical family in Table 9.1 under the new social security system, and the net income under the current system.

Net income rises steadily, although slowly, under the proposed system, and is lower than under the current system at gross incomes below £100 per week and then higher until £145 per week. The solution to the poverty trap chosen by the Government is illustrated in Figure 9.3 as the line ZBD. Net incomes are lower for those between Z and B, and higher for those between B and D. Marginal rates are lower for those between A and C, and higher for those between Z and A and between C and D. Thus although the maximum marginal rate has fallen, the number with marginal rates in excess of 80 per cent rises substantially, from just over 250,000 to almost 700,000. The rise is this great because not only has the band of income over which such high marginal rates operate widened, but also the range of the income distribution into which they now stretch is much denser than at lower incomes.

6. Tax Cuts in the New System

The new benefit system will react differently to changes in the direct tax system. Benefit entitlements under the current system are unaffected by changes in the amount of tax paid, while under the new system, a reduction in tax will lead to an increase in net income, and thus a reduction in benefit entitlement which will offset the original tax reduction. For someone

Table 9.5 Number of tax units in the poverty trap (in thousands): the effect of a 30 per cent rise in allowances under the current and proposed systems

	Marginal tax rate		
	60–80%	80–100%	Over 100%
Current system	310	150	115
—with allowance rise	350	100	70
Reformed system	1,400	700	0
—with allowance rise	1,475	400	0

Source: IFS tax and benefit model. See Davis and Dilnot (1985) for full details.

receiving both family credit and housing benefit for rent and rates, all but 6 per cent of any tax cut will be absorbed by reduced entitlement to benefit. So for people who continue to be entitled to benefit, net income will be almost unaffected by a change in the tax system. Marginal rates are also insulated from the tax system. If someone receiving family credit and housing benefit, and paying income tax and National Insurance,[3] were to be taken out of tax by an increase in allowances, his marginal rate would fall from 96.2 per cent to 94.4 per cent. The smallness of this reduction is the result of the high withdrawal rates of the new family credit and housing benefit.

Families in the poverty trap will gain very little in net income from a reduction in the direct tax burden, and families taken out of tax will face a negligible reduction in their marginal tax rate. There is one group which can both gain net income and see a substantial reduction in the marginal tax rate they face. Families with small entitlements to either family credit or housing benefit can be floated off benefit altogether by tax cuts, and would thus see a substantial reduction in their marginal rate. Increasing allowances under the current system takes a small number of people out of the lower end of the poverty trap. Increasing allowances under the proposed reformed system will take a larger number of people out of a less extreme version of the poverty trap, but they will be a different group—those at the top end of the poverty trap income range affected. Table 9.5 illustrates this point. A 30 per cent rise in tax allowances, which would cost some £6 billion,[4] would reduce the number facing marginal rates in excess of 80 per cent by around 100,000 under the current system, and by 300,000 under the reformed system.

[3] Say at a rate of 7 per cent.
[4] The net cost under the Fowler system will be slightly lower, since benefit entitlements are now reduced.

7. Conclusion

The poverty trap arises from the complex interaction of the direct tax and means-tested benefit systems. Under the current system, a small number of families with children face marginal tax rates in excess of 100 per cent. The problem of high marginal tax rates in some region of the income distribution is essentially intractable if a social security system at or above the current level is to be maintained; in particular, raising tax allowances is a very ineffective means of alleviating the poverty trap. The proposed reforms of the social security system will make it impossible for marginal tax rates in excess of 100 per cent to be faced, but many more people will face a less extreme form of the poverty trap, with marginal tax rates over 80 per cent. Raising allowances under the new system will take more people out of the less extreme version of the poverty trap, but they will be a different group from those taken out by increased allowances under the current system. Nevertheless, using the tax system to manipulate problems caused by the social security system will continue to be very expensive and relatively ineffective.

10

The Take-Up of Supplementary Benefit: Gaps in the 'Safety Net'?

VANESSA FRY AND GRAHAM STARK*

1. Introduction

Non-take-up of social security benefits—the fact that not all of those eligible for benefits claim them—is widely acknowledged to be one of the most serious problems facing the social security system (see, for instance, Atkinson (1984) and Dilnot, Kay, and Morris (1984)). It means that the welfare system is to some degree ineffective in delivering the assistance its own provisions acknowledge as necessary. Non-take-up of supplementary benefit (SB) has caused the most widespread concern and attention, both within and outside government, as a result of the critical role of SB in the social security system. SB (formerly called National Assistance) has frequently been termed a 'safety net' benefit because it provides a minimum standard of living to those (in eligible categories) who have either no or very low incomes from other sources—including other benefits. The analysis of SB non-take-up therefore seems central to an understanding of poverty and a pre-condition for the design of effective social security reforms.

In 1981 (the most recent year for which figures have been published) the Department of Health and Social Security (DHSS) estimated that 1.4 million families did not claim a total of £760 million of SB entitlement (an average of £10.50 per week each—or approximately £15 in 1987 prices). This represented a take-up rate of 71 per cent of those entitled. The first purpose of this article is to provide estimates of SB take-up that are at once both more recent and more detailed, using data from the 1984 Family Expenditure Survey (FES). This in itself will, we hope, provide some contribution to the debate about the current extent and seriousness of the problem.

* At the time of writing this article, Vanessa Fry was a lecturer at the University of Essex and a Research Associate of the Institute for Fiscal Studies, and Graham Stark was a Research Officer at IFS.

This paper was first published in *Fiscal Studies*, November 1987.

The authors would like to thank Andrew Dilnot and Ian Walker for helpful comments. All remaining errors are their own. Finance for this research provided by the Department of Health and Social Security and the Economic and Social Research Council under project B02250004 is gratefully acknowledged.

The second purpose is more far-reaching. Consideration of the possible reasons for non-take-up makes it apparent that the take-up rate is unlikely to remain constant as not only the benefit system itself but also other economic circumstances change. Two of the most widely discussed explanations for non-take-up are lack of information and perceived social stigma (see, for instance, Atkinson (1984) and Cowell (1986)). We can think of claims for benefit as having associated costs—which may include time and effort as well as information and stigma—and the likelihood that a given eligible individual will claim as the likelihood that for them these costs are outweighed by the expected value to them of the benefit (see, for example, Moffitt (1983) and Blundell, Fry, and Walker (1988)). It follows that, other things being equal, we might expect to see lower take-up rates among groups who were entitled to relatively small amounts of benefit, who expected not to be eligible to claim for very long (because the fixed cost of claiming would seem higher relative to the total value of the benefit stream), who had relatively little access to information about the benefit system, or who felt particularly strongly that there was some stigma attached to being a benefit claimant. Two important consequences follow. First, since both lack of information and stigma are likely to diminish as the number of claimants rises (Cowell (1986)), take-up rates may increase with unemployment—and conversely remain lower among groups in which there are relatively few entitled to claim. Second, and most important, an increase (decrease) in average entitlement levels is likely to increase (decrease) the take-up rate, with important effects on the income distribution and revenue implications of any proposed change to the system (Blundell, Fry, and Walker (1988)). The second aim of this article is therefore to examine how far our analysis of SB bears out these conjectures and to provide estimates of the determinants of SB take-up which can be used to help forecast take-up and social security expenditure as circumstances change.

Section 2 describes the structure of SB and how entitlement calculations are made from the 1984 FES by the IFS tax and benefit model. Section 3 presents the results of comparing calculated entitlement to SB with receipts, examines take-up rates among different groups, and makes a preliminary assessment. Section 4 presents econometric estimates of the determinants of SB take-up and discusses their implications. Section 5 summarizes our conclusions.

2. Supplementary Benefit and the Calculation of Entitlement

SB is the major income-related benefit in the UK, representing an expenditure in 1984–5 of £6.5 billion (18 per cent of benefit expenditure) to 4.7 million families. SB provides those who are entitled with the shortfall of

Table 10.1 The extent and costs of the SB system

	1979–80	1984–5	1987–8 (estimate)	Percentage change 1979–80 to 1987–8 (real in parentheses)
Number of recipients (millions)	2.9	4.7	4.9	+69
Total expenditure (£ million)	2,440	6,472	8,300	+240 (+79)

Source: HM Treasury (1983 and 1987).

their income from a pre-defined level of 'need' and entitles them to have their rent and rates met by 'certificated housing benefit'. The predecessor of SB, National Assistance, which existed from 1948 to 1966, was originally intended to be a relatively minor part of the UK benefit system, providing a 'safety net' for those few claimants not eligible for (full) National Insurance (NI) benefits (mainly unemployment benefit, state retirement pension, and sickness benefit). However, this was never really the case and in recent years a combination of persistent high unemployment and the limitations—both in coverage and in level of benefit—of the NI benefit system has caused SB to grow rapidly in importance. Today, approximately one in every five families in the UK depends at least in part on SB. Table 10.1 gives an idea of the extent and costs of the SB system, and of its rapid growth in recent years.

Not everyone—even if they have a low income—is eligible for SB. However, in general all pensioners, and non-pensioners not in full-time work or education, are eligible provided they do not own capital (apart from their homes and personal possessions) of more than £3,000. As mentioned above, for those who are eligible, entitlement to SB is the difference between income and 'needs'. 'Needs' are defined by family size, with special heating additions for the very old, the very young, and the sick, and include mortgage interest and a home maintenance allowance for owner-occupiers. Those whose incomes fall short of their needs, and who are therefore entitled to SB, also automatically qualify for 'certificated housing benefit', which covers all of their rent and rates. They may also qualify for a number of one-off payments—for example, for clothing and furniture—and for various 'passported' benefits—benefits in kind such as free school meals and NHS prescriptions—although SB receipt is not a prerequisite for these. A fuller description of the SB system as it was in 1984, which was (and is) very much more complex than the above abbreviated outline suggests, can be found, for example, in Child Poverty Action Group (1984).

SB was replaced in 1988 by income support (IS), as part of the 'Fowler reforms' of the benefit system. Broadly the same people are eligible for IS as were eligible for SB, but IS has many fewer special additions, replaces one-off payments with discretionary loans, and is less generous to many single people than SB.

Both today and in 1984, the main groups likely to be entitled to SB are pensioners, the unemployed, single parents, and sick people and those caring for them.

Pensioners are likely to qualify because the basic state retirement pension has for some years been very close to their basic SB 'needs' level, and so qualification for a small heating or dietary addition can be enough to tip the balance. This means that many pensioners are entitled to small sums of SB. However, those who qualify are usually also entitled to greater sums of certificated housing benefit.

Unemployed people may be entitled to SB either to top up their income from unemployment benefit (UB, which like the pension is close to the SB scale) or more frequently because they are not eligible for UB—they have been unemployed for over a year or have not worked sufficiently to build up a contribution record (this may be the case, for example, for school-leavers or those suffering repeated spells of unemployment).

Many of those who qualify or just fail to qualify for SB could qualify for standard housing benefit (SHB, formerly rent and rate rebates and allowances). In cash terms, they would be unambiguously better off on SB, if they qualify for it, since under SB they would get all their housing costs paid under certificated housing benefit, plus some actual SB, whilst under SHB the most that they could get would be all their housing costs. This 'overlap' of benefits proves to be a great complication in what follows.

The analysis of SB take-up undertaken in this article is based on a comparison of calculated entitlement and recorded receipt for each benefit and for all tax units in the 1984 Family Expenditure Survey. Entitlement data are drawn from the IFS tax and benefit model, which calculates the tax and benefit position of each of the households interviewed in the FES. (See Davis, Dilnot, Stark, and Webb (1987) for a full description of the model and Stark (1987) for more detail on the modelling procedures used here.)

It would be unrealistic to expect calculated entitlement to be wholly accurate. Various details needed both to establish eligibility and to calculate the amount of entitlement are missing from the FES. So, in some cases, is the amount of receipt itself (see Stark (1987)). Moreover, some of the information that is included—in particular, some income data—may contain errors. This is particularly true of self-employment income, which is known to be unreliable (see Atkinson and Micklewright (1983)), and so the self-employed are excluded from the present analysis. Problems of missing and erroneous data appear to be especially important for pensioners, for whom we provide separate results.

An additional difficulty is that the FES provides us with details of house-

Table 10.2 Estimates of SB take-up

Study	Year	Data	Take-up rate		
			Pensioners	Non-pensioners	All
DHSS	1977	ASE[a]/FES	.72	.79	?
DHSS	1979	ASE/FES	.65	.78	.70
DHSS	1981	ASE/FES	.67	.75	.71
Fry and Stark	1984	FES	.87	.81	.83
Fry and Stark[b]	1984	FES	.66	.78	.74

[a] Annual statistical enquiry of SB claimants.
[b] Estimate on 'DHSS basis'.
Source: HM Treasury (1984).

holds' circumstances in a particular fortnight, with very limited information on their 'history'. For instance, suppose that the head of a household has lost his/her job just prior to the FES interview. He/she may not yet have got around to making a benefit claim (though intending to) or may have made a claim which has not yet been processed, and so no benefit has yet been received. Any time-lag in the processing of claims in particular means that for groups such as the unemployed, whose circumstances change periodically, we are never likely to observe 100 per cent take-up (when we measure this by current receipt of benefit). These points will become important when we come to interpret the results in Section 3.

3. The Take-Up Rate

Most previous studies of benefit take-up, and most popular discussion, have focused on 'take-up rates'—ratios of the number of people receiving a benefit to the number who are entitled. Here, we present our own estimated take-up rates. Although there is no unambiguously correct take-up measure (Atkinson (1984)), we prefer what we feel to be a natural definition—namely, the proportion of those thought to be entitled to benefit who actually claim it. However, the definition is not as unambiguous as it might appear, so that care must be taken in making comparisons with other estimates.

Table 10.2 shows some previous estimates of take-up of SB produced by the DHSS. These define take-up as

$$\frac{\text{Number actually receiving SB}}{\text{Number actually receiving SB} + \text{Estimate from FES of number entitled but not receiving}} \quad (1)$$

Table 10.3 Supplementary benefit, standard housing benefit, and non-take-up in the 1984 FES

	Receiving SB			Entitled to SB but not receiving it	
	Entitled to SB	Entitled only to SHB	Entitled to neither SB nor SHB	Receiving SHB	Receiving nothing
	(1)	(2)	(3)	(4)	(5)
Non-pensioners					
Number in sample	790	35	32	58	180
'Grossed-up' figure (thousands)	2,579	110	106	183	584
Pensioners					
Number in sample	314	72	8	157	49
'Grossed-up' figure (thousands)	1,137	238	29	559	176

Apart from the complications arising from the use of two sources of data (administrative statistics on the numbers actually claiming SB and the FES sample for non-take-up), this differs in two respects from our figure. First, the number receiving SB may include some people who in their current circumstances are not entitled (for example, they have just got a job or an administrative error has been made). This will tend to make the DHSS figure larger than ours (by inflating the number of recipients included in both the numerator and denominator of (1)). Second, a number of those who appear to be entitled to SB in the FES in fact appear to be claiming SHB instead. By 1984, following the 1983 housing benefit reform, the number of non-pensioners in this category was relatively small. We have excluded all those who appear to be receiving the 'wrong benefit' from our calculation of the take-up rate, and return to the reasons for this below. The DHSS estimate of the numbers not taking up SB includes those taking up housing benefits instead, as well as those not taking up anything. This, of course, tends to reduce its estimate of the take-up proportion. Table 10.2 therefore includes an estimate from the 1984 FES on an approximation to the DHSS basis for comparison. Our estimate is quite close to the published DHSS figure. A substantial proportion of non-take-up in pre-1983 estimates was thought to consist of those receiving housing benefits, and Table 10.2 suggests this is particularly the case for pensioners.

Table 10.3 illustrates these differences using our 1984 data. Our 'DHSS basis' figure is {columns (1+2+3)}/{columns (1+2+3+4+5)}, whilst our own figure is {column 1}/{columns (1+5)}. Those in columns 2 and 3, who are receiving SB without any apparent entitlement, are clearly anomalous and indicate shortcomings in the data and/or the benefit administration. If such errors were random, we might expect to see similar figures for column 4—those apparently entitled to SB but receiving housing benefit (HB); however, for pensioners the figure is much larger. This is one indication that there may be problems with our pensioner estimates, and Table 10.3 also shows other evidence that there are problems with the pensioner figures. The figures in the second and fourth rows show the 'grossed-up' population totals suggested by the sample numbers (see Atkinson (1983) for methodology and Stark (1987) for the weights used here and in Table 10.5). Compared with administrative totals for the year, we have approximately the right number of non-pensioners receiving SB (in columns 1, 2, and 3) but too few pensioners, whilst we have a startlingly large number of pensioners who are apparently taking up HB whilst being entitled to SB.

As discussed in Stark (1987), grossed-up 'raw' FES figures contain only about 67 per cent of the number of pensioner SB recipients that would be needed to match the administrative totals for that year. By scrutinizing the data for possible misrecording of SB receipts (especially as state retirement pensions), Stark shows how this can be improved to around 80 per cent, and it is these figures that are used in this analysis. However, it remains true that some SB receipt by pensioners still appears to be missing from the FES, and this may well account for around 200,000 of the cases in column 4 of the table. At present, it is not possible to tell which of the cases in column 4 are in fact receiving SB and belong in column 1, which are in fact not entitled to SB and therefore do not belong in the table at all, and which are genuinely taking up the 'wrong' benefit. Given this uncertainty, we exclude them from the statistical analysis of the next section. Most of these cases are 'borderline' anyway—the financial difference between their calculated SB entitlement and actual SHB receipt is small. Both from the viewpoint of poverty analysis and from the viewpoint of expenditure forecasting, it is the determinants of non-take-up which are our primary concern.

We have already noted that there is a degree of inaccuracy in our calculations that makes it difficult to be precise about the exact level of take-up (and consequently also whether it appears to be increasing or not). They do indicate that, overall, take-up rates for SB are higher than those for other means-tested benefits;[1] on the other hand, because of the large

---

[1] For 1979, official estimates of take-up were: rent allowances 50%, rent rebates 72%, rate rebates 70%, and family income supplement (1978–9) 50% (*Hansard*, 1 December 1980, col. 88; *Social Security Statistics*, 1981).

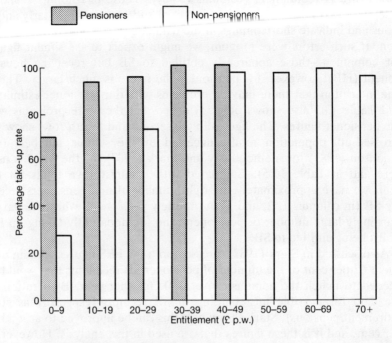

[a]Includes certificated housing benefit.
[b]An extremely small number of pensioners in our sample
are entitled to more than £49 p.w.; all of them take it up.

Figure 10.1   Take-up rates for SB by range of entitlement[a,b]

numbers concerned (and their poverty), the 17 per cent non-take-up in
1984 indicated in Tables 10.2 and 10.3 may still be cause for considerable
concern. Moreover, overall averages may conceal the experience of particular groups.

Figure 10.1 shows take-up rates for pensioners and non-pensioners by
range of entitlement, and provides a strong preliminary indication of a
positive relationship between take-up and entitlement level. Table 10.4
breaks down our sample of entitled units according to a variety of characteristics. Even these preliminary groupings reveal substantial variation.
Among tenure groups, owner-occupiers take up considerably less than
either council or private tenants, while among non-pensioners, on average
those with children take up more than those without. There is considerably
higher take-up amongst household heads than among non-householders,
while among those in different economic positions, there is a remarkable

Table 10.4 SB take-up rates[a]

By tenure

	Pensioners			Non-pensioners		
	Entitled	Receiving	Percentage take-up	Entitled	Receiving	Percentage take-up
Tenants[b]	240	230	96	655	580	88
Owners	115	83	72	286	195	68
Others[c]	–	–	–	13	10	76

By family type

	Entitled	Receiving	Percentage take-up
Single people	503	376	75
Single-parent families	139	131	94
Childless couples	119	99	83
Couples with children	193	179	93
Single pensioners	321	282	88
Couple pensioners	42	32	76

By family relationship

	Entitled	Receiving	Percentage take-up
Head of household	955	858	89
Son/daughter of head	286	187	65
Other relation of head	36	28	78
No relation	40	26	65

By economic position of head

	Entitled	Receiving	Percentage take-up
In work (including part-time)	94	36	38
Retired, over pension age	360	312	86
Early retired	24	19	79
Out of labour force	285	262	92
Short-term unemployed	179	116	65
Long-term unemployed	375	354	94

[a] Figures do not necessarily sum to totals in Table 10.3 because of missing data on some characteristics.

[b] Includes both council and private tenants.

[c] Mainly those in rent-free accommodation.

Table 10.5 Grossed-up figures for those entitled to SB

	Receiving SB[a]		Receiving SHB		Receiving nothing	
	No. (000s)	£m p.a.[b]	No. (000s)	£m p.a.[c]	No. (000s)	£m p.a.[d]
Single people	1,270	1,900	60	50	430	450
Single-parent families	460	1,100	30	10	30	40
Childless couples	300	800	60	70	60	120
Couples with children	540	1,900	30	20	60	100
Single pensioners	1,020	900	450	140	140	70
Couple pensioners	120	80	110	40	30	10

[a] Excludes those receiving with no modelled entitlement: this includes 260,000 pensioners.

[b] Receipts, including certificated housing benefit.

[c] Amount not taken up: difference between SB entitlement and SHB receipt.

[d] Amount not taken up: SB entitlement.

distinction between the short-term and long-term unemployed.[2] Only 65 per cent of the former take up, while of those in our sample classified as long-term unemployed, 94 per cent take up their entitlement. This is all the more noteworthy given the relatively large sample, though, as noted in Section 2, the figures may to some extent be affected by delays in the processing of claims.

Table 10.5 shows what these figures imply for the population as a whole. Grossing-up from our sample suggests that in 1984 some £700 million per annum was unclaimed by non-pensioners and a further £75 million by 176,000 pensioners.

These results are both interesting in themselves and suggestive about the (proximate) reasons for non-take-up. However, there is a limited amount that simple cross-tabulation can tell us. Do single parents have a high take-up rate because they also belong to a low-income group, or because they are entitled to relatively large amounts of benefit, or because of characteristics peculiar to single parents—for example, greater needs, less resistance to the benefit system, or greater access to information through other branches of the health and social services? It is important to be able to answer this sort of question both to understand non-take-up and to be able to predict the effect on future take-up rates of changes to the benefit rules or in economic or demographic factors. To do this we must look to the econometric analysis in the following section.

---

[2] The 'short-term unemployed' are those who have been out of a job for less than 12 months. 'Long-term unemployed' includes all those seeking work who have not worked in the last 12 months, not only those who have been unemployed all that time but also, for example, school-leavers or those returning to the labour market.

Table 10.6 The determinants of SB take-up

	Non-pensioners[a]		Pensioners[a]	
Intercept	−.543	(1.05)	−.384	(.76)
log SB entitlement (£ p.w.)	.695	(5.85)	.865	(4.77)
Household income (£ p.w.)	−.005	(6.46)	−.004	(1.90)
Private tenant	−.257	(1.01)	−.314	(.85)
Owner-occupier	−.006	(.04)	−.088	(.34)
Part-time worker	−1.368	(6.26)		−
Short-term unemployed	−.566	(3.05)		−
Long-term unemployed	.356	(1.80)		−
Single parent	.849	(2.27)		−
Number of adults − 1	.192	(1.94)	−.194	(1.11)
Number of children under 6 years	.061	(.248)		−
Number of children aged 6 and over	.011	(.075)		−
Age (years)	−.006	(.85)	.001	(.07)
Education (years)	−.033	(.80)	.054	(.43)
Non-householder (relative of head)	−.063	(.25)		−
Non-householder (non-relative of head)	.041	(.13)		−
Number in sample	942[b]		356[b]	

[a] Figures in parentheses are t-statistics. A figure greater than 2 is a conventional indicator of statistical significance.

[b] See note (a) to Table 10.4.

4. The Determinants of Take-Up of SB

In this section, we report the results of estimating equations that attempt to explain take-up, so that we can distinguish the separate effects of income, benefit entitlement, and various demographic characteristics on take-up behaviour.

While all that we can observe is whether an individual takes up or not, what we predict is a probability that that individual takes up (or, equivalently, the proportion of identical individuals that we expect to take up), which must, of course, lie between 0 and 1. Table 10.6 reports the results of estimating equations for those above and below retirement age, which describe how the probability that an individual takes up relates to that individual's characteristics, entitlement, and income. For more detail on the generation of the take-up probability and underlying theory, see Blundell, Fry, and Walker (1988).

For non-pensioners, the most statistically significant effects are those associated with the level of entitlement and the level of income. A distinction between the short-term and long-term unemployed is apparent, with the short-term unemployed having a substantially lower probability of taking up their benefit than either the long-term unemployed or non-participants in the labour market (the reference category of individuals). This may well reflect the effects of duration and expected duration of eligibility on take-up behaviour—the longer individuals are unemployed, the greater may be their awareness of benefit availability, the lower may be their own resources, such as savings, and the lower may be their expectations of finding a job in the near future. Turning to family characteristics, the results reveal that, although from the group averages in Table 10.4 both single parents and couples with children appear to have similarly high take-up rates relative to other groups, the estimates in Table 10.6 show that children have little impact on take-up rates when we control for other factors, including in particular the level of entitlement. Single-parenthood has a substantial positive effect on take-up. Similarly, once we have controlled for income, entitlement, family size, and economic position, there are no perceptible differences between householders and non-householders, or between different tenure groups.

For pensioners, the main determining factor is the level of entitlement, and the effect of additional income is similar to that for non-pensioners. The number of adults has a small negative but insignificant effect, again suggesting that the overall difference between single and married pensioners shown in Table 10.4 is attributable to other factors.

To gain some feel for the magnitude of the effects reported in Table 10.6 on the probability of take-up, in Table 10.7 we show the impact of an additional £5 of SB entitlement and an additional £5 of other income (for example, as a result of increasing other non-means-tested benefits) for households in different circumstances.

The first column shows the probability predicted by the model for various hypothetical household types at the average income and entitlement levels in the sample; the second column shows how the predicted probability would be affected if SB entitlements were increased by £5, and the third if (non-SB) income were increased by £5 (but entitlements were unaffected).

5. Conclusions

Supplementary benefit provided income support to some $4\frac{1}{2}$ million families during 1984–5; the FES-based calculations presented here suggest that it failed to reach a further $\frac{3}{4}$ million, who were entitled to claim approximately £20 per week each.

This should cause us considerable concern about the living standards of those with very low levels of other income. But it is also worrying because of the degree of resistance to the means-tested benefit system it could indi-

Table 10.7 The effects of income and SB entitlement on predicted take-up[a]

	Predicted take-up probability		
	Mean income and entitlement	Additional £5 SB	Additional £5 income
One-parent family, unoccupied, aged 25, one child under 6, in council accommodation	.986	.990	.985
One-parent family as above, but with a part-time job	.794	.832	.785
Couple aged 35 with one child under 6, one child over 6, in council accommodation and head short-term unemployed	.821	.855	.813
Couple as above, but head is long-term unemployed	.967	.976	.965
Couple, early retired, aged 60, private tenants	.844	.875	.837
Couple, pensioners, aged 70, private tenants	.851	.910	.846

[a] All examples have the mean level of education—10.5 years for non-pensioners and approximately 9 for pensioners.

cate. The estimates presented of the determinants of SB take-up show that the single most important factor is the level of entitlement itself. Provided people know that they are entitled, this implies that there are costs to claiming which in some cases can outweigh the value of the benefit; the hypothetical short-term unemployed family of Table 10.7 would only be more likely to take up than not at entitlement levels above about £9 per week, which in some sense represents the 'price tag' it puts on being a claimant. Our estimates cannot, of course, distinguish the extent to which such costs represent feelings of social stigma or other elements of the hassle associated with making benefit claims. But they do indicate that non-take-up of SB can have serious implications for the welfare of both claimants and non-claimants.

The importance of income and entitlement levels in determining the take-up of SB confirms that it is essential to take changes in take-up behaviour into account when assessing proposed reforms to the means-tested benefit system, both in forecasting their public expenditure implications and in judging their overall impact on the welfare of all those who are intended to benefit.

11

The Reform of Social Security:
A Government View

MICHAEL PORTILLO[*]

May I start by thanking the Institute for inviting me to address this important and distinguished audience. As a mere politician I confess to finding it a somewhat daunting occasion, because I know this audience includes many people who have spent far longer than I on the topics under debate today and whose depth of knowledge is profound. I am also well aware that the Institute has established itself as one of the leading authorities on the analysis of fiscal issues in the UK, and now has a growing international reputation. It has concerned itself deeply with discussions on how both the tax and social security systems should be reformed, and with the more detailed appraisal of specific policy options. Indeed, it is fair to say that through the efforts of IFS, these debates have been widened and carried forward and that this has raised the overall level of understanding and appreciation of the issues and the complexities involved.

This conference takes place, of course, at a particularly well-chosen time, in the very week in which the biggest single overhaul of the welfare benefits system for forty years comes into effect. I know that this audience will be deeply knowledgeable about these changes. So I will not bore you by describing them in detail or the reasons why they have been introduced. They follow several years of public discussion and debate. Taken together, the changes have introduced a structure—particularly for the income-related benefits—which is simpler and more straightforward, so helping claimants to be better aware of what they may be entitled to; a system which is fairer between different people on low incomes, whether they are on benefit or working for modest pay; a system which can be more responsive to changing need: in particular, we are putting in extra help to families with children; and a structure which will do more to encourage personal independence and intitiative and return to the old notion of a benefit sys-

* Michael Portillo is Parliamentary Under Secretary of State for Social Security.
This article forms the text of a speech given at a conference on 'The Economics of Social Security', organized by the Institute for Fiscal Studies, held on 15 April 1988. It is reproduced here with the permission of the Controller of Her Majesty's Stationery Office.

tem which provides a floor on which individuals can build instead of a ceiling which locks them into indefinite dependency.

But I am sure that even this audience will not be surprised if, in a week when the reforms have been subjected to a massive barrage of political abuse and criticism, I take the opportunity today to make a few remarks in reply to some of the criticisms which have been made. For I take grave exception to the campaign of misrepresentation which has been launched particularly by the Opposition this week. Of course, I recognize that with any major reform on this historic scale there will be difficulties and apprehension at the moment of transition. Such problems and fears must, of course, be looked into and, where possible, resolved. But what is wrong, and indeed, irresponsible, is to seek to whip up a hysteria of fear, which may often be unwarranted and unnecessary, by portraying the changes in the manner the Opposition has sought to do in the last few days.

It is difficult to believe in the sincerity of those who claim to be concerned with the disadvantaged, when they indiscriminately scare and agitate millions of claimants who stand to lose nothing in the reforms. It is hard to take lectures in compassion from those who drag families into the glare of publicity to score political points. Those families should know that when the camera lights have dimmed, their new-found political friends will have moved away, on to another shock-horror story.

What should a nation spend on social security? The question is unanswerable. In Britain today we commit a third of all taxpayer spending. We provide one of the most extensive safety nets in the world. People can qualify for help on a wider range of grounds than in most systems, and can go on receiving it for longer, indeed usually without time limit. Our income-related benefits do not provide a high standard of living. They cannot. They cannot because every penny paid to claimants comes from the working population and the product of their industry. But those benefits do relieve poverty and lift people above it. Over time their value has increased in real terms. For example, supplementary benefit scale rates have doubled in value since 1948 and were worth more in 1987 than in 1979. As society has grown more prosperous, as the luxuries of yesterday have become the essentials of today, so benefit rates have risen.

That brings with it its dangers and its problems. One is that it is not sensible or possible to look at the value of income-related benefits in isolation. We have to consider the wider implications. For example, we have to look to the relationship between such benefits and the value of the contributory benefits, which should provide a proper return on the contributions which pensioners and others have paid all their working lives. Nor can we ignore the relationship between the rewards from work and the rewards out of work. Work must be seen to pay. And there is always the underlying question—particularly in provision for pensioners—of the ratio of the working to the non-working population and the burdens we can impose on the former without undermining growth itself.

One cannot wish away these problems. Neither can one from these broad principles arrive at a right level of social security spending. But I certainly feel no penny-pinching shame about a system which currently costs an average of over £40 a week to each and every working taxpayer.

Social security remains by far the largest element in taxpayer spending. The level of public expenditure as a whole remains a vital element in determining the prospects for growth in our economy. For as long as we maintain control of the rate of growth of public spending, we can enjoy rising levels of social security spending and our problems remain essentially problems of success: a debate about how the fruits of growing prosperity should be distributed. But if we lose control of public spending then our problems would revert to a more familiar type in post-war British history: how to wind down expectations and find real reductions. The ambitions of every lobby group are unrealizable without the assumption of continued economic growth.

In these reforms we have worked within a planned rise in social security spending of £2 billion this financial year. This year, after the reforms, we will still be spending on the income-related weekly benefits what we would have spent under the old system, had it continued. But I believe this spending will be far better directed.

Those opposed to the reforms sometimes seem to believe that in moving from one system to another, nobody should be left with a lower entitlement than they had. In other words, they want all the gains from the new system, whilst fully preserving in perpetuity the position of those who did better under the old. That is unrealistic. One cannot simplify the system by grafting onto the old structure a new one and then running the two side by side. One cannot sort out anomalies by preserving them. What we can do is provide cash protection for most people at the point of change.

But the system has changed and the entitlements of today are different. I would like to highlight just a few points from the reforms on which there has been debate.

First, different rates of benefits for different ages. We were absolutely right to build these in. It seems to me absurd to erect a system on the basis that the rate of benefit for a 17-year-old must assume that the person could start a family, leave home, and set up independently, all at the taxpayers' expense. Or that the rate of benefit of an 18-year-old who has never worked should be the same as that of a 55-year-old with 40 years' work experience. The 18-year-old's job prospects are better and what he can expect to earn should be lower; and the benefit system must reflect that.

Second, the Social Fund replaces single payments. Those payments grew about fivefold in real terms in 5 years at a time when the numbers on benefit rose by about two-thirds. In one office 2,500 applications for furniture were received in a few days. The availability of these grants to those out of work caused resentment amongst those in work who might have an income no higher but who had to budget. The payments were part of the unemployment trap. I do not believe that any government would have left this system unchanged.

Third, with regard to the capital limit for the three income-related benefits, I believe that it is universally accepted that benefits paid to people in need should take account of what they own as well as what they earn, of their capital as well as their income. The only question is at what level one applies the cut-off. I find it hard to justify asking taxpayers who may have nothing put away for themselves to pay the rents and rates of their neighbours with substantial sums in the bank. Our record on saving and thrift is unassailable. We saw pensioners' income from savings rise in value by 52 per cent in our first 6 years alone. But talk about encouraging thrift from politicians who when in office destroyed pensioners' nest-eggs in building societies by inflation so that their value fell by a third, is humbug. The income which pensioners got from their savings fell by 16 per cent in real terms.

But a conference like today's is an opportunity to raise our sights beyond the current political debate. I would like to touch briefly on some issues which will continue to dominate the agenda in the field of social and fiscal reform when the dust has settled on this month's changes.

One of the questions which I am sure will be raised today is whether we should go further in the future towards the closer integration of the tax and benefit systems.

This was, of course, the theme of this very Institute's major contribution to the debate some years ago when the reform process was starting. Some recent commentators have seemed to regard tax and benefit integration as a cure-all. For example, high marginal tax rates on people with low earnings, they say, can be removed by integrating the separate systems we now operate. The advent of modern computers, it is said, will open the way to a brave new world in which the poverty trap is eliminated, good work incentives are guaranteed, and the interests of taxpayers and beneficiaries are no longer seen to conflict.

I have to say that I retain severe doubts about many of those types of proposals. IFS set out clearly the effects of its proposals, recognizing the disadvantages as well as the possible improvements. But too many commentators do not seem to really think through the implications of their apparent panacea.

Depending upon the scheme, tax and benefit integration could possibly involve:

- ending or radically redefining the contributory principle;
- withdrawing entitlement to pensions and other benefits from people with higher incomes, despite the taxes or the contributions they have paid through their working life;
- calling on all taxpayers to fill in a return each year (when presently only one in five employees need do so);
- large increases in the burden of tax on earnings and huge increases in the numbers confronting high marginal tax rates;

and it could create:

- a system of benefits which might respond less quickly and adequately to changes in needs amongst the poorest members of society;
- a system which might do irreparable harm to work incentives.

On this last point the American experience seems to have lessons for us which I hope will be touched on in the discussions today.

The long series of detailed and expensive negative income tax experiments undertaken in the United States in the 1960s and 1970s were intended in part to help in identifying possible behavioural effects on families and individuals. The simple notion of giving everyone a lump sum and then withdrawing it progressively as income rises appeared particularly attractive. But in practice the results seem to have been disappointing. I understand that a recent symposium organized by the Brookings Institution in order to appraise these experiments showed the results on behaviour to be complex and not entirely obvious. On balance, it appeared that:

- husbands' hours of work, if anything, tended to fall;
- women's hours of work were more adversely affected.

The sheer complexity of the experiments seems now to have led in the United States to widespread political disillusion. Whilst academics may debate legitimately the true significance of, say, labour supply effects, politically, the idea is thought by many to be unworkable—at least for some considerable time. As a result, politicians, administrators, and indeed many eminent academics are now looking for more straightforward, direct, and simpler approaches, based above all on enabling and encouraging more of those in need to support themselves.

Given the problems which have arisen through the sheer complexity of existing arrangements, it is worth noting that on a widespread international scale—including in most major European countries, the United States, Canada, Australia, and New Zealand, for example—the broad drive is towards simpler tax and benefit systems. But, so far as I am aware, no one is now proposing fully to integrate their tax and their welfare systems.

I would draw three lessons from this. First, I think we should be sceptical about the kind of root-and-branch change implied by some of the more grandiose integration ideas. There *are* different objectives in policy, and there *do* have to be trade-offs and compromises. Any scheme which seems to offer perfection on one criterion is almost certainly deeply flawed on another.

Second, we must remember that we never start with a blank piece of paper, and that getting from where we are to some ultimate ideal is bound to prove difficult. And even despite the rapid spread of computers, total integration would take so long that the underlying policy imperatives might well have changed and moved on by the time anything serious was achieved.

Third, we should aim at goals which carry us forward and are achievable, even if they fall short of providing a universal solution to all problems. This is what we have done in the area of work incentives. If we look at the system before this month's reforms, pay rises could leave people *worse* off because marginal rates of tax and benefit withdrawal in some cases exceeded 100 per cent. That was a disincentive to work or to work harder but—perhaps more importantly—it was extremely unfair. It helped lock people into the culture of dependency.

Take a married couple with three children aged 3, 8, and 11 who have average local authority rents and rates. Under the old scheme their net income after housing costs at gross earnings level of £75 per week was £108.78.

At £100 per week gross earnings, their net income would have fallen to £106.55.

At £120 it would have fallen to £104.75.

At £130 it would have fallen even further still to £103.28.

Indeed, it was not until this family's gross income was over £150—more than double my starting-point—that net income actually increased.

This was totally indefensible and it has now been ended. Basing all income-related benefits on net incomes rather than gross and putting more money into family credit ensures low-income working families have the opportunity to increase their living standards by their own efforts. I recognize that one consequence of this straightening out of marginal tax rates is to raise the number affected by the withdrawal of benefit as well as paying tax. But that is the mathematical consequence of giving more help to low-income families with children. The only practical or affordable alternative to our policy would be to cut the amount of help we give such families. No one, of course, wants that.

Nor, in thinking about these issues, can we overlook the changing context in which tax policy in particular is seen. This includes the growing realization, in a number of countries, that lower rates can have a dynamic effect not just on individuals but also in terms of economic efficiency and even net revenue; and that no country can afford to look at its fiscal arrangements in isolation from those of its competitors. In other words, we need to consider future policy options not in static but in dynamic terms, looking not just at the distributional effects of change on particular individuals at particular moments, but also at what the behavioural effects may be and the possible implications for such things as dependency, initiative, effort, and international competitiveness.

Before concluding, Mr Chairman, I would like to raise one other issue which will, I hope, be of interest to many here today: the way in which we analyse the changing incidence and characteristics of those on relatively low income.

For there is no dispute that good policies first require good analysis. That is why bodies such as IFS are so essential. But it has become increasingly clear that one of the main regular analyses published by government, the so-called Low Income Statistics, has suffered from some serious weaknesses. For example:

- the use of the supplementary benefit scale rates as a yardstick for 'low income'. This means that we have been using one of the main policy instruments for alleviating low incomes as the yardstick by which low income is measured. This creates the well-known paradox that increases in the real value of benefit will lead to an apparent increase in the numbers on 'low incomes';
- the scale rates themselves were ambiguous; they were, in fact, two rates of very different values; and
- the use of the word 'family' was similarly ambiguous: it was used in this context to describe a benefit unit, which may have no children, or there may be two or more benefit units in a family as commonly understood.

Despite these very serious drawbacks, these figures have come to be widely described as the official 'poverty' figures. In 1986 my predecessor announced a technical review of the methods and assumptions on which the tables are based. The report of the review team has now been published (DHSS (1988a)). Apart from drawing attention to the weaknesses of the current analysis, and the imminent end of the supplementary benefit scheme itself, the report recommends the introduction of a number of new analyses based on income measures which would be broadly independent of the social security rules and rates. They would provide a wider range of more meaningful and relevant data. And they could continue unaffected by this year's benefit changes themselves.

I have welcomed the report's proposals which will put the series on a more robust footing and extend the range of data published on a regular basis. Accordingly, we intend to publish within the next few weeks a final edition of the previous tables, covering 1981, 1983, and 1985, together with the first edition of the new tables for the same years (DHSS (1988b)). I hope that these improvements in the analytical basis against which policy can be considered will be widely welcomed.

I will now draw my contribution to a close. We have concentrated, lightly, exclusively on the business of social security. We must not, however, lose sight of what really underpins our ability to make future improvements to benefits, improvements we all wish to see. This foundation must be the continued success of the country's economy. That is why there is no contradiction between the benefit reforms and the Budget changes. The Budget will undoubtedly build upon our achievements:

- GDP is at a highest ever level;
- 1987 was the first year for a generation that the rate of growth exceeded the rate of inflation; and
- we are now in the eighth successive year of sustained growth averaging 3 per cent.

With this in mind, I hope that this conference will encourage people to look forward to the possibilities of tomorrow. We need to move on from the sterile arguments of comparing new with old. We need now to focus our efforts on the policy of the future. I am confident that today's discussions will carry that process forward, and I look forward to hearing the outcome of these discussions.

12

The Politics of Social Security: An Assessment of the Fowler Review

RUTH LISTER*

1. Introduction

The reforms set out in the Bill are fundamental. They follow the most comprehensive review of social security since the last war and the most detailed consultation with the public. (Fowler (1986))

These two claims—to the most substantial examination of social security since Beveridge and full public consultation—were a recurrent theme of what came to be known as the Fowler Review. In attempting to assess their validity, it is difficult to disentangle the content of the Review's outcome from the processes that led to it—the more so because the Review cannot be understood without reference to the wider political, ideological, and economic concerns that helped to shape it.

This paper therefore starts by setting the Review in context. It then looks at the process of reform (in so far as it is known in our secrecy-obsessed democracy) from the announcement of the Review through to its implementation, paying special attention to the parliamentary lobbying it provoked. It assesses the extent to which it inspired the 'great debate on the welfare state' sought by Norman Fowler and its claim to emulate the Beveridge Report. It concludes by looking at the lessons that can be learnt from the whole exercise.

2. The Agenda for Reform

In an essay published shortly before the Green Paper (DHSS (1985a)), Ward (1985) identified three interrelated agendas for reform: those of the DHSS, the Treasury, and the ideologues of the Right. The short-term DHSS agenda was prompted by a 'crisis in administration' of the two largest means-tested benefits: supplementary benefit and housing benefit. The 1980 reform of the supplementary benefit scheme, daughter of the pre-

* Ruth Lister is Professor of Applied Social Studies at the University of Bradford.
This paper was presented at a conference on 'The Economics of Social Security', organized by the Institute for Fiscal Studies, held on 15 April 1988.

vious administration's nil-cost review, had failed to deliver 'the great advance in fairness' promised by Patrick Jenkin (1980). More importantly from the Government's point of view, it had not 'resolved some central problems' (Fowler (1984a)), in particular that of complexity, with its implications for the number of Civil Servants required to administer the scheme. A reduction in the size of the Civil Service was also a primary motive behind the transfer of responsibility for housing costs to local authorities in 1982–3 under the new housing benefit scheme, dubbed by *The Times* (20 January 1984) as 'the biggest fiasco in the history of the welfare state'.

In both cases, reform was blighted by under-resourced and over-hasty implementation, at a time when the numbers claiming the benefits were rising rapidly, largely as a result of economic policies leading to higher unemployment and higher local authority rents.

The DHSS's own agenda was thus shaped to a large extent by that of the Treasury. But the Treasury also had its own explicit agenda for the Review. The importance of this cannot be overemphasized for, whichever party is in power, the Treasury is a principal actor in the process of social security reform. From interviews with officials and politicians, Whitely and Winyard (1987, p. 127), in their study of the poverty lobby, observed that central government has become 'fragmented into competing issue-communities'. They were told by one DHSS official that 'it's us against the Treasury'. In this author's own experience, even Conservative DHSS Ministers have been prepared to enlist the support of the Child Poverty Action Group (CPAG) in this battle with the Treasury.

The ludicrous lengths to which the Treasury itself has been prepared to go were illustrated in an extraordinary intervention recorded by David Donnison. In a response to the Supplementary Benefit Commission's critical draft report on the Social Assistance review, a Treasury official wrote:

I understand that there is a suggestion that this document should be published. There are some serious problems about the provision of paper and HMSO are likely to be exhorting Departments to economise in the use of paper, particularly during 1979–80. It is therefore for consideration whether this document of 60 pages—which reproduces in shriller tones what has already been incorporated in the Commission's annual reports for 1975, 1976, and 1977—should be published at the taxpayers' expense. (Donnison (1982, p. 149))

The 'wolves in the Treasury, always ranging abroad in hopes of bringing down a social benefit' (Donnison (1982, p. 209)), had tasted blood in 1980 with the Social Security (No. 2) Act (which, among other things, abolished the earnings-related supplement and cut the real value of a number of National Insurance benefits) and with a cut in the real value of child benefit. But, despite the ineffectual parliamentary opposition to what was perceived inside Whitehall as a watershed in social security policy, when the Treasury wolves came back for more, they were thwarted in their attempts at further full frontal cuts in the real value of income maintenance benefits, thanks largely to the rallying of the Tory 'wets' under the social security banner. Instead, the Treasury had to engage in a steady war of attrition in which housing benefit was identified as the soft underbelly (although it proved to be not that soft, as potential Conservative supporters were affected) and minor cuts were made in complex bits of the system with incomprehensible names. As Johnson (1985, p. 33) observed, 'the incrementalism that allowed the welfare system to grow so silently is now used to effect its quiet contraction'.

With the return of a Conservative government and a new Chancellor, the stakes were raised again and the received wisdom was that Norman Fowler put forward the reviews partly to buy off the Chancellor's demands for social security cuts in the 1983 and 1984 public expenditure rounds. So once more the DHSS was to embark on a review within a nil-cost remit imposed by the Treasury—a handicap not faced by Beveridge. Norman Fowler made clear to Parliament that options for change were to be restricted to those that could be contained 'within the present overall level of social security expenditure' (Fowler (1984a)), a message reinforced in the subsequent consultation documents. This inevitably placed restrictions on what was presented as a thorough and comprehensive review.

A particular focus of criticism from both Right and Left was that, as observed by the economics correspondent of *The Daily Telegraph*, 'the reviews have tackled only one side of the modern welfare state equation, that of benefits paid through the social security system. They have ignored the "hidden welfare state"—the allowances through the tax system for mortgage interest, pension contributions and so on which go largely to the better off' (Williams (1985)). Indeed, mortgage interest tax relief was explicitly excluded from the housing benefit review team's terms of reference—not that that stopped those submitting evidence, including the Social Security Advisory Committee and the Social Services Select Committee, from drawing attention to it.

As in the 1978 Review, the nil-cost remit effectively marginalized concerns about the adequacy of benefits and the ever-increasing dependence on means-tested benefits. But this time round, the Treasury went further and was reported to be seeking cuts of between £2 billion and £4 billion, whereas Mr Fowler wanted to be able to use any savings to restructure social security and claim the mantle of Beveridge. Although Mr Fowler was perceived as having won the battle, with smaller cuts in the short term and the much larger cuts staved off until the end of the century, the package that emerged still bore the mark of a cost-cutting exercise.

The Treasury's public spending agenda was closely intertwined with that of the ideologues who were seeking to reduce the role of the State and price the unemployed into low-paid work. The thumb-prints of both were clearly identifiable on the objectives set out in the Green Paper: the enhancement of personal independence; a social security system 'consistent with the Government's overall objectives for the economy'; more effective targeting of resources on those in greatest need; and, perhaps less obviously, a system which is 'simpler to understand and easier to administer' (DHSS (1985a, Cmnd 9517)).

3. A Model of Public Consultation

At each stage of the reform process, Ministers were at pains to legitimize the Review by emphasizing its fundamental nature, thoroughness, and the extent of the consultation undertaken. Norman Fowler's preface to the Green Paper painted a glowing picture of democracy in action. The White Paper took it a stage further:

The process of consultation began in the Autumn of 1983. Since then Ministers, helped both by an independent committee and by outside advisers, have examined the major parts of social security. Prior to the Green Paper there were 19 public sessions in which 62 organisations and individuals gave oral evidence. Over 40,000 consultation documents were issued and nearly 4,500 pieces of written evidence received. Since publication of the Green Paper there have been a further 7,000 written responses. The aim was to ensure that no points of legitimate public concern were overlooked in preparing for change. (DHSS (1985b, para. 1.3))

As we trace the consultation process described by Mr Fowler and follow it through and beyond the Bill's passage through Parliament, a number of questions need to be borne in mind in order to assess whether the rhetoric of public consultation and debate and of fundamental reform signified very much in reality:

1. the extent to which the Government was genuinely responsive to outside views in shaping its proposals at each stage from the initial setting of the agenda and production of the Green Paper, through the Bill's parliamentary passage, to finally the more detailed questions surrounding implementation;
2. the depth and breadth of the analysis and proposals contained in the Green Paper and the extent to which the public was allowed access to the information and thinking which informed them;
3. the extent to which a genuine public debate about the future of the social security system was stimulated;
4. the extent to which the Government achieved the consensus behind its reforms that it claimed to be seeking; and

5. the validity of Mr Fowler's claims to the Beveridge mantle.

But first, we need to ask what the motives were behind the enthusiasm for public consultation. As Donnison (1982) had observed, the DHSS was not exactly renowned for open policy debate. The decision in 1978 to carry out an exercise in open government was, according to Walker (1982, p. 19),

based primarily on practical and instrumental considerations arising from the main objective, to provide continuity and impetus in the policy-making process to ensure urgent reform of the supplementary benefit scheme. It was primarily a public relations exercise designed to educate a public, including such diverse interests as politicians of all parties, staff, claimants, and pressure groups, into the need for change and to create an atmosphere in which change was a natural outcome.

In this it succeeded, in that the review survived a change of government. But the views expressed in response to the Social Assistance consultation document 'had only a modest impact on the reforms introduced and apparently no influence on the Government's perception of the *role* of supplementary benefit' (Walker (1982, p. 21)). Whether the outcome would have been very different had Labour remained in power, given the Treasury's iron grip on the proceedings, is doubtful.

This time round, the decision to hold a public review appears to have been prompted, at least in part, by the lesson learnt from the abortive think-tank exercise: that, as Deakin (1987, p. 132) put it, 'lasting reforms could not be achieved by *coup d'état* behind the closed doors of the Cabinet room'. According to *The Sunday Times*, the procedures adopted showed 'a sophisticated approach to the public presentation of what is both an inevitable and painful reassessment of the principles laid down by Sir William Beveridge . . . by soliciting evidence from the public, the review committee will be able to "think the unthinkable" about welfare reform in a way that a secret Whitehall inquiry would find politically explosive' (Jones and Kettle (1984)).

Consultation Prior to the Green Paper

'The most substantial examination of the social security system since the Beveridge Report' (Fowler (1984a)) was announced in April 1984. In fact, the review of pensions had been announced the previous November and that of housing benefit in February. The April announcement of the supplementary benefit and children and young people's reviews plus a survey of people with disabilities was followed a month later by a further review of maternity benefits (to be conducted by Civil Servants, taking written evidence only). The impression given was of 'a hotch-potch of overlapping inquiries, some looking to specific groups of claimants and others at specific benefits' (Bennett (1984, p. 38)) with important parts of the system left out completely.

It took another 6 weeks from the April announcement for the membership of the housing and supplementary benefit and children and young people's review teams to be published, together with brief and rather vague consultation documents. While membership of the housing benefits review team was completely independent, the other two were an unusual mixture of independent members with Ministers in the chair. It was not long before critics were asking how independent the independent members were. There was also considerable criticism of the rushed nature of the consultation process which allowed only 10 weeks over the summer for responses.

Scepticism about the genuineness of the consultation exercise was heightened as information about the review process trickled out. In response to press reports that a central team of Civil Servants would be addressing in secret wider issues than those contained in the consultation documents, a joint letter to *The Times* (26 June 1984) from a number of charities asked for 'a clear and definitive list of the real issues under consideration'—but to no avail. In fact, some of these wider questions emerged unexpectedly at the public hearings of the children and young people's review as witnesses were asked their views on the scope and purpose of social security provision. It was as if, having set up a number of disparate reviews, the DHSS realized that it had not provided a forum for discussion of underlying questions such as these. The manner in which the questions were asked, however, did not inspire confidence in the openness of the review team's minds. The answer they were interested in was the 'relief of poverty', and attempts to expound social security's other wider roles were cut short.

It also became clear that there was no intention of publishing the review teams' reports to the Secretary of State (other than, it transpired, that of the housing benefit review). As *The Economist* (24 November 1984) observed, this suggested that 'the exercise is not quite the advertisement for open government which it might seem'. Similarly, the Government refused to publish the evidence that had been submitted, in contrast to the 1978 review when incoming Ministers had agreed, albeit reluctantly, to the Civil Service review team's request to publish a summary of responses.

Once the review teams had reported to Norman Fowler, a shroud of 'almost paranoic secrecy' enveloped this 'open review of the social security system' (Timmins (1985)). According to one press report, a top secret 10-day conference in a rural retreat was carried out in a cloak-and-dagger atmosphere usually reserved for issues of national security, with Civil Servants reduced to exchanging information in the gentlemen's lavatory. (Were there any women there, one wonders?)

There then followed a period of uncertainty as the final report made its way through a Cabinet subcommittee and the Cabinet itself. The full extent of the involvement of the Cabinet subcommittee and of the Prime Minister's Policy Unit is not clear. At the time, it was very much played down; now they appear to have played a pretty central role. Nor was it clear until late in the day whether it would be a 'White Paper with green edges' or a 'Green Paper with white edges'. After a series of delays (and numerous leaks, of which more below), a Green Paper was finally published at the beginning of June, again in a cloak-and-dagger atmosphere of security vans arriving at the Elephant and Castle in the middle of the night before publication.

The Green Paper

The first wave of protest around the Green Paper focused on the exclusion of any figures either at the global level of overall expenditure or at the level of individual gainers and losers. The Social Services Select Committee criticized the decision to exclude figures (apparently taken at the last minute) as 'unwise and unhelpful' (Social Services Committee (1985, para. 8)). Ministerial protestations that they wanted the debate to concentrate on structures at this point cut little ice and they were eventually forced to concede that illustrative figures would be provided with the White Paper.

Leaving aside questions around the substance of the Green Paper's proposals (which is not the subject of this paper), criticisms of the quality of the analysis gradually emerged. Two years later, in an article on the policy-making process, Sir Douglas Wass (1987) used the social security reforms as

an example of a policy decision having been reached and presented with less than the thorough public analysis I think desirable. . . . many would say that the review should have been fundamental and that is what the Secretary of State's review purported to be. But even the most casual reading of the Green Paper reveals how far the standard of that review fell short of the standard I have suggested. . . . It was heavily party political, as some of the language of the Green Paper reveals. It was weak on defining the objectives which the social security system seeks to achieve (though it was admittedly quite strong on the costs which it imposes). There was little evidence of how other countries were tackling the problems. But, worst of all, the Green Paper presented only one set of options.

Contemporary criticisms of the Green Paper's analysis focused on the absence of any assessment of the needs that social security is designed to meet and of how far benefits actually meet them—'a black hole at the centre' in the words of Townsend (1985)—a criticism later echoed forcefully by Francis Pym during the Bill's Second Reading debate; the inadequacy of the analysis of social trends since Beveridge, including, as the Social Security Advisory Committee (SSAC) noted, changes in the position of women; and the failure to learn from the lessons of history, particularly in relation to nil-cost attempts at simplification of supplementary benefit and the discretionary Social Fund. Berthoud (1986) later dubbed the lurch from discretion to rigid entitlement and back again as 'the windscreen wiper' approach to policy-making.

There were also gaping holes. The 'tangle' of benefits for young people identified by Rhodes Boyson was left undisturbed. More fundamentally, despite Norman Fowler's earlier assurance that 'the Government is considering and will consider their proposals in conjunction with tax; that has never been at issue and it would be absurd to do otherwise' (Fowler (1984c)), any consideration of the relationship between social security and tax was left to a subsequent Inland Revenue Green Paper (1986).

An attempt by CPAG to analyse evidence submitted to the Reviews (in the absence of a published official analysis) (Bennett and Tarpey (1984–5)) suggested that the main thrust of the Green Paper's proposals was out of tune with most of the submissions. The main cut proposed in the housing benefit scheme had been explicitly opposed by the housing benefit review team both in its report and in its letter to the Secretary of State. And it soon emerged that the abolition of the State Earnings-Related Pension Scheme (SERPS) had not been recommended by the pensions review team and that its members were not happy with the proposal.

Press reports suggested that the abolition of SERPS was Norman Fowler's own personal decision, even though he had assured the Commons when announcing the review that the purpose was 'not to call into question the fundamental pensions structure that was established in the 1970s with all party agreement and to which I was a party' (Fowler (1983)). It was, it appeared, the product of his failure to make other broad radical structural changes. In particular, despite clear early indications that the child benefit scheme was under serious threat, the Green Paper reasserted the Government's commitment to the principle of a universal child benefit (though making it clear that it would have lower priority than the new family credit). Political realities—in the form of the strong support for child benefit among the powerful Conservative Women's Advisory Committee and many Conservative MPs on both sides of the Party—had helped ensure that targeting was not taken to its logical conclusion.

From Green to White Paper

The strength of the commitment to child benefit (and public consultation) soon became clear when, within 2 weeks of the Green Paper, a cut in its real value was announced, together with a number of other cuts that were seen as the first step towards implementation of the Green Paper's proposals.

Responses were due in September, again giving rise to accusations of undue haste, and whereas Social Assistance had been free, the cost of the Green Paper seriously diminished any potential claimant participation in the consultation process.

The White Paper emerged, after some delay, just before Christmas. The 'reprieve' for SERPS in the face of opposition from the National Association of Pension Funds, the CBI, and the insurance companies obscured the extent to which the rest of the White Paper was virtually identical to the Green, notwithstanding Norman Fowler's earlier assurances that the proposals were not 'set in concrete'. There were some concessions, such as the abandonment of the proposed presence test and of a combined rent and rate rebate taper, and a slight modification of the treatment of young people. The point was also taken that implementation in 1987 was courting trouble, the main bulk of the reforms being delayed until 1988.

The White Paper was written in bland language that, while conceding 'concern' had been expressed about a number of specific proposals, tried to give the impression that the overall thrust of the reforms had broad support and that serious consideration had been given to those criticisms that had been made. An analysis by CPAG of 60 responses from a wide range of bodies told a different story. Of the 60, only 2 gave uncritical support to the proposals as a whole. These were the Institute of Directors and the Monday Club. It is difficult to believe that this is what Mr Fowler had in mind when he later declared that 'we must make sure that at every step we carry the great bulk of commonsense opinion with us' (Fowler (1985)). How different from the response to the Beveridge Plan when Beveridge (1943) was able to write 'the main result of studying [the published volume of evidence] is to show how much agreement there was, even before my Report was made, upon all its main principles'.

4. From Bill to Implementation

The Passage through Parliament

The Bill that was presented to Parliament in January was very much a skeleton Bill leaving the detail to be filled in by regulations and, in the case of the Social Fund, the Secretary of State's directions and guidance. Concern was expressed about this and about the speed with which the Government pushed ahead with the legislation by the Social Services Select Committee.

The relegation of the details of social security legislation to regulations has become increasingly common. It means that effective parliamentary scrutiny is reduced, particularly when, as in this case in contrast to the 1980

Bill, the Notes on Clauses supplied to Standing Committee members did not give a clear indication of how the regulation- and direction-making powers would be used. Scrutiny of the legislation was further reduced by the extension in the Bill of the Secretary of State's right not to consult the SSAC on draft regulations in a period from 6 months to 12.

When the Bill returned to the Commons for its Third Reading in May, Norman Fowler observed that it had been 'subject to the longest scrutiny by a Standing Committee of any social security legislation since the original Beveridge proposals' (Fowler (1986)). This scrutiny helped to clarify the Government's intentions, although the tabling of too many amendments meant that some important issues were not addressed at all.

Apart from what Mr Fowler himself admitted privately was 'a close shave' on the payment of family credit through the pay-packet, the Government was, however, never in serious trouble, even though Ministers did not always have the total support of their back-bench colleagues. The only significant amendments to the Bill were those introduced by the Government itself—after it had imposed a guillotine on debate. Most controversial of these was the doubling of the disqualification period for unemployment benefit from 6 to 13 weeks without justification or any prior warning in either the Green or White Paper or even when the issue had been discussed the previous week in Committee.

As a concession to demands for an independent right of appeal on the Social Fund, provision for an internal social fund review inspectorate was made at Third Reading. The most significant development, though, was the unexpected climb-down on the payment of family credit through the pay-packet. Like Paul on the road to Damascus, Norman Fowler suddenly saw the light, with the help of concerted pressure from his own back-benchers. At the last moment he announced that the issue would be reconsidered in consultation with a number of bodies—to the surprise of the Whips who had been expecting a vote on a Conservative back-bench amendment. Early in the Committee Stage in the House of Lords, it was announced that family credit would be paid directly to the mother, and Ministers conceded privately that they had been caught in a pincer movement between the poverty and women's lobbies on the one hand and the small business lobby on the other.

The only other unmitigated success for opponents of the Bill was the extension of invalid care allowance (ICA) to married and cohabiting women the day before their exclusion was ruled unlawful by the European Court. This was one of the few occasions when the Government had to bow to defeat in the courts. The strength of the campaign to extend the ICA meant that it did not, as had been feared, try to move the goal-posts by tightening up the qualifying rules for everybody.

The Government did have a difficult time of it in the Lords. It suffered three defeats, two of them with sizeable majorities. One of these led to the introduction of a severe disability premium which went only a small way to meet the Lords' concern, and to improved transitional protection for those with severe disabilities. The other, which introduced an independent right of appeal and regulations into the Social Fund, placed Ministers in a quandary. The eventual 'compromise' was a Social Fund Commissioner with no real power and an independent right of appeal limited to decisions on maternity and funeral expenses.

At the end of the day, the Government was able to overcome the Lords' misgivings by sheer power of numbers. *The Daily Telegraph* (1 August 1986) painted a graphic picture of the scene:

Last week the chamber filled to overflowing as the Government marshalled all its forces to ensure that it rubber-stamped earlier decisions by MPs to overturn the defeats suffered on the Social Security Bill. Urgent messages were sent out to Tory backwoodsmen to turn up and support the Government. Dukes, earls and viscounts duly arrived—and when the vote was taken there were more than 350 peers voting, compared to a normal turn-out of around 160. 'I have never seen so many peers before', admitted one bemused Minister. 'They were all perched all over the Throne, almost clinging to the rafters.'

There were tales of Lords who did not know where the lavatories were and even of one who was unsure how to vote.

The Economist (28 June 1986) described the defeats in the Lords as 'a testimony to the lobbying power of organisations which represent every conceivable group of the unfortunate and deprived'. One of the potentially significant developments during the passage of the Bill was the way in which the members of the 'poverty lobby' really did act as a single lobby. Co-ordinated by CPAG, a number of voluntary organizations, together with the Association of Metropolitan Authorities, the Association of County Councils, and a coalition of trade unions, came together to work on the Bill. By the time it reached the Lords, what had been fairly loose co-ordination had been tightened up and the Social Security Consortium was born. The Consortium issued a series of joint briefings and amendments which clearly helped to shape the course of the debate in the Lords.

Although at the end of the day, the Bill was passed relatively intact, the general view was that the Consortium's work had not been in vain. It had forced some concessions and had made the Government very vulnerable on some key issues. In particular, the significance of the family credit climb-down should not be underestimated. Ministers and Civil Servants had been adamant that no concession would be made because of its ideological importance as a key element in the strategy to price the unemployed into low-paid jobs and underpin low wages. The coalition that had finally squeezed the concession out of the Government had not formed spontaneously and until then Ministers had made it clear they were willing to ride out the opposition to the proposal.

Taking the review process as a whole, Whitely and Winyard (1987, p. 152) conclude that 'the poverty lobby *did* play an important role in "holding the line" against some of the more extreme proposals for radical restructuring of the social security system'. Moreover, the very establishment of the Social Security Consortium, and the degree of co-operation involved, marked an important step forward in the development of the poverty lobby. Since the Bill reached the statute-book, the Consortium has continued to grow and provide a focus for lobbying on social security issues. Given the ease with which governments can play off different groups against each other, such co-operation has helped to strengthen the position of the poverty lobby in these adverse times.

That more was not achieved can be attributed to a number of factors. First, the odds against achieving significant concessions were always stacked against the lobbyists, given the size of the Government's majority and the importance of the Bill to the Government's broader objectives. Second, the number of different changes contained in the Bill meant there could not be a single focus of opposition. Generalized opposition to 'the Fowler Bill' did not cut much ice at Westminster. This, together with MPs' traditional lack of interest in social security matters (confirmed by Peter Taylor-Gooby's recent work of their attitudes to social security), meant that many MPs were not fully aware of the Bill's significance. There were also other more fundamental factors at work, the implications of which will be considered in the final section.

Legislative Tippex and the Flesh on the Bones

Since the 1986 Social Security Act reached the statute-book, MPs have been called upon to apply 'legislative tippex' (as Frank Dobson put it) through two Bills which corrected errors relating to the Government's powers under the Social Fund. To misquote Oscar Wilde, one such amending Bill may be regarded as a misfortune; two look like carelessness. Moreover, regulations were being amended less than a fortnight before implementation and again within weeks of it, in one case repeating a mistake made in 1980 that similarly had to be rectified.

There were also a number of details that had to be sorted out outside the parliamentary arena. The most significant of these related to the Social Fund. The White Paper (DHSS (1985b, paras. 4.15 and 4.16)) expressed the Government's gratitude for the

thoughtful contributions which have been received from bodies such as the Select Committee on Social Services and the Social Security Advisory Committee. They raise real issues for consideration. . . . The Government will continue to refine the detail in the period between this White Paper and the introduction of the scheme and will continue to be ready to modify its structure in the light of further experience and comment.

The DHSS did circulate the draft Social Fund Manual, containing the Secretary of State's directions and guidance to a limited number of bodies. But it then virtually ignored the unanimous criticisms made of it, including those of the SSAC which declared it 'unfair and unworkable' (SSAC (1987a)). In a letter of 25 August 1987 to the Chair of the SSAC, Nicholas Scott made clear that

the social fund will go ahead as planned. We have given full and careful consideration to the objections raised by the Committee and other bodies we consulted, to some of the principles of the social fund; and we have appreciated the thought and effort which the Committee put into devising an alternative approach. But these issues of principle were well exposed and discussed when the social fund provisions were being debated in Parliament in 1986 and we have concluded that the case for the social fund is just as strong now as it was then.

(Newspaper reports, in fact, suggested that the new DHSS Ministers were themselves keen to drop the Fund.) The SSAC's response was to take the unprecedented step of sending an open letter to the Minister placing on record that the Government proceeded with the Social Fund substantially as planned 'without our support' (SSAC (1987b)). What the Minister had omitted to say was that all the SSAC's careful constructive suggestions had had no more impact on the final shape of the scheme than the outright rejection by the poverty lobby and local authority associations.

It is too early to say whether the prediction of the SSAC and others that the fund will be unfair and unworkable will be borne out. But what is clear already is the gap between some of the original claims made for the fund and the reality of the (far from simple) Social Fund Manual and the application procedure. For example, one of the alleged advantages of the fund was that 'there will be less need for detailed scrutiny of an applicant's circumstances' (Major (1986)). Recently Michael Portillo justified the requirement that applications must be made on the lengthy prescribed form as follows:

It is desirable that we should have the form because . . . we are moving away from a regulated system. . . . It is rather different when we are dealing with priorities and discretion. In that case, there is a whole range of information that the social fund officer will wish to have to ensure that he knows all there is to know about the application in order to have a full appreciation of what its priority should be.

When challenged, he continued:

whether it is an application for single payments or a social fund application, some of the questioning is bound to be intrusive because it will be about means and resources. However, a letter applying for a single payment—which was a regulated system—might contain sufficient information for it to be decided whether the regulation was satisfied. In the case of a social fund application, it is obviously desirable that there should be a range of information so that the priority of the application can be judged. (Portillo (1988))

Put that statement beside those made when the Bill was going through Parliament and we are entering into the world of *Alice through the Looking Glass*.

Slightly more impact was made by the local authority associations through their negotiations on the housing benefit changes—not on the substance of the changes but on the subsidy arrangements and on the timing of the proposed board and lodging changes (not included in the original Green and White Papers). But local authorities were offered only about half of the money they estimated was necessary to cover start-up costs (for the scheme is in some ways more complicated to administer than the previous one), and the delay in issuing the regulations and guidance manual has increased the danger of a repeat of the problems that beset the introduction of housing benefit. According to the Institute of Housing, over half of local authorities may not be properly prepared for the changes (*The Guardian* (28 March 1988)). Further problems were predicted by the Institute as a result of the concessions announced after the new scheme's implementation, when it had evidence that about 200 local authorities were already in difficulty. The DHSS itself did not know how it would reimburse those affected, and it was predicted that the system of reimbursement would not be working until well into the summer.

One particularly problematic area for the DHSS has been the position of income support claimants with severe disabilities who will suffer as a result of the abolition of additional requirements, in particular the domestic assistance addition. The introduction of the severe disability premium (the details of which had to be quickly amended when the DHSS had to admit that the disability organizations had been correct in challenging official estimates of the numbers who would qualify) did not satisfy its critics. Eventually, after a great deal of agonizing, and nearly a year after Parliament was told that discussions were taking place with disability organizations in an attempt to resolve the problem, Nicholas Scott announced an independent £5 million trust fund that would be responsible for administering discretionary grants. Further details were announced little more than a week before the new scheme was due to be introduced. Reaction to the Independent Living Fund was almost universally hostile. Of the charities approached, only the Disablement Income Group has been prepared to cooperate in its establishment. The impression left is of a government forced to concede too little too late, doing nothing to placate its critics who are suspicious of what is widely regarded as the privatization of part of the social security safety net.

One important concession—made during the General Election campaign having earlier been dismissed out of hand—was to provide for a degree of compensation for the payment of 20 per cent rates in the means-tested benefit scale rates. Although only an average figure, it was clearly better than nothing. However, when the actual benefit rates came to be announced in October, it became clear 'that a large part of the compensation is being clawed back through cuts in the personal allowances under the new scheme, and through a further increase in the rate of withdrawal of help with rent [the "taper"]' (Social Security Consortium (1987, p. 5)). It also became clear that assurances to MPs that consideration would be given to their concerns about the level of the proposed premiums, especially the family premium, had had no impact on the final premium rates.

A new set of gainer and loser tables was published at the same time as the benefit rates. Unfortunately, they do not paint a complete picture of the impact of the reforms overall, because of the phased implementation of some of those reforms and because they exclude the impact of the abolition of single payments and cuts in child benefit. Moreover, as the Social Security Consortium observed in a letter to the Secretary of State on 7 April, in public debate Ministers have 'been tending to isolate the positive effects of specific benefit changes on claimant groups . . . without taking into account other simultaneous changes which may have a more negative impact. And the presentation of the figures of gainers and losers has been characterised by a concentration on the *cash* position at the point of change'—an odd stance for a government that has set such store by the reduction of inflation.

The presentation of global expenditure figures has been equally unsatisfactory: Ministers repeatedly compare the Social Fund budget with current expenditure on single payments, rather than with expenditure levels before the cuts paving the way for the Social Fund were made. And attempts through parliamentary questions to ascertain whether the implementation of income support will mean an increase or decrease in expenditure have been met by veils of obfuscation in the form of confusing statements concerning transitional protection and compensation for the 20 per cent rates payment. (The answer would appear to be that there has been a cut of £60 million (House of Commons Debate (1988a)).)

Analysis of the effects of the actual benefit rates both in parliamentary answers and by independent commentators reveals once again the gap that can exist between the objectives of policy reform and actual outcomes. Two key objectives—to target resources more effectively, especially on low-income working families with children, and to improve work incentives—are not being realized. Parliamentary answers have revealed that some of the poorest working families will be worse off and that the number of low-paid workers facing effective marginal tax rates of 60 per cent or more will nearly double to over half a million (House of Commons Debates (1987 and 1988b)). As Parker (1988, p. 30) concludes,

the peaks and troughs of the poverty trap will be removed, but in most cases this is done by cutting disposable incomes at the bottom. The poverty trap is rationalised but not significantly improved. Despite living standard cuts at nil earnings, the unemployment trap remains more or less as before . . . Given the terms of reference for the social security review these results are not surprising. They show that 'poverty relief' through improved targeting is a mirage. Poverty cannot be removed simply by redistributing benefits within the low income population. Nor can social security reform on its own restore incentives.

Similarly, although there is a degree of simplification (at the expense of a good dollop of 'rough justice'), as Norman Fowler admitted at the outset of the Review, 'by their nature [means-tested] benefits are complicated to legislate for, administer and understand' (Fowler (1984b)). Assessment of resources remains as complicated as ever. Even the simplification derived through the premiums structure is marred by the need to graft on the Independent Living Fund to cater for those who do not fit into the neat new scheme of things.

It remains to be seen how the various reforms work in practice. Given that in the case of the Social Fund in particular, they introduce new principles into social security policy, it is disappointing that there has not been the same DHSS commitment to supporting an independent programme of research as there was when the 1980 Act was introduced. Nor was heed taken of relevant independent research in the framing of the proposals. Bill Daniel, Director of the Policy Studies Institute, has commented that 'it is extraordinary that the Government gives so little weight to independent research in its domestic policies. This only weakens its capacity to fulfil its own objectives' (Daniel (1988))—a lament echoed by the SSAC in its most recent report. Although it now looks as if there will be some kind of research programme following implementation, one cannot but suspect that the lack of enthusiasm this time round reflects the extremely critical results emanating from the research programme commissioned in 1980. These may have also helped to precipitate the new powers of veto attached by the DHSS to research that it does fund.

A System Capable of Meeting Demands into the Next Century?

There is a widespread view that monitoring of the Social Fund will confirm the fears of the SSAC and others that it will be unfair and unworkable. In the absence of an independent right of appeal, MPs could find themselves providing an important channel of information to Ministers about how the fund is working. Barclay (1988a) has predicted that 'individual cases of what anybody would regard as hardship will emerge and the degree to which the volume of these cases grows and MPs' surgeries are full of detailed case histories will perhaps result and I hope will result in second thoughts'. In the case of housing benefit, the second thoughts were sooner than anyone would have anticipated, as concessions were made within less than a month of the Act's implementation.

The original vision was of a social security system 'capable of meeting the demands into the next century' (DHSS (1985a, Cmnd 9517, para. 1.4)). The more the details of many aspects of the new scheme became clear, the less convincing that claim became. But an even more serious challenge to it has come from Mr Fowler's own successor, John Moore. Far from a set of reforms designed to see the country through to the next century, Mr Moore seems to see the Social Security Act 1986 as the catalyst to a period of permanent revolution in the DHSS. In his widely reported speech in autumn 1987, he observed that 'it has been suggested that when history comes to consider this review it may decide the most important fact about it was that it happened at all. . . . With the passage of the Social Security Act 1986, it at last has been accepted that change is possible and indeed that in a fast-moving modern society social policies should probably remain under continuous review' (Moore (1987)).

Ministers have made clear that child benefit, in particular, in view of its cost and its 'ill-targeted' nature, is to be kept constantly under review. Little more than two years after the completion of a supposedly fundamental review of financial support for children (of which child benefit is the main element), the scheme is once more under scrutiny. But this time it is an internal Civil Service review and outside bodies are not being asked for evidence as there is plenty of evidence for the Civil Servants to scrutinize from last time round, if they so wish.

Other changes have already been legislated for since the 1986 Act reached the statute-book; in particular, the raising of the normal age of entitlement to income support from 16 to 18; a further doubling of the unemployment benefit disqualification period; and further tightening up of the contribution conditions. In the view of David Willetts of the Centre for Policy Studies, Ministers are now prepared to start asking 'the real world questions' about the 'problem of welfare dependency' that are high on the agenda in the United States. As the presenter of the *File on Four* programme in which Willetts was interviewed emphasized, 'the agenda for the welfare revolution is ambitious. The aim is to change our attitudes to work and benefits'. John Moore has made clear that he regards the Social Security Act 1986 and its objective of targeting to be 'crucial as part of the long term effort to change the climate of opinion on welfare' (Moore (1987)).

As part of the revolution of reducing expectations, no DHSS statement is complete these days without its reference to 'reducing dependence on the benefit culture'. In this context, the Social Fund, although representing only a fraction of total spending on social security, marks 'the one great symbolic change' in the Act; according to Nicholas Timmins of *The Independent*, this 'cultural change, with the shifts implied by the Social Fund and its clones, is one we are likely to see more of' (Timmins (1988)).

5. A Great Debate on the Welfare State?

In some ways, it looks as if the implementation of the Social Security Act 1986 marks the beginning rather than the end of the great debate on the Welfare State called for by Norman Fowler shortly after announcing the pensions review. But how far was the Fowler Review itself successful in inspiring such a debate?

There is no doubt that it helped to put social security on the political agenda for a time in a way that the poverty lobby had signally failed to do. The summer of 1984 saw the publication of a series of grand plans for the reform of social security. The rushed timetable for the submission of evidence, with a closing date that coincided with the onset of the media 'silly season', helped to ensure decent publicity and a lively debate in the more serious Press over the summer. As Deakin (1987, p. 138) observed, 'some at least of the conditions for a comprehensive·debate accordingly seemed satisfied; vigorous and informed advocacy of a wide range of alternatives had ensured that the main issues were now in the public arena'.

Once the review had disappeared behind the closed doors of the Elephant and Castle, however, Ministers were able to set the pace and direction of media interest and consequent public debate through the skilful flying of kites and, as the Green Paper grew closer, judicious leaking of its more controversial proposals. By the time the Green Paper was published, little of its contents came as a surprise; indeed, one of the biggest surprises was the non-appearance of a cut in the duration of unemployment benefit which had been confidently predicted. Whether this was last minute cold feet or deliberate manipulation of expectations so that the final package appeared less drastic than expected was never clear.

The Government's success in setting the initial agenda for debate around the Green Paper has to be understood against the backcloth of 6 years of successive benefit cuts and of the denigration of public expenditure which had helped to shape expectations and had forced the poverty lobby and the Opposition into the defensive politics of the finger in the dike. There was always a danger, which the Green Paper exploited, of appearing as defenders of the status quo—a bitter irony for those who had been campaigning for reform of the social security system for many years.

Ministers appeared to be particularly successful in selling the concept of targeting in the run-up to the Green Paper. It was not just the political commentators on the Right who were enthusiastically embracing it as if it were some newly discovered, modern concept rather than simply the old wine of means-testing served up in new bottles. For CPAG and a number of other groups, this was one of the main causes of concern during this period. It was felt that the portrayal of the Fowler Review as just an exercise in cutting was too simplistic, and obscured the more fundamental questions it was likely to raise about the purpose and future of the social security system. The Green Paper, CPAG argued in a briefing published shortly before it, 'will be important not just for the specific proposals it puts forward but also for the general ideology about the role of the welfare state upon which those proposals are based' (Lister (1985, p. 1)).

It was an uphill struggle. As Deakin (1987, pp. 145, 162, and 163) observed, 'the wider debate that both Norman Fowler and his critics were hoping to see was not taking place'. Missing was the 'sustained discussion of the concept of welfare and the objectives it should seek to satisfy' that CPAG attempted to stimulate. Deakin continued: 'there are politicians on the left—and indeed, in the centre—of British politics who might in other circumstances be prepared to engage in sustained debate at this level; but the relentless running battle around the theme of "cuts" and the political importance of attacking or defending in detail all the individual elements in the complex benefits system has pre-empted their energies'.

In the event, as noted above, the Green Paper betrayed a faltering of purpose. With one or two exceptions, the potentially radical implications of its objectives for the future role of social security were not followed through to their logical conclusion in the specific proposals put forward.

This created something of a tactical dilemma for groups like CPAG. Should they burst the bubble of Mr Fowler's pretensions to the Beveridge tradition and underline that the Green Paper, beneath its handsome packaging, amounted to 'little more than a jumble of inconsistent elements' (Deakin (1987, p. 150))? Or should they accord it more status in order to demonstrate the perceived dangers of the direction in which the Green Paper was taking the social security system, even if with faltering steps?

This dilemma, together with the media's desire for more tangible news items, also probably helped to focus the ensuing political and media debate on issues of figures rather than principles. Although anticipated, the abolition of SERPS attracted the lion's share of media and political interest, which was indeed considerable at the time of the Green Paper. But it did not last. The White Paper, published just before Christmas, was completely overshadowed by the Westland affair even though, for the first time, the Government had put figures to its proposals which showed the number of losers would exceed the number of gainers. With the 'reprieve' of SERPS, interest in the reforms diminished and it was extremely difficult to generate much media or parliamentary interest as the Bill went through the Commons. Campaigning at the local level, which had been unusually strong, also subsided to some extent as the Bill disappeared into Parliament and the main proposals were postponed for a year—almost certainly until after the general election. It was easier for many people to comfort themselves with the delusion that it would never happen.

The social security reforms did not figure as an issue in the election campaign itself. But suddenly, about a month before they were due to be implemented, politicians and the media woke up to them and it was subsequently virtually impossible to turn on a radio or television or pick up certain newspapers without seeing some mention. John Moore felt it necessary to write to every Conservative MP to remind them of the main changes and the Government's justification for them, for, in the words of the political correspondent of *The Independent*, 'at Westminster the Conservative whips are talking about "putting on the steel hats" and taking cover . . . and the Opposition has woken up to the potential danger the benefit changes could do Mrs Thatcher' (Marr (1988)). The Leader of the Opposition returned to the issue day after day in Prime Minister's questions. The timing of the Act's implementation, a month after the announcement of what was widely recognized as a Budget for the rich, served to heighten political awareness. It seemed as though many MPs (including, we are told, the Prime Minister) only belatedly grasped what the changes are about and the implications for their constituents. For those who tried, without success, to impress on the media and politicians the significance of the reforms when the Bill was going through Parliament, this belated interest was frustrating indeed. Although it did produce some concessions, these go only a very small way towards meeting the widespread criticisms of the Act.

6. Conclusion

An Assessment

Five questions were posed earlier in this paper. They concerned the responsiveness of the Government to outside views in shaping its proposals, the depth and breadth of the analysis that shaped them and public access to this analysis, the Government's success in stimulating public debate and in achieving the consensus behind the reforms it claimed to be seeking, and the validity of the claims to follow in the footsteps of Beveridge. The verdict is overwhelmingly negative. The Fowler Review was strong on the language and trappings of public consultation and fundamental reforms but short on the true substance. From beginning to bitter end, Ministers repeatedly confused the two so that the fact that the product of the lengthy deliberations was ignored became irrelevant.

Consultation was rushed at each stage and access to key documents was denied. The Green Paper itself was a narrowly conceived affair that put forward only one set of options on the basis of limited analysis and without reference to the tax system. It failed to address what were widely seen to be the underlying problems of inadequate benefit levels and over-dependence on means-tested support. The Review did put social security on the political agenda for a time, but genuine public debate about alternative avenues of reform was short-lived and much of the subsequent debate was dominated by disputes over the numbers of gainers and losers. This hardly added up to the great debate about the future of welfare heralded by Mr Fowler.

Widespread and intense opposition to most of the main proposals had little impact on the final outcome—the main exceptions being where the Government did not want to alienate the business and pensions lobbies. It is therefore hardly surprising that Ministers signally failed to 'carry the great bulk of commonsense opinion' with them or to achieve even a modicum of political consensus behind the reforms. Complaints that MPs had spent more time debating the Act than was spent on debating Beveridge only served to underline the contrast between the degree of political support achieved for the two measures.

The widely perceived gap between the outcome of the Social Security Act 1986 and the promise when the Fowler Review was launched with a fanfare back in 1984 is illustrated nicely by a recent *Financial Times* editorial:

The installation of tough floor-to-ceiling barriers to protect staff in British benefit offices and a storm of protest from groups representing the disadvantaged constitute, by any standards, a disappointing reception for reforms which the Thatcher Government once claimed were as radical and exciting as those outlined by Sir William Beveridge in the 1940s. The social security changes being implemented this month have certainly not caught the popular imagination . . . Historians are likely to regard the 'Fowler' social security reforms as little more than a penny-pinching stopgap. They do not address the real problems, not least because of the narrowness of their scope. The hope must be that a future government will work on a larger canvas and not try to draw an artificial line between benefit reform and tax reform . . . We are still awaiting a 'new Beveridge'. (*Financial Times* (1988))

Lessons for the Future

As argued by the *Financial Times*, a key lesson for any future would-be Beveridge must be that social security reform cannot be carried out in splendid isolation. The case was made over a decade ago by the Central Policy Review Staff for a joint approach crossing departmental boundaries. In particular, social security reform must be co-ordinated with tax reform and the fiscal Welfare State must be scrutinized as closely as the cash-benefit Welfare State. If such a scrutiny is to be effective, it must be accompanied by reform of 'the Treasury's antique accounting methods which count cash benefits as public expenditure (and therefore bad) and tax relief as negative income (and therefore good)' and which, as Parker has persistently pointed out, 'are not only absurd but dangerous' (Parker (1985)).

Genuine open government and public consultation would require a number of reforms in the institutions of government. As Sir Douglas Wass has argued, there should be a statutory right of access (subject to considerations of national security) to government papers as they are produced so that outsiders can see the same information as that on which government takes its decisions. In the case of the Fowler Review, this would have included the reports of, and a summary of the evidence to, the review groups and any background papers. Genuine public debate would also be facilitated if a number of options for reform were presented, with clear indications at the outset of their respective costs and their likely impact on different claimant groups and family types, and without the strait-jacket of a nil-cost remit. The gainers and losers tables should have been made available at the Green Paper stage and, as Parker (1985) has argued, should have been accompanied by some model family analysis. Although this is only as good as the assumptions on which it is built, it has only been through such analysis that the targeting of cuts on some of the poorest working families with children has become clear.

Sir Douglas also suggested that policy proposals of this kind should first be referred to the relevant select committee before being debated by Parliament as a whole. An alternative, put to the Government at the time, would be to make use of the procedure which allows a standing committee to take evidence before its line-by-line scrutiny of a Bill. Where details are left to subordinate regulations and rules, MPs on the standing committee should be given a clear indication as to how it is intended to use such powers.

The experience of the Fowler Review also contains lessons for the poverty lobby. In particular, it has to address what emerged as a fundamental weakness during the Bill's passage through Parliament; namely, the gap between the strong local campaigning and the sophisticated national lobbying. Even sympathetic Conservative MPs observed that they had not received much mail on the issue from their constituents, in contrast to the bulging post-bags on, for example, Sunday trading and animal rights. CPAG is now attempting to address this weakness through the development of a network of Poverty Watch constituency contacts whose main job

will be to provide a local lobbying focus for the Group's national parliamentary work. Already, nearly 300 constituencies are covered by over 400
contacts. Thought has to be given as to how the implications for individuals
can be got across before rather than after legislation is implemented. As
Barclay (1988b) observed in the wake of the political furore once the cuts
started to bite, 'individual cases of hardship will in the end be more powerful to move our hearts than mere numbers'.

There is, though, a more fundamental problem reflected in those empty
Conservative post-bags. Notwithstanding the poverty lobby's attempts to
get across the message that the future of the social security system is an
issue that concerns us all, the Social Security Act does, in the shorter term,
primarily affect only poor people in receipt of means-tested benefits. The
'sharp elbows of the middle classes' (Field (1982, p. 90)) do not come to the
defence of benefits in which they have no stake. Poor people themselves
are not, by and large, people who write to their MPs. Those who did in the
end complain to their MPs were in the main not the poorest claimants but
those with savings of over £6,000. Active campaigning takes energy and
money, and many claimants are isolated and often unaware of what is
going to hit them until too late. (In this case, the belated outcry did force
some minor concessions after Conservative MPs woke up to the implications of parts of the legislation for some of their potential supporters,
including, in particular, those living in Finchley.) Moreover, as Robin
Cook (1987) has observed, 'a key element in our failure to resist the Fowler
offensive against social security was the impossibility of mobilising the vast
army of claimants to defend a DHSS by which they felt oppressed rather
than supported'.

The Politics of Social Security

Whitely and Winyard (1987, p. 153) have suggested that 'the tremendous
growth of state dependency in recent years has produced a situation where
claimants are a significant, possibly pivotal, voting block if they could be
mobilised around income maintenance issues'. It is, however, a big if. The
1983 British Election Study quoted in Whitely and Winyard showed that
those in receipt of supplementary or unemployment benefit are less likely
to vote than the population as a whole, a situation likely to be exacerbated
by the poll tax.

Growing polarization into what has been described as 'a one-third/two-
thirds' society (Gamble (1987)), combined with the cleavages in the elec-
toral map, points to the increasing political marginalization of the poor. On
the one side, as the Conservative historian Lord Blake (1987) has
observed, 'for long years past Conservatives in office or Opposition have
behaved nervously and cautiously on the assumption that they are the

party of the "haves" who are a minority, always under threat from the "have nots" who are a majority . . . Mrs Thatcher has instinctively realised that this dichotomy is no longer true. The "haves" are in one sense now the majority'. The 1988 Budget is the clearest expression yet of this realization. On the other side, Labour's election post-mortem focused on the need for the party to address itself to the 'have somes' as well as the 'have nots'. These developments take place against a background of traditional lack of interest in social security policy, amongst politicians. People living in poverty do not necessarily identify themselves according to the categories used by the poverty lobby and many do not wish to wear the label of poverty. This creates a dilemma for the poverty lobby, anxious on the one hand not to alienate poor people themselves and on the other not to adopt the sanitized language of the Green Paper which denies the reality of poverty.

The unexpectedly loud and widespread outcry once the Act was actually implemented does open a potential window of opportunity. As *New Society* (1988) observed, 'an important question is whether the unaccustomed limelight that the poor are now enjoying will have any longer term consequences . . . It is a large task to convert public outrage into political choice . . . This week's exposure of the poor's plight could be the last for another decade. Or it could, just possibly, provide the first step towards a different social vision'. Whether or not it does depends on whether politicians and the poverty lobby are willing and able to rise to the challenge.

In conclusion, assessment of the reform process leading up to (and beyond) the Social Security Act 1986 has to be set in the context of these wider factors that help shape the politics of social security. It is doubtful whether any institutional reforms would have made any significant difference to the outcome of this particular review. The Green Paper made absolutely clear that the Government's objectives for social security were closely intertwined with its wider political, economic, and ideological objectives. It was hardly going to sacrifice these in the interests of genuine public consultation and consensus.

13

The New Pension Scheme in Britain

JOHN CREEDY AND RICHARD DISNEY*

1. Introduction

In 1985, the Government proposed to abolish the State Earnings-Related Pension Scheme (SERPS), just 7 years after its introduction. This proposal was made in a Green Paper (DHSS (1985a, Cmnd 9517)) which followed what was claimed to have been 'the most fundamental examination of our social security system since the Second World War'. The resulting 'new approach' to social security involved a 'partnership between the individual and the state' in which it was argued that it is an 'altogether more sensible division of responsibility for government to concentrate on providing as good a basic pension as possible' while leaving the earnings-related component to the private sector. In fact, the Government quickly retreated from such a radical change and accepted the need for at least a residual earnings-related component in its White Paper (DHSS (1985b)). Nevertheless, the White Paper proposed numerous alterations to the state pension scheme, many of which were subsequently implemented in the Social Security Act 1986 and its associated legislation. These reforms are described in more detail in Section 3 of the present paper.

Apart from describing the new pension scheme, the paper also examines some of the economic implications of the new arrangements. As part of the background to the reform, and in view of the large number of changes to the pension scheme made in recent years, it is useful first to ask what kind of arguments have been made by the present government to justify its policies, and then to examine their internal consistency; this is done in Section 2. The main changes are then outlined in Section 3, while Section 4 examines some of the economic issues raised by pension reform. These are threefold: the likely effects on consumer choice and on the capital and labour markets. Somewhat surprisingly perhaps, these issues, especially

* John Creedy is the Truby Williams Professor of Economics at the University of Melbourne, Australia, and Richard Disney is a Professor at the University of Kent at Canterbury.
This paper was first published in *Fiscal Studies*, May 1988.
The authors would like to thank Andrew Dilnot and Ian Walker for useful comments on an earlier draft.

the impact on capital and labour markets, have been largely ignored in previous commentaries on the pension proposals.

2. The Rationale for Government Policy

Future Costs

Much recent policy has been motivated largely by the desire to reduce the share of government expenditure in national income. Social insurance expenditures are no exception. Reform of SERPS has only a minor short-run impact on public expenditure, because costs do not build up significantly until the end of the century. Nevertheless the Government became alarmed by the expected rise in costs under existing arrangements and the possible lack of flexibility when such large sums were committed. It suggested that the total cost of the pre-1986 state pension scheme would rise from £15.4 billion in 1984–5 to £45 billion in 2033–4 in real terms if the basic pension were adjusted in line with prices, and to £66.5 billion if adjusted in line with earnings (DHSS (1985a, Cmnd 9519, Table 2.10)). These forecasts alone were regarded as persuasive evidence of the need to change the scheme.

Although future costs rather than future tax rates have received the bulk of the attention, there is some discussion of the latter in government documents. For the pre-1986 scheme, the Government suggested that a combined employer and employee National Insurance rate of 18.6 per cent of earnings would be required by the year 2033–4 to finance the pensions component of social insurance, assuming a 6 per cent unemployment rate, average real earnings growth of $1\frac{1}{2}$ per cent per year, and with the basic pension indexed to prices.[1] Adding in expenditure on other contributory benefits, plus current rates of contributions to the National Health Service and to the Employment Protection Allocation, would raise the rate to 24.9 per cent. If the unemployment rate were to continue to be around 10 per cent, the joint contribution rate would be around $1\frac{1}{2}$ percentage points higher than this figure (Government Actuary's Department (1984)). Indexing the basic pension to earnings would also raise the contribution rate significantly.

The modifications proposed in the White Paper are expected to reduce the joint contribution rate by about 4 percentage points by 2033–4. The revised rate is described as 'one which future generations should be able to afford' (p. 20). This aspect was not discussed further in the White Paper,

[1] See DHSS (1985b, Appendix, Table 1). If real earnings growth is 1 per cent per annum, the contribution rate rises by about 3 percentage points. The impact of an unemployment rate change is described in the text. Indexing the basic pension to earnings raises the contribution rate by 5 percentage points.

although the idea of 'willingness to pay' taxes usually involves the basic idea of majority voting; a government that imposes excessive taxes will lose votes. But despite the fact that several pension schemes have been aborted by newly elected governments, 'willingness to pay' has by no means been the central political issue in British pension policy. Several commentators have pointed out that higher pension burdens have been absorbed in the past and may be sustainable in the future under alternative assumptions concerning retirement age, real earnings growth, and the unemployment rate (Piachaud (1985), Hammond and Morris (1986), and Nobles (1986a)).

An alternative way of interpreting the emphasis on total costs is that it reflects the view that the extent of inter-generational redistribution created by the state pension scheme will be excessive; future generations of working people will not be held by the implicit social contract involved. But this cannot be assessed simply by considering future contribution rates. The 'willingness to pay' of a generation in part depends on its perception of the signal which that sends to the next generation, who will in turn be obliged to underwrite its pensions. Thus a minimum of *three* generations must be taken into account in examining redistribution between generations.

In general, in a pay-as-you-go scheme such as the UK scheme in which present contributors finance present pension recipients, all generations will be better off under such an arrangement so long as the real rate of interest is less than the sum of the growth rates of population and real wages. Future generations can pay current commitments because they are richer. So even if the ratio of contributors to pensioners becomes more unfavourable, as is predicted to occur in the early part of the next century, a viable pay-as-you-go scheme can be sustained so long as real wages are growing steadily. Maintaining a high level of labour force participation and a low rate of inflation are therefore just as important as demographic factors in the long run.

On the other hand, the Government's intention that the private sector should play a greater role in pension provision raises the issue of the viability of fully funded schemes. A basic requirement for such a scheme, if it is to be able to maintain the living standards of pensioners, is that the real rate of interest should be positive. This allows the real value of the fund to be maintained. In the latest review of the contracting-out rebate by the Government Actuary's Department (1987), it is suggested that real interest rates, as measured by the 20-year return on equities minus increases in earnings, have averaged just under 3 per cent in recent years. Investment in long-dated fixed interest gilts has yielded a somewhat lower return. Therefore so long as real wages maintain a growth rate of around 2 per cent, the case for a pay-as-you-go scheme as opposed to a fully funded scheme is evenly balanced.

Other Criteria

In addition to total cost considerations, the Government briefly discussed the basic role of the State in providing contributory social security. It argued that the State 'must recognise the responsibility of government to establish an underlying basis of provision' (DHSS (1985a, Cmnd 9517, p. 1)). This 'underlying basis' is, however, difficult to decipher from the discussion in the Green Paper. It is not limited simply to cases where individuals are unable to obtain private insurance through some kind of market failure, for it is stated quite explicitly that 'the objective of relieving need does not lead simply to the conclusion that the state should provide *only* where all else fails' (Cmnd 9517, p. 3).

An alternative underlying basis for state provision would be for the State to provide a minimum income during retirement at or above the poverty level and dispense altogether with any formal requirements as to what form, if any, individual arrangements would take for additional pensions above this level. But this is disavowed in the Green Paper where, in considering the allocation of the contracted-out rebate, it is argued that:

there is a danger that some employers and employees would take a short-term view, preferring more take-home pay to the possible distant prospect of security in retirement. The government believes that it is important for everyone in work to have that security by building up a minimum additional pension to add to what they will receive from the state . . . Those with only the basic state pension would too often have to fall back on income-related benefits. (DHSS (1985a, Cmnd 9518, p. 4))

This is an interesting remark because it admits that the basic pension may continue to be inadequate for many people when compared with the standard of need laid down by the income support system. It also confirms that the Government has actually taken a strong paternalistic view in pension provision in the recent reform, in particular by limiting the free choice available to individuals concerning the allocation of their contracted-out rebate. In particular, the possibilities that a state scheme implies compulsory over-saving, and that individual welfare might be higher if there were greater freedom concerning the allocation of earnings over the life cycle, remain. On balance, however, the Government believes that potential under-saving is the greater problem, not least because inducing individuals to save sufficiently to raise them above the poverty threshold would reduce the expenditure on means-tested benefits for the elderly, currently running at some £3 billion annually and likely to rise as the number of pensioners increases.

In contrast, an important issue in pension policy which has been little discussed in recent initiatives is the redistributive impact of alternative pension schemes within generations. State pension schemes are rarely distributionally neutral: that is, different pensioners receive a different 'return' on their contributions. On the benefit side, state pension schemes involve non mutual eligibility conditions and entitlements such as the '20 best years' rule in the pre-1986 scheme and provisions for widows and widowers. On the finance side, the tax and National Insurance contribution schedules have both regressive and progressive segments, and interact in a complex manner. Add to these factors the contracting-out conditions and differential mortality of various income groups and it is clear that measuring lifetime redistribution is a complex issue. Nevertheless it is feasible to attempt to do so (Creedy (1982) and Creedy and Disney (1985)). Yet the Green Paper limited itself to the almost apologetic statement that 'we must accept that this [proposed change] involves some redistribution between different groups of people' (Cmnd 9517, p. 18). No further details were given.

Overall, therefore, the principles underlying the current pension reform appear confused. A desire to reduce future costs is clear, but there is little discussion of why this should be the guiding principle. In contrast, some issues which might be expected to underpin the extent and nature of public provision of pensions are only cursorily discussed. These issues include the extent to which some individuals are unable to obtain pensions, or annuities offering similar characteristics (notably some form of price indexation) in private markets, as well as the optimal degree of income transfer implied by a pension scheme, both between individuals of the same generation and between generations. Finally, although there is an expressed desire to allow greater choice of pension arrangement and to introduce greater flexibility into the system, there is a strong paternalistic element underpinning the reform. Of course, this confusion concerning motivation does not necessarily mean that the actual changes do not improve the system, and it is to the details of these changes that the next section turns.

3. The Main Changes to the Pension Scheme

The main elements of the new pension scheme can be summarized as follows:

1. SERPS entitlements are now based on an individual's average lifetime earnings rather than earnings in the best 20 years (although special arrangements will continue to be made for mothers who spend time out of the labour force, those with home responsibility, and those with incapacity credits). Earnings in each year continue to be adjusted using an index of average earnings.
2. Benefits paid out under SERPS are subject to a maximum of 20 per cent rather than 25 per cent of pensionable earnings. This reduced ceiling

will not affect those retiring in the state scheme until the next century, when the ceiling will be reduced by half a percentage point per year from the year 2000. Existing contracted-out schemes must now provide at least a guaranteed minimum pension (GMP) based on average life-time earnings at the new rate of earnings.

3. Previously, widows and widowers could inherit the whole of their spouse's state earnings-related pension, subject to the condition that the total pension could not exceed the amount which would have been paid to the deceased member. However, after 2000 only one-half of this pen-sion can be inherited, and therefore the upper limit on the total pension is less likely to be binding.

4. The complex contracting-out conditions will be relaxed so that occupa-tional schemes will only have to pay the GMP to members and surviving spouses. However, there is an important change to the indexation arrangements. Under the pre-1986 SERPS arrangements, the GMPs were not adjusted for inflation during the post-retirement period. Hence the state scheme had to pay the difference between the GMP and the value based on the best 20 years' earnings, in addition to financing the full amount of the inflation adjustment. Contracted-out schemes must now provide GMPs with inflation adjustment of up to 3 per cent per year, with any excess inflation adjustment financed by the Govern-ment.

5. It is now possible for further occupational schemes to contract out by providing a defined contribution plan, rather than the defined benefit plan involved in GMPs. Such 'money purchase' schemes need to pro-vide a guaranteed minimum level of contributions (GMC), set by the amount of the contracted-out rebate on National Insurance contribu-tions, which is 5.8 per cent from April 1988. For those who contract out into such schemes, the hypothetical value of their GMP will be deducted from their SERPS payment, although there is of course no guarantee that these contributions will secure the GMP. There is also an overall limit on contributions to such schemes, of 17.5 per cent of earn-ings, and up to 25 per cent of the accumulated fund can be taken as a tax-free lump sum on retirement.

6. Alternatively, individuals can contract out of SERPS (from July 1988) or their occupational scheme (from April 1988) and have their rebate paid, via the DHSS, into a personal pension (along the lines of Individ-ual Retirement Accounts in the United States). As with defined contri-bution plans, the accumulated value of contributions will be used at retirement to purchase a whole-life annuity from an insurance com-pany. Banks, unit trusts, and building societies can also operate such policies. Tax relief will be given on contributions and interest income, and the same rules concerning tax-free lump sums and maximum

contributions apply as with occupational pension schemes. Benefits can be available from as early as age 50 or indeed if retirement is due to ill health.

7. From October 1987, individuals who remain in an occupational scheme can choose to supplement these contributions with a free-standing additional voluntary contribution (AVC) to a personal pension plan. Occupational pension schemes must also provide facilities for AVCs. These contributions must not exceed 15 per cent of earnings excluding any contribution to the company scheme, and total benefits must not exceed the Inland Revenue maximum upon retirement (there is some controversy as to who is to monitor this ceiling).[2]

8. There is an incentive for new contracted-out occupational schemes and for personal pensions, in the form of an additional 2 per cent rebate on all earnings between the upper and lower earnings limits. This extra rebate will be given until April 1993 and is of course designed to make contracting out of SERPS a more attractive option. In 1983, some 9.6 million individuals were in contracted-out occupational pension schemes. The Government Actuary assumes that this extra rebate, as well as the greater variety of schemes on offer, will lead to an extra 1 million individuals contracting out of SERPS during the period (Government Actuary's Department (1987, no. 38)).

9. Under the pre-1986 arrangements, if someone left an employer after less than 5 years, the pension rights did not need to be preserved and the contributions could be returned to the individual. From April 1988, these rights must be preserved after only 2 years, or transferred to a new scheme, a personal pension, or a deferred annuity. This is designed to 'ensure that more people kept their pension savings invested for their retirement' (DHSS (1985b, p. 16)). If the pension rights are preserved, they must be indexed in line with prices up to 5 per cent per year until retirement.

10. Members of private schemes must receive 'relevant information' about pension rights and the size of the fund. Specific arrangements for investor protection are being reviewed (see also Nobles (1986a)).

This brief outline indicates that substantial changes to the operation of SERPS have been implemented, reflecting the aim of reducing future costs both by reducing benefits available under SERPS and by extra inducements to contract out. The Government Actuary's Department estimated that these changes would reduce the cost of SERPS by the year 2033–4 by one-half, allowing the combined National Insurance rate to be about 4 per-

---

[2] See *The Observer*, 18 October 1987. Apart from the maximum sum which can be taken tax-free, from March 1987 new entrants to occupational schemes are limited in their pension benefits to a certain fixed multiple of final year salary.

centage points lower than otherwise, as mentioned earlier. Notwithstanding the anticipated increase in contracting-out, the major source of this reduced contribution rate is the reduced benefits available under SERPS.

4. Economic Issues

Although there was a certain amount of debate both before and after the Green Paper concerning the merits or otherwise of maintaining SERPS, the economic consequences of the changes actually implemented in the 1986 Act have received little attention. This is not just because of the relative novelty of the new arrangements, but also stems from the complexity of choice now available and the difficulty in predicting the likely degree of switching between pension schemes as a result of the new arrangements. Nevertheless, some general issues can be raised, under the three broad headings which follow.

The Scope for Rational Choice

In principle, individuals now have the scope for several pension strategies: remaining in SERPS; remaining in or joining an occupational scheme, with or without AVCs; or leaving a group scheme entirely in order to purchase a personal pension. Defined contribution as well as defined benefit plans will be able to contract out. Finally, there are, of course, existing supplementary insurance policies on offer, with different regulations concerning tax-free lump sums and the age of benefit availability from those governing the new schemes (although some of these, such as so-called S226 self-employed pensions, cannot be newly taken up after July 1988 once personal pensions are on offer). However, the incentives available to switch between pension schemes are not uniform; for example, the extra 2 per cent contribution rebate is not available to individuals in an occupational scheme at January 1988 who leave their scheme in order to rejoin SERPS, or who switch from one occupational scheme to another.

One important point is that complex regulations have been introduced fairly rapidly. Consequently, the implications of the changes have not been fully assimilated by the public: a Gallup survey conducted at the end of 1987 for Abbey Life showed that only one in four respondents had heard of the forthcoming changes.[3] This corresponds with earlier findings, when the official survey of public attitudes to social security undertaken in 1984 by Gallup in preparation for the Green Paper proposals (see Cmnd 9519, Paper 4) showed that 41 per cent of employees did not know how much

---

[3] See 'Time to plan pensions', *The Observer*, 29 November 1987.

they paid in National Insurance contributions, only 31 per cent believed that these contributions paid, in part, for the state retirement pension, and 55 per cent of respondents had never heard of SERPS. This degree of ignorance is consistent with the long history of paternalism in social insurance provision but has serious implications.

The present reform presumes that competition among alternative types of pension will both force down administrative costs and generate the type of information needed to make rational decisions. Some companies do indeed offer free guides to the changes. But the Occupational Pensions Advisory Service, which offers free advice on pension matters, has decided to exclude all queries about personal pensions from its service. In general, the acquisition of full information will be costly, and rational individuals will trade the uncertain gains from better information against the costs of acquiring it. A substantial degree of inertia in pension arrangements can therefore be predicted as a result. This in itself is not irrational and may indeed be the best outcome for many individuals; most analysts suggest that contributors in SERPS aged over 40 should probably stick with SERPS, while those of similar age in occupational pension schemes should perhaps supplement their scheme by AVCs rather than shift to a personal pension. In contrast, younger individuals, particularly those in occupational schemes based on final earnings, may find a personal pension attractive in the light of the extra rebate. However, such shifts between pension schemes as do occur will have implications for both the capital and the labour markets.

In the case of SERPS, the expected individual pension depends not just on forecasts of future earnings and price inflation, but also on the type of indexation arrangements in operation. Unlike personal pensions, where benefits can be taken at any time from age 50, the state pension cannot be received until the retirement age, although receipt can be deferred for up to 5 years. Thus the age of initial state pension receipt is not wholly a decision variable. Nevertheless the value of reckonable earnings to accrue is one choice variable that will depend on a number of other variables, only some of which are within the control of the Government.

The tax structure and tax rates might be regarded as variables over which the Government does have influence and which should affect this decision, albeit not directly since contributions are levied on gross not net-of-tax earnings. Moreover, expected tax rates will affect work effort. Unfortunately the tax system and the social insurance system continue to be treated as quite separate issues in government policy, even though general taxes finance half of social security expenditure. The combined tax and contribution structure is now complex, given the National Insurance threshold effects, the upper earnings limit on the employee, and the shift to some degree of graduated contribution structure at the lower end of the schedule. This makes predictions of changes in work effort stemming from changes in basic tax rates difficult.[4]

The present indexation arrangements, in which the National Insurance earnings limits are indexed to prices in line with the basic state pension, also make calculation of present values difficult for the individual contributor. For if earnings continue to grow faster than prices, then the segment of the individual age–earnings profiles being cut off by the upper earnings limit may well increase steadily over time. The magnitude of the pensionable earnings which are used to calculate pension entitlements will increasingly be determined by the real value of the upper earnings limit, rather than the underlying age–earnings profile of the individual. This problem will be alleviated if the earnings limits are indexed to earnings, as indeed is assumed by the Government Actuary in calculating the future cost of state pensions (Cmnd 9519, Paper 2, Annex B), but this means breaking the link between the lower earnings limit and the basic state pension; this has not been done as yet.

Effects on Capital Markets

There are several potential effects on the capital market which may be briefly mentioned. These concern the viability of existing pension and related insurance schemes, the effect on total private savings, and the problem of indexation.

The first has been raised by some commentators, such as Nobles (1986b). If personal pensions prove particularly attractive to younger workers because of the extra rebate and the fact that the structure of benefits in occupational schemes benefits older workers, those occupational schemes may find their long-term future in doubt; they may be left with older workers accruing the more expensive pensions. So long as more senior workers have a dominant voice in defined benefit plans, the structure of benefits is unlikely to alter. Hence, it is argued, employers will have an incentive to shift to providing defined contribution plans. On the other hand, it can equally be argued that in so far as the changes concerning the preservation of pension rights (which is referred to as vesting) favour remaining in occupational schemes, and so long as inflation forecasts and pension fund asset accruals allow schemes to offer incentives to contributors, the viability of existing schemes is not to be seriously doubted.

The second issue concerns the rate of saving, and here the outcome is also difficult to forecast. The introduction of personal pensions and AVCs may raise the rate of personal saving, so affecting such economic variables as the rate of interest and the level of aggregate demand. The aggregate

---

[4] But see, for example, Blundell, Meghir, Symons, and Walker (1986).

private saving rate may also rise if contracting out of SERPS (a pay-as-you-go scheme) increases significantly.[5] The impact on economic variables, notably aggregate economic activity, resulting from these changes is difficult to quantify, for an increase in saving may reduce consumption directly but raise it indirectly through lower interest rates and other wealth effects. To the extent that these types of saving substitute for other types of private saving, such as life insurance and direct purchase of equities and bonds, there will be limited effects on aggregate consumption. But there may be an impact elsewhere, such as on the ease of borrowing to finance the public sector borrowing requirement (PSBR). Moreover, even if there is full offset on private saving, the reform may have non-neutral effects if wealth holders with differing portfolios respond in disparate ways to changes in relative asset prices.

Some evidence on the likely impact of the new arrangements on private saving exists from the parallel experience of North America. Work by Venti and Wise (1987) on the introduction of Individual Retirement Accounts (IRAs) in the US suggests that most saving in IRAs was net new saving rather than substituting for saving in other financial assets. This is perhaps a surprising result, although a similar experience is reported in Canada, where IRA-type schemes were promoted in the early 1970s, after which the Canadian savings rate rose sharply relative to the US. In the long run, however, even if saving for personal pensions does not lead to substitution effects among other financial assets, it may well substitute for wider kinds of asset purchase (notably housing). In addition, in the UK context, the capital market will be affected by the reduction in compulsory saving through National Insurance contributions, given the downgrading of benefits available under SERPS.[6]

Third, there is the effect of the changes in indexation provisions, in particular the new requirement that occupational schemes must provide for up to 3 per cent inflation. The rationale for post-retirement indexation of private benefits has been hotly debated in the United States (see, for example, Pesando (1984) and Feldstein (1985)). There is some evidence that the greater the degree of benefit indexation in individual schemes, the lower the starting level of benefits (Allen, Clark, and Sumner (1986)). Essentially individuals are being offered a hedge against future inflation, or

[5] Calculations by the Government Actuary (Government Actuary's Department (1987)) suggest, however, that the degree of contracting-out makes little difference to National Insurance contribution rates in the long run. By 2033–4, the contribution rate will only be 0.2 per cent lower if additional numbers contracted-out rise from 500,000 to 5 million. This is because the contracted-out rebate will have fallen significantly by that time.

[6] In general, there are pitfalls in estimating substitution effects using data on contributions to private pension schemes derived from studies of household expenditure, particularly where not all occupational schemes are contributory or fully funded. See Hemming and Harvey (1983).

an 'implicit contract' in which the scheme bears some of the risk of unanticipated price fluctuations in exchange for lower starting pensions. A compulsory indexation provision can be justified if it can be shown that individuals are significantly risk-averse, that pension funds have better information than individuals, or are able to operate portfolio strategies which yield better returns or better hedging opportunities than individuals. However, the fact that many occupational schemes already provide some degree of inflation protection suggests that at least one of these conditions is satisfied. Finally, it would seem likely that pension funds would require some degree of reinsurance in such circumstances through the purchase of index-linked bonds or other assets. If such assets exist, however, the issue is again raised of why individuals are unable to utilize such opportunities themselves (see Diamond (1977)) and the case for compulsory indexation rests on the hypothesis of significant capital market imperfection.

Effects on Labour Markets

A central concept here is that of pensions as deferred pay, although this aspect was ignored in both the Green and White Papers. Essentially a pension scheme is a device for shifting earnings to a later stage of the life cycle. Individual employees may wish to take advantage of tax and other benefits available through company pension schemes which cannot be obtained through other methods of private saving. They may also wish to shift earnings from periods when they face high marginal tax rates to periods when such rates are lower (a strategy which the Government usually seeks to limit by imposing a maximum limit on the proportion of earnings which can be saved through pension contributions).

Employers may also find pensions attractive as a form of deferred pay in reducing personnel turnover and its associated costs, especially when a long period of training is required. Such arrangements can therefore be regarded as forming part of an implicit long-term contract, the attraction of which to employees depends on their rate of time preference, their attitude towards risk, the reputations of firms for fulfilling such long-term agreements, and the regulations governing pension portability. Nevertheless not all firms find a strategy of deferred pay attractive, especially where turnover costs are low and training costs minimal.[7] This raises the possibility that there are individual employees who are constrained, in the sense that they would wish to take advantage of the opportunities for deferring pay in

[7] Not surprisingly, Green, Hadjimatheou, and Smail (1985) find that entitlement to a private pension among individuals depends on occupational group and positively on length of job tenure.

an occupational pension scheme but are unable to do so because their employer does not offer one. The assumption that such a group exists was among the explicit reasons for the original introduction of an earnings-related state pension scheme, and it will be interesting to see whether the development of group money purchase schemes and personal pensions will also be taken up by individuals not currently in occupational schemes.

The opposite argument may also have some credence, however. Just as the post-retirement indexation arrangements offer a trade-off between initial annuity value and protection against unanticipated price changes, so the existence of pension schemes offers the choice of a trade-off between current and deferred pay. Current pay will be lower to the extent that a pension scheme is an additional pecuniary advantage of the job. This is, of course, a compensating differential. In such circumstances, the stimulus of an extra rebate to newly contracted-out individuals may provide an undesirable distortion and it is not obvious that use of this particular subsidy is optimal.

A similar argument can be used concerning the reduction in the vesting period from 5 years to 2. In defined benefit plans, employees pay the bulk of their contributions at an early age (whereas the employer's cost increases with age) so that earlier vesting, combined with the restriction that mobile workers cannot take a lump sum, will mainly limit the individual's choice over the allocation of their own contributions. Furthermore, delayed vesting is commonly used by firms as an incentive for workers to remain with an organization so that the costs of training may be recovered. If vesting is obtained much earlier, one possible implication is that age–earnings profiles will become steeper and it is not obvious that workers will be better off in general (see Pesando and Rea (1977)).

Finally, there is the development of defined contribution (money purchase) plans in addition to defined benefit plans. If there are individuals who would wish to take advantage of pension plans but are unable to do so at present through a defined benefit plan, the introduction of such plans is desirable. There is some evidence that new plans of this type are being introduced as a result of the reform (Industrial Relations Service (1987)). Nevertheless it would be useful to ask why defined contribution plans have not proved more popular in the past, and it may well turn out that the uncertainty with such plans as to whether the GMP will actually be achieved is important. In particular, if some firms are tempted to substitute defined contribution plans for defined benefit plans in order to limit defections among younger workers, then welfare will be lower for other individual employees who are significantly risk-averse. However, to the extent that contribution schemes can on average yield a greater surplus over the GMP than defined benefit plans, these individuals will be compensated for the greater risk involved.

5. Conclusions

This paper has given a brief guide to the motivations underlying the reform of the state pension scheme, to the reform itself (primarily the provisions of the Social Security Act 1986), and some preliminary ideas as to the impact of these new arrangements on individual choice and on capital and labour markets.

Section 2 argued that long-run cost considerations underpinned the changes to SERPS and that these changes are expected to halve its costs by 2033–4. It suggested that other motives for state intervention in the pension field had been only cursorily discussed by the Government, although it was revealing that the Government anticipates that the basic pension by itself will continue to be insufficient to raise most individual pensioners above the income support level. Furthermore, although the reform offers the individual a much greater choice of pension plan, which has generally been welcomed, there continues to be a strong paternalistic bias to government intervention.

Section 3 described the provisions of the reform in some detail. The most significant are the changes to the benefits available under SERPS, notably the shift to lifetime average earnings rather than the '20 best years' rule in calculating benefits, and the new provision for widows and widowers; the relaxation of rules in order to allow defined contribution schemes and individual pension plans to contract out; the requirement that contracted-out schemes must contain some degree of post-retirement indexation of benefits against price changes; and the alteration to the minimum vesting period.

Some implications of the reforms were discussed in Section 4, these issues being the implications for consumer choice and for the capital and labour markets. Considering first consumer choice; it was suggested that the wider variety of schemes allowed to contract out would enhance this, but that the Government was relying on the private sector to provide adequate information. Although inertia in pension strategy might in fact prove rational for many individuals given their expected lifetime income and consumption plans, there was a potential problem in the cost of acquiring impartial information concerning available choices. The difficulties of forecasting future benefits under SERPS, especially given present indexation arrangements, were also mentioned.

The impact on capital markets would be determined by a number of factors. First, the question of the soundness of existing occupational schemes was raised, given the types of individual who might take up the personal pension option. The effect of the wider range of choice on the rate of private saving was discussed, and evidence from other countries suggested that the introduction of such schemes might in the short run raise the rate of private saving (assuming sufficient take-up of the new schemes) rather than substitute for other forms of financial asset saving. In the long run, other asset holding, notably housing, might be affected, and account should be taken of the reduction in contribution rates associated with the downgrading of SERPS benefits. It was also suggested that the new indexation arrangements implied lower starting values of annuities and rested on the implicit assumption that capital markets are to some degree imperfect.

In the labour market, it was argued that pensions were a form of deferred pay, and that compensating differentials might exist by which individual employees traded lower current earnings for higher future benefits. To the extent that employees faced an unconstrained choice between alternative current/deferred pay mixes, an extra rebate to encourage contracting-out was a suboptimal use of resources. But to the extent that individuals were constrained (i.e. wanted deferred pay schemes which firms were not prepared to offer), the establishment of new forms of contracted-out schemes would increase welfare. It would have been useful had the official survey of attitudes to social security asked directly whether individuals were constrained in the choice of occupational pension scheme on offer. Last, it was suggested that if firms wished to switch from defined benefit to defined contribution schemes (although they would not receive the extra rebate), the shift in the notional incidence of risk-bearing would not prove attractive to all individuals. There is clearly much scope for further interesting and useful research on all these issues.

14

The 1988 Social Security Reforms

ANDREW DILNOT AND STEVEN WEBB[*]

1. Introduction

The Social Security Act 1986 represented the culmination of more than 2 years of consultation and debate about the future of social security in the UK. The Act introduced major changes to the system of income-related benefits which were only fully implemented in April 1988, as well as changes to the structure and level of both state and private pension provision in the UK. In this paper we set out the Government's case for these reforms, and outline the principal measures contained in the 1986 Act. Concentrating mainly on the changes to income-related benefits, we move on to provide a detailed analysis of the impact of the structural changes on various groups in the benefit-receiving population. Finally we present an evaluation of the changes, noting the improvements that have been made, but highlighting the limitations of the changes and the areas where serious problems still remain.

2. The Government's Case for Reform

The 1985 White Paper *Reform of Social Security* (DHSS (1985b)) identified five 'clear and fundamental' defects of the social security system as it then stood. These related to the complexity of the system, the failure to give effective support to particular needy groups, the problems faced by those 'trapped' in poverty or unemployment because of the tax and benefit system, the effects of the system on individual freedom of choice, and the implications of present social security policies for future generations of taxpayers. We consider each in turn.

* Andrew Dilnot is a Programme Director and Steven Webb a Research Officer at the Institute for Fiscal Studies.

This paper was first published in *Fiscal Studies*, August 1988.

The work is part of the IFS project on the distributional implications of fiscal policy, which is supported by the Economic and Social Research Council and the Gatsby Foundation.

Complexity

One of the Government's principal aims in reforming the UK social security system was to reduce its complexity. It argued that the system as it stood in the mid-1980s was too complex, both for claimants and for administrators. The result was that the public was left, in the words of the White Paper, 'dissatisfied . . . and at times bewildered'.

The main source of complexity identified by the Government was the piecemeal way in which the social security system had developed since the Second World War. The Green Paper of June 1985 (DHSS (1985a, Cmnd 9517)) refers to 'forty years of tinkering', and the Government's own proposals are presented as a new approach designed to help a wayward system to find its way.

The description of the existing social security system as complex was largely uncontentious. The system encompassed thirty separate benefits, with differing structures and rationales, and cost over £2 billion annually to administer. An example of the lack of coherence which particularly concerned the Government was in the structure of income-related benefits. Though entitlement to supplementary benefit (SB), family income supplement (FIS), and housing benefit (HB) was related to income, the definition of income used in each case was different, and the rules relating to capital also differed between SB and the other benefits. Furthermore, the increases in each benefit allowed for dependants varied considerably, creating problems when particular claimants moved from one benefit to another.

A different source of complexity which also attracted the Government's attention was the way in which some benefits, and SB in particular, had been very closely tailored to meet individual needs. Under SB, in addition to basic payments of benefit which depended on family composition, age, and housing status, regular weekly additions were available for specific items such as heating, laundry, and special diets. One-off 'single payments' were also made to cover particular occasional needs such as for cookers, bedding, etc.

The Government argued that this tailoring had gone too far and that 'the basic purpose of the scheme [tended] to be swamped by the extra additions to it' (Green Paper, Cmnd 9517, p. 31). Its case was that the basic purpose of the benefit was to provide a regular weekly income for claimants. It argued that having a range of additions meant that some entitlement often went unclaimed by those who did not understand the system, required an 'undesirable degree of intrusion into claimants' lives', and led to administrative complexity' (p. 31). Both the Green and White Papers pointed out that SB alone required 38,000 staff to administer it, and the most recent published figures confirm the administrative burden of SB. In 1985–6, SB cost £839 million to administer, or 11 per cent of expenditure on that benefit, compared with £148 million or 3 per cent for housing benefit, and £233 million or 1.4 per cent for retirement pensions.

Failure to Support those in Greatest Need

The Government's second argument for reform of the social security system was that it had failed to respond to changing patterns of need. Analysis in the Green Paper showed that whilst the share of the poorest 20 per cent in total net income had remained broadly constant since the early 1970s, the composition of that group had changed considerably. It was the Government's contention that the system had failed to respond adequately to this change.

The group with which the Government was particularly concerned was families with children, both in and out of work. The proportion of those in the poorest fifth of society who were either couples with children or single parents had risen from around 48 per cent in 1971 to 58 per cent in 1982, compared with a fall in the proportion of pensioners in the poorest fifth from 35 per cent to 19 per cent over the same period. This growth in poverty amongst families with children had occurred despite the introduction in 1971 of family income supplement—a benefit available only to those with children—and the Government argued that more needed to be done for this group.

The same analysis also showed that the proportion of single people of working age amongst the poorest fifth had risen from around 10 per cent in 1971 to nearly 16 per cent in 1982. It was, however, argued that this group was less of a priority since many members of the group would be nonhouseholders living in households with higher incomes. The implication of this reasoning was that the State should not be the first source of support when alternative sources of help were available. This is a view which has underpinned many of the Government's changes in the field of social security.

The Poverty and Unemployment Traps

The third perceived defect of the old system identified by the Government related to the anomalous interaction of the various benefits both with one another and with the tax system. The Government noted that because of such interactions, individuals could find themselves 'trapped in poverty'. Such a situation would arise when a pay increase or a move to a better-paid job brought little or no net financial gain, because of higher taxes and National Insurance (NI) contributions and lower benefit receipt. Similarly, individuals might be 'trapped' in unemployment where the loss of benefits and increase in tax from taking a job at all could largely offset the extra income from employment. Both of these situations were regarded as creating undesirable disincentives to 'work and self-help' (Green Paper, Cmnd 9517, p. 24), and it was an aim of the Government in the reform to lessen the extent of these perceived disincentive effects. The Government argued that it was already making progress on these problems by means of its tax-cutting policy, but that reform of the social security system was also required to remove the worst anomalies.[1]

The most extreme form of the poverty trap, where a marginal increase in gross income could actually leave an individual worse off, principally affected low-income families in work with children. It was through a combination of withdrawal of FIS and HB, and increases in income tax and NI that such families could find themselves losing out. Only through a lower combined rate of withdrawal of FIS and HB could the extent of the poverty trap be reduced.

It was also families with children who typically suffered most from the effects of the unemployment trap. Benefits for larger families and those with older children in particular were significantly more generous when the parents were out of work than in work, and this created a potential financial disincentive for such parents to seek a job. A solution to this 'trap' thus required an adjustment in the relative level of benefits for those in and out of employment. In both of these cases, it was clear that reform of the structure and extent of benefits to families with children would be central to the Government's plans.

Restriction of Individual Freedom

This criticism of the existing social security system was concerned with the area of pension provision, and in particular with the extent to which individuals were free to make their own provision for retirement rather than relying solely on state provision. The Government's contention was that the scope for individuals to make their own provision for retirement was too restricted and that this was an infringement of individual freedom which led to an unnecessary encroachment of the State on the private sector.

As it stood in 1985, the structure of pension provision was that individuals made National Insurance contributions (NICs) throughout their working lives, and on retirement received a state pension. This pension had two components: a basic flat-rate pension (with additions for dependants) paid either in full or at a reduced rate to all who satisfied certain minimum contribution requirements, and an earnings-related component dependent upon the amount of NICs that had been paid. Participation in the earnings-

---

[1] See Dilnot and Stark (Ch. 9, this volume) for a discussion of the role of tax policy in reducing the poverty trap.

related part of the state pension scheme was not, however, compulsory, and individuals could 'contract out' of the state scheme provided they joined an approved occupational pension scheme. The individual and his employer would then be allowed to pay a lower rate of NICs.

There were, however, considerable restrictions on the type of occupational schemes which an individual was allowed to join in place of the state earnings-related scheme. Furthermore, the returns to such employer-specific schemes for those who changed jobs frequently were often unattractive. The Government argued that these restrictions and limitations were now discouraging individuals who would otherwise wish to make their own provision, and also discouraging employers who might be prepared to offer a scheme. They cited as evidence the fact that the percentage of the work-force covered by occupational schemes had remained stagnant over the last two decades, standing at just 51 per cent in 1983 compared with 49 per cent in 1963. The Government thus argued that measures were needed to provide a further incentive to private pension provision.

Finance in the Next Generation[2]

This fifth problem of the social security system as detailed by the Government related specifically to the State Earnings-Related Pension Scheme (SERPS). The Government was concerned about the likely growth in cost of the scheme and in particular about the impact of this growth on taxpayers in the next century.

SERPS was introduced in 1978 and was structured so that entitlement to pension would depend on an individual's contributions to the scheme over the best 20 years of their working life. It was also to be an unfunded scheme—that is to say, the entitlement of a given year's pensioners would be met out of general government revenues from the NI contributors of that year rather than from the accumulated contributions of the pensioners themselves.

One consequence of the 'best 20 years' rule was that the full cost of the scheme would not be seen until well into the next century. This was because it would be 1998 before any person had 20 years of contributions into the scheme, and the cost would continue to grow beyond then as more people had 20 years of contributions and as people with more than 20 years of contributions would be able to choose their best 20 years. At the same time, because of the unfunded nature of the scheme, those costs would have to be met by the taxpayers of the next century.

The amounts of money involved were very large indeed, as is inevitably the case when state pension schemes are discussed. The Green Paper

---

[2] For a more detailed discussion of this issue, see Creedy and Disney (Ch. 13, this volume).

suggested that the cost of the state pension scheme, both basic and earnings-related, would rise from £15.4 billion in 1984–5 to £45 billion in 2033–4 in real terms if pensions were uprated in line with prices, and to £66.5 billion if they were uprated in line with earnings. The Government believed that previous assumptions about the cost of the scheme had been too optimistic. It argued that this, combined with a drop in the proportion of people of working age in the population in the next century, would place an intolerable burden on the next generation's taxpayers. These figures were seen to be worrying enough to make reform necessary.

3. The 1986 Social Security Act

The programme of social security reform overseen by the then Secretary of State for Social Services, Mr Norman Fowler, culminated in July 1986 with the passing of the Social Security Act. In this section we describe the main measures contained in the Act, considering first the changes to the structure of income-related benefits and then the changes relating to pension provision.

The Changes to Income-Related Benefits

The 1986 Act set out plans for a major restructuring of the system of income-related benefits. Some of the measures were implemented soon after the passage of the Act, but the main changes finally came into effect in April 1988. Here we present an overview of the main features of those changes, before looking in more detail at the individual benefits concerned.

One of the main features of the new benefit system was that the relationship between the three principal income-related benefits was rationalized. For the first time, entitlement to income support (which replaced supplementary benefit), family credit (which replaced FIS), and housing benefit was on the same basis.

In the first place, the needs allowances for families of different sizes were brought into line between the various benefits. Previously, each of the main income-related benefits used a quite different approach to reflect the varying needs of families of different sizes. The definition of income which applied to all three was to be net income—that is, income after the deduction of income tax and NI. Previously, entitlement to SB had been based on net income, whilst entitlement to FIS and HB had been based on gross income. The rules relating to capital were also unified so that claimants with capital above a specified ceiling would be disqualified from receiving any income-related benefit. Previously, only SB had had such a capital cut-off. Altogether, the structure of income-related benefits was made more uniform and the relationship between the benefits more coherent.

A second principal feature of the changes was that they involved a shift in resources away from housing benefit and into the new family credit and income support. The effect of the structural changes alone was to reduce expenditure on housing benefit by around £650 million compared with the old scheme, and to increase expenditure on family credit and income support by around £220 million. There was also an initial allocation of around £200 million (later increased by a further £70 million) to provide transitional protection for those recipients of income support or family credit who would otherwise have found themselves worse off as a result of the changes. These figures do, however, also reflect the requirement that all ratepayers should pay a minimum of 20 per cent of their rates, which might alternatively be seen as part of the reform of local authority finance. To exclude this change from the above figures would reduce the cut in housing benefit by around two-thirds. However, the increase in expenditure on income support reflects compensation for an average 20 per cent contribution to rates, and if this compensation is similarly excluded (for consistency) then there is probably a small net reduction in overall expenditure on income support.

Overall, the reforms represented a shift in benefit payments from those dependent primarily on housing benefit, such as pensioners, to recipients of family credit (by definition families with children), and also to recipients of income support. Again, amongst the main beneficiaries from the changes for those on income support were families with children.

A third main feature of the reforms was that they involved a good deal of structural simplification. The precise measures are described in detail in the sections on the individual benefits below, but housing benefit and supplementary benefit in particular are substantially simplified as part of the reform package.

We turn now to the measures relating to the individual benefits.

Family Credit   Family credit is designed to supplement the incomes of low-income families in full-time work with children. It is a more extensive benefit than the family income supplement which it replaced, going to around 470,000 recipients in 1988–9 compared with the 210,000 recipients of FIS in 1987–8.

The basis of assessment for family credit is the net income of the claimant, together with that of the spouse where the claimant is married. Each claimant is entitled to an allowance known as an adult credit, with additional credits for each child, depending upon the age of the child. If the claimant's net income exceeds a specified threshold, family credit entitlement is reduced by 70 per cent of any such excess. Claimants with capital in excess of a given limit are not entitled to family credit. The children of families in receipt of family credit are not entitled to free school meals.

A structural improvement contained in the new benefit is that the additions for children available under family credit are linked to those available under income support. This means that the increase in overall benefit for each child is the same regardless of whether the parent is unemployed (and on income support) or in work (and on family credit).[3] This reform is designed to end the disparity between benefits for those in and out of work which led to the unemployment trap. For similar reasons, the threshold for family credit above which benefit starts to be withdrawn is the same as the basic personal allowance (see section on income support below) for a married couple on income support.

The switch from gross to net income as the basis of assessment for family credit also represents a structural improvement, designed in this case to end the worst cases of the poverty trap. Where a pay increase results in higher income tax and/or NI payments, this will now be taken into account when entitlement to benefit is reassessed, and the resulting fall in benefit will, for taxpayers at least, in general be smaller than under the old family income supplement. (Family income supplement was withdrawn at a rate of 50 per cent of any increase in gross income.) This change, together with a similar change in the basis of assessment for housing benefit, will ensure that an increase in gross income will always leave an individual better off overall, although the gain may still be very slight.

Housing Benefit   The single housing benefit scheme set out in the 1986 Social Security Act replaced the two previous schemes of housing benefit, one operating for recipients of SB and the other for all others on low incomes. The new benefit operates on a smaller scale than the benefit which it replaces, with expenditure of around £650 million less as a result of the restructuring alone.

Housing benefit meets up to 100 per cent of the rent and up to 80 per cent of the domestic rates of claimants. Payments of mortgage interest are not covered by housing benefit, but those not in full-time work may get assistance with these costs under income support. In common with the other income-related benefits, entitlement to benefit is based on net income, and benefit is not available to those with capital above a specified limit.[4]

---

[3] The child credit available under family credit when added to the value of child benefit is equal to the allowance for a child under income support plus the value of free school meals.

[4] This limit was originally set at the same level (£6,000 in 1988–9) as for the other benefits, but when the scheme was introduced in April 1988 the limit was quickly raised to £8,000 when it became clear that some pensioners in particular stood to lose heavily from the introduction of a capital limit into the housing benefit scheme.

The needs allowances and premiums under housing benefit are in general the same as those available under income support.[5] For claimants with net income above this level, help with rent and rates is steadily reduced. The Green Paper proposed a single taper for reduction of housing benefit as income rose, but this suggestion was dropped in favour of a dual taper. Where net income (after disregards) exceeds the needs allowance, help with rent is reduced by 65 per cent of any excess, and help with rates by 20 per cent of the excess. Deductions are made from benefit when there are 'non-dependants' in the household who are deemed to be making some contribution to housing costs.

One of the major structural improvements in the reformed housing benefit is the consistent basis of assessment for all claimants, whether they are in or out of work. Previously, those in work received less generous help, and an extra benefit, housing benefit supplement, had to be introduced to help those who would otherwise have had net incomes after housing costs which were below the supplementary benefit line. As a result of the restructuring, the need for housing benefit supplement is removed.

The system of tapers for withdrawal of housing benefit as income rises has also been radically simplified. Under the old system there were six separate tapers at which help could be withdrawn, and the move to a dual taper system marks a move to a more rational structure for the benefit. As noted above, the switch to net income as the basis for assessment will also help to relieve some of the worst problems of the poverty trap.

The introduction of a capital cut-off into housing benefit improves the coherence of the system by bringing HB into line with income support. The change will, however, hit groups such as pensioners particularly hard.

Income Support   Income support, which replaced supplementary benefit, is the main benefit for those with low incomes not in full-time work.[6] The basic benefit is comprised of a personal allowance with increases for dependants, and this may be supplemented by one or more 'premiums' available for particular groups of claimants (families with children, single parents, the elderly, and the sick and disabled). There are no additions for specific needs such as heating or laundry, and 'residual' housing costs such as water rates are no longer met under the benefit. Those with savings in excess of a given ceiling (£6,000 in 1988–9) are not eligible for the benefit. (This compares with a limit of £3,000 under supplementary benefit.)

The system of 'single payments' for one-off needs which was operated

[5] The exception to this pattern is lone parents, who receive a higher premium under housing benefit than under income support. This is in part a compensation for the loss of the favourable treatment which lone parents enjoyed under the old system.
[6] For the purpose of income support and family credit, full-time work is defined as 24 hours a week or more.

under the old supplementary benefit system was abolished and replaced by a scheme of grants and loans from a 'Social Fund'. This aspect of the changes is discussed separately below.

The new structure of income support represents a significant simplification compared with supplementary benefit. The distinctions between householders and non-householders and between long-term and short-term rates of benefit disappear, although a new distinction has been introduced between single claimants under and over the age of 25. The abolition of regular payments for additional requirements will bring a significant administrative saving, given that more than 3 million of the 5 million SB recipients in 1986 were receiving such payments.

The structure of premiums for particular claimant groups contained in income support will result in a redistribution of benefit receipts amongst the poorest benefit recipients. In particular, the new premiums for families with children and for lone parents favour these groups at the expense of childless couples and single people, whilst the significant extra needs of the oldest claimants are recognized for the first time by a higher premium for the over-80s. These changes should, however, be seen in the context of the abolition of payments for additional requirements which might also have gone to many members of these groups.

Social Fund The main income-related benefits outlined above are designed to provide a guaranteed income to cover the regular needs of claimants. However, when exceptional needs arise which may be difficult to meet from regular weekly income, help may be available from the Social Fund. The Social Fund replaced the system of single payments available for supplementary benefit recipients and the system of urgent needs payments available for others in need. It also replaced the previously separate schemes which provided help with maternity and funeral costs.

There are three main types of assistance available under the Social Fund. First, there are grants to help with funeral expenses (for any recipient of an income-related benefit) and maternity costs (for recipients of income support or family credit only). These grants are not repayable and may be claimed as of right by those who satisfy the necessary conditions. Second, there are 'community care grants'. These payments are intended principally to assist those coming out of residential care or to assist people in trying to remain in the community. They are not repayable but are available only at the discretion of local Social Fund officers. Finally there are repayable 'budgeting loans' and 'crisis loans'. Like community care grants, these loans are available only at the discretion of local officers, who have to evaluate which claimants should have prior claim on resources from the local cash-limited budget.

Both budgeting loans and crisis loans are repayable by deductions from weekly benefit, typically at a rate of 15 per cent of weekly benefit and over a normal maximum period of 78 weeks. Both the rate of repayment and the period of repayment may, however, be varied according to individual circumstances, within pre-defined limits.

The Government argued that the old system of single payments was proving unsatisfactory for a number of reasons. In the first place, the cost of the scheme had been increasing rapidly. Between 1982 and 1984 real expenditure on single payments doubled whilst the number of SB recipients rose by around one-tenth. Second, it was argued that the complexity of the scheme was leading to an unacceptable inequality of outcomes. It was noted in the Green Paper that around 80 per cent of single payments in any one year were going to 9 per cent of claimants, and it was suggested that complexity might be a bar to other claimants. Third, it was argued that the regulated basis of entitlement to single payments was too rigid and that this created a lack of flexibility and meant that resources were being poorly targeted. For all of these reasons, the Government sought to restructure the whole system of help for those with exceptional needs.

A major distinguishing feature of the Social Fund is the discretionary nature of many of the payments. This change is intended by the Government to improve flexibility locally and to ensure that resources are targeted more effectively. The discretionary elements of the Fund are cash-limited, which is designed to improve financial control. The new role for loans is also expected to reduce overall expenditure. As early as 1989–90, the loans element of the Fund is expected to be self-financing as new loans are made out of the repayments of previous recipients.

The Changes to Pension Provision

It is probably in the proposed changes to State Earnings-Related Pension Scheme provision that we see the greatest differences between the Green Paper of June 1985 and the subsequent White Paper and Social Security Act. Almost all of the main benefits were in the end reformed in a slightly different manner from that proposed in the Green Paper. However, the Green Paper's proposed reform of SERPS was abandoned completely.

In the Green Paper, the Government proposed the complete abolition of SERPS, only 7 years after its introduction. The argument was put that an 'altogether more sensible division of responsibility for government [was] to concentrate on providing as good a basic pension as possible' (p. 22). Transitional arrangements to protect those who had already started to contribute to the scheme were proposed, as were incentives for the much wider provision of occupational and personal pensions. Opposition to the abolition of SERPS came quickly from a large variety of groups, and the Government abandoned the idea of abolition in the White Paper issued in late 1985. However, while no longer proposing its removal, SERPS was to be subject to a number of reforms, the main aim of which was to reduce its cost in the long term. Alongside these changes to SERPS were a set of proposals to encourage private and individual pension provision.

The main changes aimed to reduce the generosity, and thus cost, of SERPS were three. First, the SERPS pension was to be based on average *lifetime* earnings rather than the average of the best 20 years. Second, 20 per cent rather than 25 per cent would be the maximum proportion of pensionable earnings to be paid under SERPS. Third, whereas under the original scheme widows and widowers could inherit all of their spouse's SERPS entitlement, in future only one-half of the pension can be inherited. The impact of all of these changes will be cushioned by transitional arrangements which will protect those already retired and those near to retirement now.

Further changes were made to the rules governing non-state pensions in an attempt to encourage their spread. Prior to the 1986 Act, a rebate on National Insurance contributions was available to employers and employees if the employer provided a pension scheme with a guaranteed minimum pension (GMP) during retirement. The GMP was deducted from any future SERPS entitlement, as the quid pro quo for reduced contributions. This process was known as contracting out of SERPS. The 1986 Act allows guaranteed minimum contribution (GMC) or money purchase schemes to receive the same rebate. Such schemes, which make no commitments on final benefits, are more attractive in some ways to smaller firms. A second change is that individuals will be able to contract out of SERPS, or their company's occupational scheme, and have their rebate paid directly into their own personal pension. A third change is that individuals who are members of an occupational pension scheme will be able to take further advantage of the tax privileges available to pension saving by supplementing their occupational scheme with free-standing additional voluntary contributions (AVCs) into a personal pension plan. To encourage a rapid switch from SERPS to occupational and personal provision, an extra 2 per cent rebate will be given to all new contracted-out occupational schemes and personal pensions for the period 1988 to 1993.

4. The Impact of the 1986 Act

In this section we describe the impact of the 1986 Act. We begin by examining the effects of the changes to income-related benefits on various groups in the population. It should be noted that in all the analysis that follows, we are concerned only with the underlying structural changes to the system. We thus ignore any purely transitional protection which some

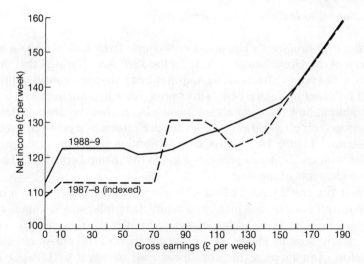

Figure 14.1 Net income under the old and new systems: married couple with two children

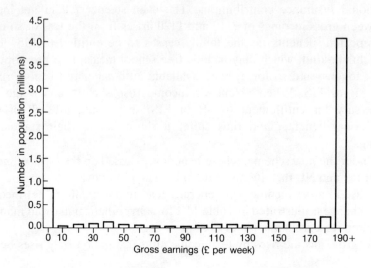

Figure 14.2 Distribution of earnings: couples with children

claimants will receive. It should also be stressed, however, that the hypothetical examples that are given are no more than illustrative. The precise effects of the changes may vary greatly from case to case according to personal circumstances. A wide diversity of outcomes is in practice observed even for members of the same group in the benefit-receiving population.

The Changes to Income-Related Benefits

Families with Children   The position of couples with children was a major concern of the Government in framing the 1986 Act. The way that the tax and benefit system affects this group has been changed considerably and this is reflected in Figure 14.1. This shows, for a hypothetical couple with two children, how the couple's net income before housing costs varies with changes in their gross earnings under the pre-reform and post-reform benefit systems.[7] Figure 14.2 shows the distribution of gross earnings of all couples with children and provides a guide to the numbers affected by the various elements of the changes.

A first key consequence of the changes is that the extreme form of the poverty trap, where net income actually falls following an increase in gross income, has been all but eliminated under the new system. This is most clearly seen in Figure 14.1 for a couple on £100 per week. Before the reform, an increase in gross income of as much as £50 per week would have left the couple worse off, because of offsetting falls in family income supplement and housing benefit, and increases in income tax and National Insurance contributions. The even steeper fall in net income between gross incomes of £110 and £120 arises from the loss of so-called 'passported' benefits, as the family ceases to be entitled to FIS. These benefits-in-kind, which may include free school meals, free prescriptions, milk tokens, and so forth, were available automatically to those receiving SB or FIS. When a family's income rose slightly above the level necessary for entitlement to SB or FIS, they could lose all of these additional benefits, and thus suffer a sharp fall in their standard of living.[8]

Under the new scheme, where benefit is assessed on the basis of income after tax and NI, the effective rate of benefit withdrawal is lower and so an increase in gross income will generally lead to some gain in net income.[9] This change is illustrated in Table 14.1 for a hypothetical married man with children on a gross income of £100 per week.

As gross income rises by £1, income after tax and NI only rises by 68p.

---

[7] In order to provide a fair comparison, the old system has been uprated in line with inflation.

[8] In Figure 14.1 *et seq.*, we show only the effect of the loss of free school meals, valued at £2.50 per week per child. The value of free prescriptions, free dental treatment, etc. would vary greatly from family to family.

[9] An exception may occur when the couple moves from income support onto family credit. In the diagram we assume that this occurs at gross income of £60 per week. In this case the loss of free school meals and of the family premium available under income support more than offsets the increase in gross income.

Table 14.1 Marginal tax rates under old and new benefit systems (withdrawal per additional pound of gross income)

Old system		New system	
Income tax	25p	Income tax	25p
National Insurance	7p	National Insurance	7p
Family income supplement	50p	Family credit	48p
Housing benefit	23p	Housing benefit	17p
Total withdrawal	105p	Total withdrawal	97p

The family thus lose 70 per cent of 68p (or 47.6p) from their family credit. Income for housing benefit purposes has then risen by 20.4p and the family loses 85 per cent of this (17.3p), giving an overall marginal tax rate of 97 per cent. More typically (and as in Figure 14.1), a family with this sort of income would probably be receiving only family credit, and so would have a marginal tax rate of 80 per cent. In either case, the system is designed to ensure that an increase in gross income yields some increase in net income. Even at the point where family credit is finally exhausted, the marginal tax rate remains below 100 per cent. This is because passported benefits such as free school meals have been replaced by a cash equivalent for recipients of family credit. This cash equivalent is then steadily withdrawn as income rises, in the usual way, thereby avoiding a sharp drop when entitlement to family credit ceases.

Whilst this change reduces the marginal tax rates of those in the extreme form of the poverty trap, the extension of family credit means that more people will face marginal rates in the region of 80 per cent. In Figure 14.1, couples with earnings of around £140–£150 per week have been brought into the income-related benefits system and so face marginal rates of around 80 per cent, rather than the 34 per cent withdrawal rate of tax and NI under the old system.

Combining this analysis with an examination of the income distribution shown in Figure 14.2, we see that the number of couples with children affected by marginal rates in excess of 100 per cent under the old system was in fact relatively small. The price of reducing the marginal rates of this group has been to extend the range of incomes over which relatively high rates of withdrawal operate to include a slightly denser part of the income distribution.

It is worth noting, however, that the shape of the income distribution may not itself be independent of the benefit system. The fact that there are relatively few people in the poverty trap may in fact imply that high marginal rates *are* important and that individuals have adjusted their labour supply accordingly. This is a difficult hypothesis to test, because of the very small number of individuals involved.

On the implications of the changes for the net incomes of couples with children, it is clear from Figure 14.1 that the majority of such couples will be better off as a result of the reforms. For unemployed couples, the new family premium available under income support will generally produce some gain compared with the outcome under supplementary benefit, although it should be stressed that the outcome will vary considerably with individual circumstances. The Government's own figures suggest that amongst couples with children dependent on income support, gainers will outnumber losers by about six to one. These figures do not, however, reflect the loss of 'single payments' (which do not appear to be compensated for in higher basic rates of benefit), and couples with children would typically have been amongst the principal beneficiaries of that scheme.[10] Further up the income distribution, gains also occur for those who previously had little or no entitlement to family income supplement but who benefit from the more extensive family credit.

The principal losers within this group are those in low-paid full-time work, with gross incomes in the range £80–£100 in our example. Although they will be receiving significantly more in family credit than they received in family income supplement, the cuts in housing benefit will in most cases more than offset this gain.

To have protected the net incomes of this group whilst at the same time reducing the overall rate of benefit withdrawal would have been very expensive and would not have been consistent with the Government's aim of a broadly revenue-neutral reform. Such an approach would also have significantly increased the numbers of people entitled to small amounts of family credit and thus facing relatively high marginal tax rates. This is because at income levels just above the present ceiling for family credit entitlement, the income distribution rapidly becomes denser. This trade-off is in practice inevitable within the context of an affordable income-related scheme. A fast withdrawal allows generous benefits to be paid to the poorest, but leaves them little incentive to increase their gross income; a more gradual withdrawal improves this incentive but means relatively less for the poorest and a significantly larger number facing relatively high marginal tax rates.

On the relationship between benefits out of work and benefits in work for this group, it is at once clear that the new system offers a far smoother

---

[10] The latest figures suggest that families with children, including lone parents, received around five-sixths of all single payments. The main items for which single payments were made included furniture, bedding, and maternity needs.

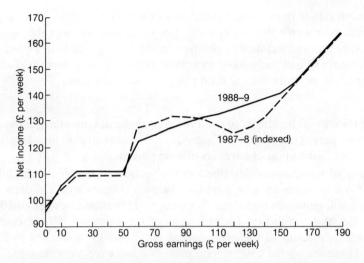

Figure 14.3 Net income under the old and new systems: lone parent with two children

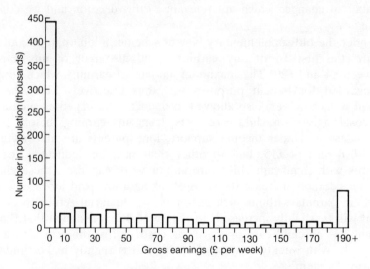

Figure 14.4 Distribution of earnings: lone parents

transition, but the effects of this restructuring on the financial incentives to seek work are ambiguous. The return to a part-time job has increased somewhat, as families of this type are now able to disregard £10 of their earnings compared with £4 under supplementary benefit. The incentive to seek the lowest-paid full-time jobs (represented in our example by gross incomes of £80–£110) will tend to have diminished since there is a smooth transition rather than a sharp jump to a new benefit regime. The range of incomes over which this applies will, however, vary considerably with the wage rate and the number of children in the family. For better-paid jobs, the return will generally have increased since benefit is now available at higher levels of gross income than was previously the case.

Lone Parents   The effects of the 1986 Act on the net income of a hypothetical lone parent are shown in Figure 14.3, together with Figure 14.4 which shows the distribution of earnings of lone parents.

Many of the changes described in the section on couples with children are also applicable to lone parents. As with couples with children, lone parents will generally no longer face marginal tax rates in excess of 100 per cent, but the proportion facing marginal rates around 80 per cent will increase as a result of the extension of family credit, as we see in Figure 14.3. However, in the case of lone parents a more frequent decision is not so much whether to work an extra hour but rather whether or not to work at all, since they are not required to sign on to receive benefit. There are a number of changes which are relevant to this decision and we consider these now.

Under the old supplementary benefit scheme, a lone parent could disregard the first £4 of any earnings, and also half of any earnings between £4 and £20. The maximum amount of earnings which could be disregarded for benefit purposes was thus effectively £12. The lone parent was, however, also allowed to deduct work expenses such as travel costs, as well as child care costs, from any earnings before benefit was assessed. Under income support, lone parents are allowed a flat-rate disregard of £15, but no other costs may be deducted. For lone parents with significant child care and/or work expenses, these changes will considerably increase the costs of taking a low-paid job. Conversely, for lone parents without such expenses, the financial return to employment will be slightly increased. In Figure 14.3 it is assumed that the lone parent has no child care or travelling costs and so the return to a part-time job (with weekly income of up to £50) is slightly higher under the reformed system.

It might be expected that a maximum net return of £12 for up to 30 hours' work by a single parent on SB would in any case discourage them from taking work, and that a change to the rules relating to disregards and deductions would be relatively unimportant. However, Figure 14.4 suggests that at least 100,000 single parents have jobs of this sort, and so changes to this element of the system may be of considerable practical importance. Furthermore, such jobs might provide single parents with a stepping-stone into full-time employment when, for example, children become old enough to go to school. For this reason also, the incentives to single parents to take part-time work might be of some importance.

With regard to seeking a full-time job, the effect of the changes on lone parents is broadly similar to that for couples with children. The financial return to a low-paid full-time job is somewhat lower under the new system, but the extension of family credit means that the return to a better-paid job is higher. However, for a lone parent the incentive to move from a part-time job into a full-time job is in general greater than that for a couple. This is because a lone parent is treated as a single person for income support purposes, but is treated in the same way as a married couple when being assessed for family credit. There is thus more incentive for a lone parent to take a full-time job and thereby qualify for the relatively generous family credit.

The pattern of gainers and losers amongst lone parents is difficult to gauge simply from a hypothetical example such as the one shown in Figure 14.3. This is because of the different ways in which lone parents could be treated under the old system. Under the SB scheme, around 70 per cent of lone parents were in receipt of the long-term rate of benefit. This higher rate was available to lone parents who had been in receipt of benefit for a year or more. The remainder received the lower short-term rate. Under income support, this distinction has been scrapped and so the gainers among lone parents will tend to be those who were in receipt of the short-term rate. It is assumed in the diagram that the lone parent was receiving the long-term rate, and when there is no other income, this person finds himself/herself slightly worse off.

All lone parents are entitled to both the family premium and the one-parent premium under income support and this will to a large extent compensate for the loss of the long-term rate. However, a long-term claimant who was particularly dependent on additional payments under supplementary benefit is likely to lose overall from the changes.[11] As noted above, the small number of lone parents with part-time jobs (see Figure 14.4) and high child care costs may well lose now that such costs are no longer deductible.

Amongst the smaller number of lone parents not on income support, the main gains come from the extension of family credit and the main losses from the cuts in housing benefit. Any widows who have inherited significant amounts of capital, or divorcees who have acquired capital sums as a result of settlements, will lose all entitlement to income-related benefits

---

[11] As an example, in Figure 14.3 it is assumed that one of the children is under 5. This would have entitled the parent to a weekly heating addition of £2.20, and the loss of this addition is not completely compensated under the new scheme.

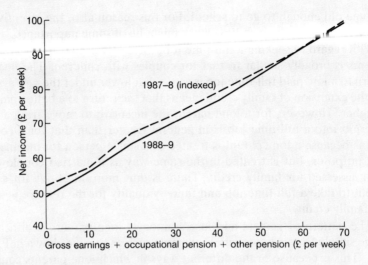

Figure 14.5 Net income under the old and new systems: single pensioner

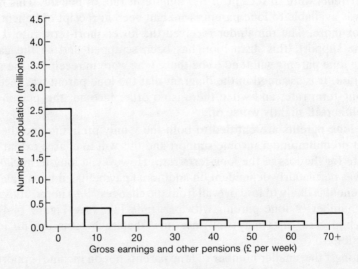

Figure 14.6 Distribution of earnings and other pensions: single pensioners

where that capital sum exceeds the newly introduced ceilings.[12] Overall, the Government estimates that within the benefit-receiving population, around 420,000 lone parents have gained from the changes, compared with 330,000 losers and 90,000 broadly unchanged.

---

[12] Accurate data on the importance of this factor are not readily available.

Pensioners Figures 14.5 and 14.6 continue our analysis for the case of a single pensioner. Here it is assumed that the pensioner is in receipt of a basic state pension and the horizontal axis measures any additional state pension, occupational pension, or earnings.

As Figure 14.5 suggests, the reforms have had relatively little effect on the marginal tax rates faced by pensioners, the principal changes coming from the reformed structure of housing benefit. Of more interest is the pattern of gains and losses among pensioners.

Our hypothetical single pensioner is, in general, slightly worse off as a result of the changes. Around 71 per cent of single pensioners are either unaffected or worse off, according to government figures. Amongst couple pensioners there are even fewer gainers, with 78 per cent either unaffected or worse off. These losses have resulted primarily from cuts in housing benefit and reflect the Government's shift in emphasis away from pensioners and toward families with children. Because the number of pensioners on benefit is large relative to the number of families with children, the Government has, however, been able to finance relatively large average gains amongst families by rather smaller average losses amongst pensioners.

Within this overall pattern, there is a wide diversity of individual outcomes. One source of gain for some pensioners is that the extra needs of older pensioners are now recognized by means of a higher premium for the over-80s under income support (and hence under housing benefit). Since the vast majority of over-80s are single, this explains in part why single pensioners fare slightly less badly in general than couple pensioners. However, where an elderly person was especially dependent on additional payments under SB for needs such as domestic assistance, heating, or laundry, the special pensioner premiums may not be adequate compensation.

The majority of losses among pensioners occur amongst those receiving only housing benefit. They may lose from the higher withdrawal rate, and also from the new capital rules. However, in response to worries about the impact of the capital rules on pensioners, the Government announced a concession in this area within a fortnight of the introduction of the new scheme, raising the capital limit from £6,000 to £8,000 for housing benefit only.

Childless Couples Figures 14.7 and 14.8 show the effects of the 1986 Act on a hypothetical childless couple, together with the distribution of earnings of such couples.

The main structural change to affect childless couples is the reform of housing benefit. The marginal tax rates faced by those in work on lower

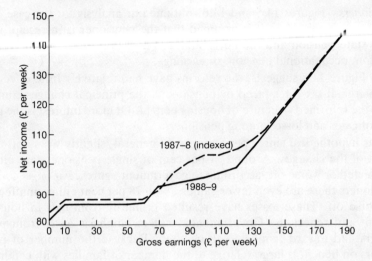

Figure 14.7   Net income under the old and new systems: childless couple

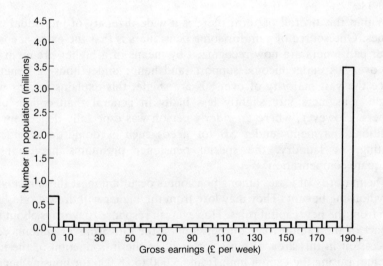

Figure 14.8   Distribution of earnings: childless couples

incomes (£70–£110) will increase, as housing benefit is withdrawn more
rapidly, but at higher incomes marginal rates will be lower, as entitlement to
benefit is exhausted. For childless couples there is some fall in the financial
incentive to seek work at all, because benefits in work have been cut, as
Figure 14.7 shows. Worries about the unemployment trap are not, however,

very great for this group, since the benefits for the unemployed without children are a good deal less generous than those for families with children.

Childless couples are one of the main groups of losers, with losers outnumbering gainers by seven to one. As Figure 14.8 shows, a major subset of the childless couples who are in any way affected by the benefit system are the 650,000 who are unemployed, and the majority of these will lose small amounts. The basic amounts of benefit available to unemployed couples before and after the changes are broadly similar, and so any couple in receipt of additions for diet, heating, laundry, etc. or with water rates to meet will tend to lose out. Similarly, couples with above-average rates will tend to lose from the requirement to pay 20 per cent of rates, since compensation is only provided in the basic allowance for 20 per cent of the average rates bill. This factor would, of course, apply to all other groups, but the effect on winners and losers might be more pronounced here because the rest of the system as it applied to unemployed couples remained broadly unchanged. Another group of losers would be couples working between 24 and 30 hours per week with low wages. Previously, supplementary benefit was available for those working up to 30 hours, but income support is only available for those working 23 hours or less.

The main gainers amongst childless couples in work would be those with relatively high rents and quite low wages (£50–£70 in Figure 14.7) who benefit from the slightly longer range of incomes over which 100 per cent help with rent is available before the taper begins. As Figure 14.8 shows, this is, however, likely to be a relatively small group of the population.

Single People   Figures 14.9 and 14.10 show the effects of the 1986 Act on two hypothetical single 19-year-olds—one who is still living at home (Figure 14.9) and one who has moved out and is living in rented accommodation (Figure 14.10). Figure 14.11 shows the distribution of earnings for all single people.

As Figures 14.9 and 14.10 suggest, the impact of the 1986 Act on single people depends very much on the housing position of the individual concerned. Under the old supplementary benefit system, there was a higher rate for 'householders' (such as those living in rented accommodation) and a lower rate for 'non-householders' (such as people living with their parents). This distinction has been abolished under income support, and so, other things being equal, non-householders will tend to gain at the expense of householders. A new distinction has, however, been introduced for single people on income support, with those aged 25 and over receiving a higher rate of benefit than the under-25s.

Taking these two changes together, we see that under-25s living away from home do particularly badly from the changes, whereas over-25s who live at home tend to gain substantially. Both of these groups are, however,

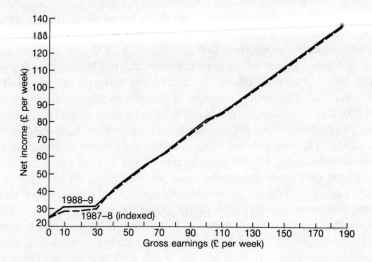

Figure 14.9   Net income under the old and new systems: single 19-year-old living with parents

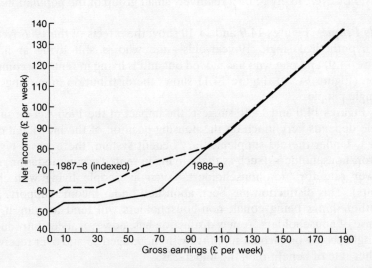

Figure 14.10   Net income under the old and new systems: single 19-year-old in rented accommodation

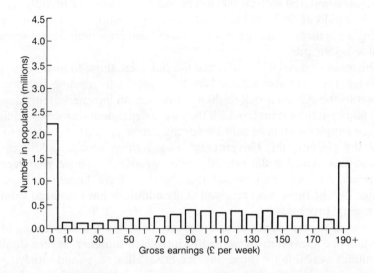

Figure 14.11   Distribution of earnings: single people

relatively atypical of their respective age groups. The picture is less clear for the majority, where an individual gains from one aspect of the change (e.g. is no longer treated as a non-householder) but loses from another aspect (e.g. receives a lower rate because of being under 25). Overall, however, the ending of the lower rate for non-householders tends to be more significant. Thus amongst single people on income support, even for the under-25s gainers outnumber losers by more than two to one, whilst among the over-25s there is an even split of gainers and losers.

For single people in work, the only change is for those with housing costs, and here there are major losses from the cuts in housing benefit. Figure 14.10 highlights the way in which housing benefit is now withdrawn much more rapidly, being exhausted in this example at a gross income of £70 per week. Under the old system, entitlement to HB continued on incomes up to £100 per week. This earlier withdrawal of housing benefit does, however, unambiguously improve the work incentives of those with incomes in the range £70–£100, by reducing their marginal tax rate whilst also reducing their average tax rate.

Sick and Disabled   For the sick and disabled, a single hypothetical example would be of little value, since the effects of the reforms are especially dependent for this group on the precise personal circumstances of the individual concerned. Overall, however, the Government estimates that around 270,000 sick or disabled claimants have gained from the

changes, compared with 80,000 losers and 70,000 who are broadly unaffected. It should again be stressed that these figures do not allow for the loss
of single payments, and these would have been important for some sick or
disabled claimants.

The main changes which affected the sick were those to income support,
although they are also affected by the changes to housing benefit. The
impact of the Act on a sick or disabled person on income support depends
very much on the extent to which they were dependent on weekly additions
to their supplementary benefit for special needs. As part of its drive to simplify the system, the Government ended these specific additions and
instead introduced a flat-rate 'disability premium'. Those who received
relatively few additions would thus tend to have benefited from this
change, whilst those who received many additions have suffered from this
'averaging' process.

It was in part in response to concerns about heavy losses arising in this
way that the Government agreed to introduce a higher 'severe disability
premium', available for those on attendance allowance (and satisfying certain other conditions). As a further concession, it has also placed £5 million
into a special 'Independent Living Fund' which will be administered by
charities for the disabled, and is designed to help the severely disabled to
go on living in their own homes.

Amongst those whose sickness or disability does not prevent them from
taking work, there are slightly more gainers than losers from the changes to
housing benefit. This group benefits from the way in which the higher personal allowances available under income support are carried over into
housing benefit. There are, however, losses from the more rapid withdrawal of benefit as income rises.

The Changes to Pension Provision[13]

It is very difficult to assess the likely impact of the proposed changes in the
pensions field. There are two reasons for this. First, the impact of the
changes will unfold over a period of many years: many of the changes to
SERPS will not begin to take effect until the next century. Second, the aim
of the proposals is explicitly to encourage individuals to leave SERPS and
move into occupational or personal pension schemes. Until the new system
has been in operation for some time, it will not be possible to know how
many individuals will switch out of SERPS.

None the less, there are a number of points which can be made. Broadly,
those who retire this century will be unaffected by the proposals, as a result
of complex transitional protection. Thereafter, the changes will begin to

[13] A more extensive evaluation of the changes may be found in Creedy and Disney (Ch. 13,
this volume).

take effect, thus reducing the average level and cost of SERPS. The cost of SERPS alone in 2033–4 is estimated by the Government Actuary to be likely to be around half of the expected cost of the pre-1986 scheme, at around £13 billion compared with £25 billion. This should allow a standard National Insurance rate of around 15 per cent, as opposed to around 18 per cent if SERPS were not reformed, to pay for National Insurance benefits. All recipients of SERPS pensions will receive less as a result of the reduction in the pension from 25 per cent to 20 per cent of pensionable earnings. The extension of the qualifying period from the 20 best years to average lifetime earnings will hit those with fluctuating earnings more heavily than those with relatively stable income profiles. The reduction in the proportion of the SERPS entitlements of a spouse which can be inherited will particularly hit elderly women, whose husbands are much more likely to die before their spouses than to outlive them.

As noted above, any estimates of the likely extent of switching from SERPS to occupational or personal provision must be highly speculative. Certainly, we can say that it is much more likely to be attractive for relatively young workers to leave occupational schemes with defined benefit provision for a personal pension than it would be for workers more than half-way through their working careers. There have been some suggestions that switching might occur to such an extent that occupational pension schemes might find themselves dangerously 'top-heavy', but this seems improbable. At present, the best strategy for those who want to know what will happen to the balance of state, occupational, and personal provision must be to wait until we have some evidence on individual responses to the new system.

5. Evaluation

We aim in this section to assess the success of the reforms in alleviating the five defects outlined in Section 2 and to analyse the reasons for any failures. Before we move on to this assessment, it is important to note that there is substantial scope for disagreement over the objectives of social security systems. The White Paper and Social Security Act probably reflect a view of social security which sees poverty prevention/alleviation as the primary goal. Other views might, however, emphasize the importance of universal provision for groups such as families with children, or of helping families to redistribute income across their life cycles, or of social insurance arrangements. Such differences in objectives must inevitably lead to disagreement over the nature of the social security system. Bearing this point in mind, we now examine the more limited question of the extent to which the reforms actually achieved the objectives for which they were designed.

The first defect identified was that of complexity. The reforms certainly reduce the amount of complexity: levels of benefit are more sensibly aligned and complexity of calculation is reduced. By abolishing single payments, the administration of income support should be more straightforward than that of supplementary benefit. However, the gains should not be exaggerated. While the DHSS's task will be made easier, it is probably still unlikely that claimants will be able to estimate their entitlements accurately. It is also worth noting that complexity is already creeping back. The Green Paper proposed a single taper for housing benefit for both rent and rates; the Social Security Act has two tapers—one for rent, one for rates. The White Paper proposed the same capital cut-off of £6,000 for both housing benefit and income support; 2 weeks after implementation of the reforms, the capital cut-off for housing benefit was increased to £8,000, while that for income support remains at £6,000. There are perhaps two reasons for this encroaching complexity. First, there appears to be a natural tendency for complexity to appear as gaps in provision are observed or as the changes have unforeseen implications. Second, and more serious in this case, introducing changes which impose losses on already poor individuals is a potentially unpopular activity. In both of the examples mentioned above, the initial simple proposal was abandoned because of the losses it would have imposed. Had more money been available to ease the introduction of structural change, greater simplicity could have been achieved. This is not necessarily an argument for higher expenditure in the long term, but for accepting that carrying out reforms without any extra expenditure, or even while reducing expenditure, is likely to limit severely the available options.

The second identified defect was the failure to give effective support to those in greatest need, especially low-income families with children. The reforms will increase the incomes of many such families, through the new family premium under income support and the increase in expenditure on family credit when compared with family income supplement. It is also the case that the new higher housing benefit withdrawal rates will concentrate HB expenditure more on those with lowest incomes.

A major gap in the proposals, however, is the failure to introduce structural improvements which will improve the take-up of means-tested benefits. The take-up of FIS was 50 per cent; the White Paper hopes that the take-up of family credit will be 60 per cent, but provides no justification for this assumption. It could be argued that a simpler system, with fewer people having simultaneous entitlement to family credit and housing benefit, will improve take-up, but there will also be a larger number of small entitlements at higher incomes, and studies suggest that this is likely to reduce the proportion who take up their entitlement.[14] Even if the Government's optimism is justified, a take-up rate of 60 per cent seems

[14] See, for example, Blundell, Fry, and Walker (1988).

inadequate if the benefit is aimed at the very poor. Increased reliance on targeting is surely only acceptable if the benefits used are received by all those entitled to them. A further cause for concern for 'those in greatest need' may be the abolition of single payments, to be replaced by the Social Fund and especially the loan element of the Fund. If income support is set at a level which is just enough to cover the needs of a particular family, reducing that level to repay a loan from the Social Fund must presumably impose hardship.

The disincentive problem in the form of the poverty and unemployment traps was the third issue identified. As noted above, the extreme form of the poverty trap where marginal tax rates can exceed 100 per cent will be virtually eliminated. The cost of this is that high marginal tax rates will affect a larger group. The new alignment of family credit and income support, together with larger earnings disregards, should ease the unemployment trap. However, it is worth noting that there is remarkably little evidence that these incentive 'problems' cause any change in behaviour. The reforms are broadly beneficial, but unlikely to have much impact. Although the importance of the traditional poverty and unemployment traps for incentives may be exaggerated, there are groups affected by very high marginal tax rates whose behaviour does seem more responsive. One such group, examined in Dilnot and Kell (Ch. 8, this volume), is women married to unemployed men. Another group might be single-parent families. For neither of these groups will there be any very major change in marginal tax rates.

Lack of choice in pension provision was the fourth problem area. Choice is being expanded and a state scheme retained. It will be difficult to assess the impact of these changes for some years. Potential problems arise if individuals are short-sighted, and thus make inadequate provision for their retirement, or if they simply do not understand the options available to them.

The final problem was the level of future expenditure, especially on pensions. The reduction in expenditure on SERPS in 2033–4 from £25.5 billion in 1984–5 prices to £13 billion is quite dramatic. However, as noted in the final part of Section 4, this corresponds to a reduction of only 3 percentage points in the National Insurance contribution rate. It may well be that the amounts of money, which are to a great extent the result of compound interest, have led to an over-reaction.

The reforms have made some progress towards alleviating the defects identified by the White Paper, but have been held back in a number of areas. One clear lesson is that structural change without some spare money to protect potential losers is difficult to achieve. It must also be recognized that some obvious defects, particularly the low take-up of means-tested benefits, are simply not addressed.

Bibliography

Akerlof, G. A. (1978), 'The economics of "tagging" as applied to the optimal income tax, welfare programs and manpower planning', *American Economic Review*, **68**, 8–19.

Allen, S. G., Clark, R. L., and Sumner, D. A. (1986), 'Post-retirement adjustments of pension benefits', *Journal of Human Resources*, **21**, 118–37.

Atkinson, A. B. (1969), *Poverty in Britain and the Reform of Social Security*, Cambridge: Cambridge University Press.

—— (1983), 'Adjustments to the Family Expenditure Survey data', ESRC Programme on Taxation, Incentives and the Distribution of Income, Research Note 7.

—— (1984), 'Take-up of social security benefits', ESRC Programme on Taxation, Incentives and the Distribution of Income, Discussion Paper 65.

—— (1987), 'On the measurement of poverty', *Econometrica*, **55**, 749–64.

—— (1988), 'Income maintenance for the unemployed in Britain: the response to high unemployment', mimeo.

——, Gomulka, J., Micklewright, J., and Rau, N. (1984), 'Unemployment benefit, duration and incentives in Britain: how robust is the evidence?', *Journal of Public Economics*, **23**, 3–26.

—— and King, M. (1980), 'Housing policy, taxation and reform', *Midland Bank Review*, Spring.

—— and Micklewright, J. (1983), 'On the reliability of income data in the Family Expenditure Survey 1970–1977', *Journal of the Royal Statistical Society*, Series A, **146**, 33–61.

—— and —— (1985), *Unemployment Benefits and Unemployment Duration*, ST/ICERD Occasional Paper 6, London: London School of Economics.

—— and —— (1988), 'Unemployment compensation, employment policy and labour market transitions', mimeo, OECD, Paris.

—— and Stiglitz, J. E. (1980), *Lectures on Public Economics*, New York: McGraw Hill.

—— and Sutherland, H. (1988), *Tax–Benefit Models*, ST/ICERD Occasional Paper 10, London: London School of Economics.

Barclay, P. (1988a), interview on *File on Four*, Radio 4, 9 and 10 February.

—— (1988b), 'The rough edges of the social fund', *Social Work Today*, 28 April.

Barro, R. (1978), *The Impact of Social Security on Private Savings*, Washington DC: American Enterprise Institute.

Bennett, F. (1984), 'Biggest and best since Beveridge?', *Poverty*, 58.

—— and Tarpey, M. (1984–5), 'The 1984 Reviews: some thoughts and themes', *Poverty*, 59.

Berndt, E. R., Hall, B. H., Hall, R. E., and Hausman, J. A. (1974), 'Estimation and inference in non-linear structural models', *Annals of Economic and Social Measurement*, **3**, 653–65.

Berthoud, R. (1980), 'Giving Fowler a human face', *The Times*, 28 January.

Berthoud, R. and Ermisch, J. (1985), 'Housing and low incomes—steps towards a long-term solution', in *Reshaping Benefits*, London: Policy Studies Institute.

Besley, T. and Kanbur, S. M. R. (1987), 'Food subsidies and poverty alleviation', *Economic Journal*.

Betson, D. and van der Gaag, J. (1985), 'Measuring the benefits of income maintenance programs', in M. David and T. Smeeding (eds.), *Horizontal Equity, Uncertainty, and Economic Well-Being*, NBER Studies in Income and Wealth, **50**, Chicago: University of Chicago Press.

Beveridge, W. H. (1942), *Social Insurance and Allied Services*, Cmd 6404, London: HMSO.

—— (1943), newspaper report quoted in R. Lister with C. Oppenheim, *The Social Security White Paper: A Plain Person's Guide*, CPAG, London, 1985.

Blake, Lord (1987), *Daily Telegraph*, 29 May.

Blank, R. (1985), 'The impact of state economic differentials on household welfare and labour force participation', *Journal of Public Economics*, **28**, 25–58.

Blundell, R. W., Fry, V. C., and Walker, I. (1988), 'Modelling the take-up of means-tested benefits: the case of housing benefits in the United Kingdom', *Economic Journal*, **98**, Conference Papers Supplement, 58–74.

——, Ham, J., and Meghir, C. H. D. (1987), 'Unemployment and female labour supply', *Economic Journal*, **97**, Supplement.

——, Meghir, C. H. D., Symons, E. J., and Walker, I. (1984), 'On the reform of the taxation of husband and wife: are incentives important?', *Fiscal Studies*, **5**, 4, 1–22.

——, ——, and —— (1986), 'A labour supply model for the simulation of tax and benefit reforms', in R. W. Blundell and I. Walker (eds.), *Unemployment, Search and Labour Supply*, Cambridge: Cambridge University Press.

——, ——, ——, and —— (1989), 'Labour supply specification and the evaluation of tax reforms', *Journal of Public Economics*, forthcoming.

Booth, C. (1902–4), *The Life and Labour of the People in London*, 17-volume edition, London: Macmillan. (Original volume on East London published 1889.)

Boskin, M. J. and Hurd, M. (1978), 'The effect of social security on early retirement', *Journal of Public Economics*, **10**, 361–78.

Burtless, G. and Moffitt, R. (1985), 'The joint choice of retirement age and post-retirement hours of work', *Journal of Labour Economics*, **3**, 209–36.

CBI (1980), 'Submission on government proposals set out in Cmnd 7864', London: Confederation of British Industry.

Checkland, S. G. and Checkland, E. O. A. (eds.), *The Poor Law Report of 1834*, Harmondsworth: Penguin.

Child Poverty Action Group (1984), *National Welfare Benefits Handbook*, London: CPAG.

Committee of Public Accounts (1985), *Statutory Sick Pay*, Tenth Report, House of Commons Session 1984–5, HC 176, London: HMSO.

Cook, R. (1987), 'The hole in Labour's heart', *Marxism Today*, August.

Cooke, K. (1987), 'The withdrawal from paid work of the wives of unemployed men: a review of research', *Journal of Social Policy*, **16**, 371–82.

Cowell, F. A. (1981), 'Income maintenance schemes under wage-rate uncertainty', *American Economic Review*, **71**, 692–703.

—— (1986), 'Welfare benefits and the economics of takeup', Taxation, Incentives, and the Distribution of Income, Discussion Paper 89, ST/ICERD, London School of Economics.

Creedy, J. (1982), *State Pensions in Britain*, Cambridge: Cambridge University Press.

—— and Disney, R. (1985), *Social Insurance in Transition: An Economic Analysis*, Oxford: Clarendon Press.

Daniel, W. (1988), quoted in *Social Services Insight*, 1 April.

Davis, E. H. and Dilnot, A. W. (1985), 'The IFS tax and benefit model', Institute for Fiscal Studies Working Paper 58.

——, ——, Stark, G. K., and Webb, S. J. (1987), 'The IFS tax and benefit model', Institute for Fiscal Studies Working Paper 87/9.

Deacon, A. and Bradshaw, J. (1983), *Reserved for the Poor: The Means Test in British Social Policy*, Oxford: Basil Blackwell and Martin Robertson.

Deakin, N. (1987), *The Politics of Welfare*, London: London University Paperbacks.

Department of Employment (1985), *Employment: The Challenge for the Nation*, Cmnd 9474, London: HMSO.

—— (1988), *Training for Employment*, (White Paper), Cm 316, London: HMSO.

DHSS (1980), *Income during Initial Sickness: A New Strategy*, (Green Paper), Cmnd 7864, London: HMSO.

—— (1985a), *Reform of Social Security*, (Green Paper), **1–4**, Cmnd 9517–20, London: HMSO.

—— (1985b), *Reform of Social Security: Programme for Action*, (White Paper), Cmnd 9691, London: HMSO.

—— (1988a), *Low Income Statistics: Report of a Technical Review*, DHSS, March.

—— (1988b), *Households Below Average Income Statistics*, DHSS, May.

Diamond, P. A. (1977), 'A framework for social security analysis', *Journal of Public Economics*, **8**, 275–98.

Dilnot, A. W., Kay, J. A., and Morris, C. N. (1984), *The Reform of Social Security*, Oxford: Oxford University Press.

—— and Morris, C. N. (1983), 'Private costs and benefits of unemployment: measuring replacement rates', *Oxford Economic Papers*, **35**, 321–40.

Disability Alliance (1986), *Statutory Sick Pay: The Failure of Privatisation in Social Security*, Disability Alliance with Leicester Rights Centre and Leicester City Council Low Pay Campaign.

Disney, R. (1987), 'Statutory sick pay: an appraisal', *Fiscal Studies*, **8**, 2, 58–76.

Dixit, A. K. and Sandmo, A. (1977), 'Some simplified formulae for optimal income taxation', *Scandinavian Journal of Economics*, **79**, 417–23.

Donnison, D. (1982), *The Politics of Poverty*, Oxford: Martin Robertson.

Ermisch, J. (1984), *Housing Finance: Who Gains?*, London: Policy Studies Institute.

Feldstein, M. S. (1980), 'International differences in social security and savings', *Journal of Public Economics*, **14**, 225–44.

—— (1985), 'Should private pensions be indexed?', in Z. Bodie and J. B. Shoven (eds.), *Financial Aspects of the United States Pension System*, Chicago: University of Chicago Press.

—— and Pellechio, A. (1979), 'Social security and household wealth accumulation: new microeconomic evidence', *Review of Economics and Statistics*, **61**, 361–8.

Field, F. (1982), *Poverty & Politics*, London: Heinemann.

Financial Times (1988), 'Lack of vision on benefits', 5 April.

Finer Committee (1974), *Report of the Committee on One-Parent Families*, Cmnd 5629, London: HMSO.

Foster, J., Greer, J., and Thorbecke, E. (1984), 'A class of decomposable poverty measures', *Econometrica*, **52**, 761–6.

Fowler, N. (1983), *House of Commons Debates*, 23 November, col. 360.

—— (1984a), statement announcing the Reviews, *House of Commons Debates*, 2 April, cols. 652–60.

—— (1984b), letter to Child Poverty Action Group, 30 May.

—— (1984c), *House of Commons Debates*, 8 November, col. 232.

—— (1985), speech made to Sutton Coldfield Conservative Association, 26 October, London: Conservative Central Office.

—— (1986), Third Reading of the Social Security Bill 1986, *House of Commons Debates*, 30 May, cols. 265 and 263.

Friedman, M. (1962), *Capitalism and Freedom*, Chicago: University of Chicago Press.

Gamble, A. (1987), 'The north–south divide', *Marxism Today*, March, quoting P. Glotz.

Garraty, J. A. (1978), *Unemployment in History*, New York: Harper and Row.

Gomulka, J. and Stern, N. (1986), 'The employment of married women in the UK: 1970–1983', London School of Economics Discussion Paper 98.

Government Actuary's Department (1984), *Population, Pension Costs and Pensioners' Incomes*, London: HMSO.

—— (1987), *Occupational Pension Schemes: Review of Certain Contracting-Out Terms*, Cm 110, London: HMSO.

Green, F., Hadjimatheou, G., and Smail, R. (1985), 'Fringe benefit distribution in Britain', *British Journal of Industrial Relations*, **23**, 261–80.

Grey, A., Hepworth, N., and Odling-Smee, J. (1981), *Housing Rents, Costs and Subsidies—A Discussion Document*, London: Chartered Institute of Public Finance and Accountancy.

Halpern, J. and Hausman, J. (1986), 'Choice under uncertainty: labour supply and the decision to apply for disability insurance', in R. W. Blundell and I. Walker (eds.), *Unemployment, Search and Labour Supply*, Cambridge: Cambridge University Press.

Hamermesh, D. S. and Rees, A. R. (1984), *Economics of Work and Pay*, third edition, London: Harper & Row.

Hamill, L. (1978), 'An explanation of the increase in female one parent families receiving supplementary benefit', Economic Adviser's Office, DHSS.

Hammond, E. M. and Morris, C. N. (1986), 'What price equality? The costs of changing the age of retirement', *Fiscal Studies*, **7**, 3, 25–40.

Harris, D. et al. (1984), *Compensation and Support for Illness and Injury*, Oxford: Clarendon Press.

Heckman, J. J. (1974), 'Shadow prices, market wages and labor supply', *Econometrica*, **42**, 679–94.

Hemming, R. and Harvey, R. (1983), 'Occupational pension scheme membership and retirement saving', *Economic Journal*, **93**, 128–44.

Hills, J. (1987), *Subsidies to Social Housing in England: Their Behavioural Implications*, London: London School of Economics.

HMSO (1944a), *Social Insurance Part I*, (White Paper), Cmd 6550, London: HMSO.

—— (1944b), *Social Insurance Part II: Workmen's Compensation*, (White Paper), Cmd 6551, London: HMSO.

—— (1984), *DHSS: Statutory Sick Pay Scheme*, Report by the Comptroller and Auditor General, House of Commons Session 1984–5, HC 45, London: HMSO.

HM Treasury (1983), *The Government's Expenditure Plans 1983–84 to 1985–86*, (Public Expenditure White Paper), Cmnd 8789, London: HMSO.

—— (1984), *The Government's Expenditure Plans 1984–85 to 1986–87*, (Public Expenditure White Paper), Cmnd 9143, London: HMSO.

—— (1987), *The Government's Expenditure Plans 1987–88 to 1989–90*, (Public Expenditure White Paper), Cm 56, London: HMSO.

—— (1988), *The Government's Expenditure Plans 1988–89 to 1990–91*, (Public Expenditure White Paper), Cm 288, London: HMSO.

House of Commons Debates (1987), 30 November, written answers, col. 464.

—— (1988a), 7 March, written answers, cols. 56–7.

—— (1988b), 25 March, written answers, cols. 243–4.

Industrial Relations Services (1987), 'Pensions: the issues', *Industrial Relations Review and Report*, 389, 2–6.

Inland Revenue (1986), *The Reform of Personal Taxation*, (Green Paper), Cmnd 9756, London: HMSO.

Jenkin, P. (1980), DHSS press release, 17 July.

Johnson, P. (1985), *The Historical Dimension of the Welfare State Crisis*, London: ICERD/LSE.

Jones, M. and Kettle, M. (1984), *Sunday Times*, 8 April.

Kanbur, S. M. R. (1986), 'Budgetary rules for poverty alleviation', Institute for International Economic Studies, University of Stockholm, Discussion Paper 363.

—— (1987), 'Transfers, targeting and poverty', *Economic Policy*, 4, 112–36 and 141–7.

—— and Keen, M. J. (1988), 'Non-linear income taxation for poverty alleviation', mimeo.

Kemp, P. (1987), 'The reform of housing benefit', *Social Policy and Administration*, **21**, 2.

Kemsley, W. F. F., Redpath, R. U., and Holmes, M. (1980), *Family Expenditure Survey Handbook*, London: HMSO.

Killingsworth, M. (1983), *Labour Supply*, Cambridge: Cambridge University Press.

—— and Heckman, J. (1986), 'Female labor supply: a survey', in O. Ashenfelter and R. Layard (eds.), *Handbook of Labor Economics*, Amsterdam and New York: North-Holland.

King, M. A. (1983), 'Welfare analysis of tax reforms using household data', *Journal of Public Economics*, **21**, 183–214.

Layard, R., Barton, M., and Zabalza, A. (1980), 'Married women's participation and hours', *Economica*, **47**, February, 51–72.

—— and Nickell, S. J. (1985), 'The causes of British unemployment', *National Institute Economic Review*, 111, 62–85.

Levy, F. (1979), 'The labor supply of female heads, or AFDC work incentives don't work too well', *Journal of Human Resources*, **14**, 76–97.

Lister, R. (1985), *Social Security Reviews: Countdown*, London: Child Poverty Action Group.

McLaughlin, E., Millar, J., and Cooke, K. (1988), *Work and Welfare Benefits*, London: Gower, forthcoming.

Maddala, G. S. (1983), *Limited-Dependent and Qualitative Variables in Econometrics*, Cambridge: Cambridge University Press.

Major, J. (1986), speech to Association of County Councils Conference, 9 December.

Mallender, J. and Ramsden, S. (1984), 'Incomes in and out of work 1978–82: some results using the DHSS cohort simulation model', Government Economic Service Working Paper 69.

Marr, A. (1988), *The Independent*, 2 March.

Matthewman, J. and Calvert, H. (1987), *Guide to the Social Security Act 1986*, London: Tolley.

Meade Committee (1978), *The Structure and Reform of Direct Taxation*, London: Allen and Unwin.

Micklewright, J. (1985), 'On earnings related unemployment benefits and their relation to earnings', *Economic Journal*, **95**, 133–45.

—— (1986), 'Unemployment and incentives to work: policy and evidence in the 1980s', in P. E. Hart (ed.), *Unemployment and Labour Market Policies*, Aldershot: Gower.

Minford, P. (1983), *Unemployment: Cause and Cure*, Oxford: Martin Robertson.

Mirrlees, J. A. (1971), 'An exploration in the theory of optimum income taxation', *Review of Economic Studies*, **38**, 175–208.

Moffitt, R. (1983), 'An economic model of welfare stigma', *American Economic Review*, **73**, 1023–35.

—— (1985), 'A problem with the negative income tax', *Economic Letters*, **17**, 261–5.

—— (1986), 'Work incentives in the AFDC system: an analysis of the 1981 reforms', *American Economic Association Papers and Proceedings*, **76**, 219–23.

—— (1987a), 'Work and the US welfare system: a review', mimeo, Brown University.

—— (1987b), 'Has state redistribution policy grown more conservative?', mimeo, Brown University.

—— (1987c), 'Survey paper', mimeo.

Moore, J. (1987), speech, 26 September, London: Conservative Central Office.

Morris, C. N. and Preston, I. (1986), 'Inequality, poverty and the redistribution of income', *Bulletin of Economic Research*, **38**, 277–344.

Moylan, S., Millar, J., and Davies, R. (1984), *For Richer, For Poorer? DHSS Cohort Study of Unemployed Men*, London: HMSO.

Narendranathan, W., Nickell, S. J., and Stern, J. (1985), 'Unemployment benefits revisited', *Economic Journal*, **95**, 307–29

National Federation of Housing Associations (1985), *Inquiry into British Housing*, NFHA.

New Society (1988), 'The hole in welfare's safety net', 15 April.

Nickell, S. J. (1979), 'The effect of unemployment and related benefits on the duration of unemployment', *Economic Journal*, **89**, 34–49.

Nobles, R. (1986a), 'Pensions: the new framework?', *Modern Law Review*, **49**, 42–67.

—— (1986b), 'Retirement provision and the Social Security Act—the prospects for radical change', *Industrial Law Journal*, **15**, 209–13.

Nolan, B. (1987), *Income Distribution and the Macroeconomy*, Cambridge: Cambridge University Press.

Office of Population Censuses and Surveys (1986), *General Household Survey 1985*, London: HMSO.

O'Sullivan, A. (1984), 'Misconceptions in the current housing subsidy debate', *Policy and Politics*, **12**, 2.

Parker, H. (1985), 'When Fowler is off-target', *The Times*, 14 June.

—— (1988), *The Effects of Mr John Moore's April 1988 Benefit Changes on the Disposable Incomes and Work Incentives of Low Income Working Age Families*, London: ICERD/LSE.

Pencavel, J. (1986), 'Labor supply of men: a survey', in O. Ashenfelter and R. Layard (eds.), *Handbook of Labor Economics*, Amsterdam and New York: North-Holland.

Pesando, J. E. (1984), 'Employee evaluation of pension claims and the impact of indexing initiatives', *Economic Inquiry*, **22**, 1–17.

—— and Rea, S. A. (1977), *Public and Private Pensions in Canada: An Economic Analysis*, Toronto: University of Toronto Press.

Piachaud, D. (1985), 'Can we afford SERPS?', *New Society*, 1172, 407–8.

Portillo, M. (1988), *House of Commons Debates*, 14 March, cols. 956–7.

Rayner Committee (1981), *Payment of Benefits to Unemployed People*, DE/DHSS, London: HMSO.

Rowland, M. (1988), *Rights Guide to Non-Means-Tested Social Security Benefits*, eleventh edition, London: Child Poverty Action Group.

Rowntree, B. S. (1902), *Poverty: A Study of Town Life*, London and New York: Macmillan.

Sen, A. K. (1985), *Commodities and Capabilities*, Amsterdam: North-Holland.

Sjoquist, D. L. (1976), 'Labor supply under uncertainty: note', *American Economic Review*, 66, 929–30.

Social Security Advisory Committee (1987a), press release, 1 July.

—— (1987b), press release, 15 October.

Social Security Consortium (1987), *Of Little Benefit*, second edition, London: SSC.

Social Services Committee (1985), *The Government's Green Paper 'Reform of Social Security'*, Seventh Report, 451, London: HMSO.

Stark, G. K. (1987), 'Supplementary benefit take-up and the IFS tax and benefit model', mimeo, Institute for Fiscal Studies.

Stern, N. H. (1987), discussion of Kanbur (1987), *Economic Policy*, 4, 136–40.

Timmins, N. (1985), *The Times*, 5 February.

—— (1988), 'A harsh way to end the dependency culture', *The Independent*, 6 April.

Tobin, J. (1965), 'On improving the economic status of the negro', *Daedalus*, 878–98.

Townsend, P. (1985), *The Guardian*, 8 July.

Treasury and Civil Service Sub-Committee (1983), 'The structure of personal income taxation and income support', 'The Meacher Report', in Treasury and Civil Service Committee, *Third Special Report*, Session 1982–3, HC 386, London: HMSO.

Venti, S. F. and Wise, D. A. (1987), 'IRAs and saving', in M. S. Feldstein (ed.), *Taxes and Capital Formation*, Chicago: Chicago University Press.

Walker, C. (1982), 'Social assistance: the reality of open government', *Policy and Politics*, 10, 1.

Ward, S. (1985), 'The political background', in S. Ward (ed.), *DHSS in Crisis*, London: Child Poverty Action Group.

Wass, D. (1987), 'A better way of governing', *New Society*, 12 June.

Whitely, P. F. and Winyard, S. J. (1987), *Pressure for the Poor*, London: Methuen.

Williams, F. (1985), *Daily Telegraph*, 3 June.

Zabalza, A., Pissarides, C. A., and Barton, M. (1980), 'Social security and the choice between full-time work, part-time work and retirement', *Journal of Public Economics*, 14, 245–76.

INDEX

Note: References are to social security in the United Kingdom except where otherwise specified.